JEWISH STATE
PARIAH NATION

JEWISH STATE
PARIAH NATION

Israel and the Dilemmas of Legitimacy

JEROLD S. AUERBACH

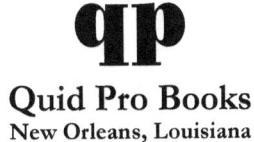

Quid Pro Books
New Orleans, Louisiana

Copyright © 2014 by Jerold S. Auerbach. All rights reserved. This book or parts of it may not be reproduced, copied, or transmitted (except as permitted by sections 107 and 108 of the U.S. Copyright Law and except by reviewers for the public press), by any means including voice recordings and the copying of its digital form, without the written permission of the publisher.

Published in 2014 by Quid Pro Books.

ISBN 978-1-61027-214-8 (pbk)
ISBN 978-1-61027-213-1 (hbk)
ISBN 978-1-61027-215-5 (ebk)

Quid Pro Books
5860 Citrus Blvd., Suite D-101
New Orleans, Louisiana 70123
www.quidprobooks.com

qp

Publisher's Cataloging-in-Publication

Auerbach, Jerold S.

    Jewish state, pariah nation: Israel and the dilemmas of legitimacy / Jerold S. Auerbach.

        p. cm. — (Contemporary society)
    Includes bibliographical references and index.
    ISBN   978-1-61027-214-8 (pbk)

1. Israel—History. 2. Jews—Palestine—History—20th century. 3. Jews—United States. 4. Arab-Israel conflict. I. Title. II. Series.
DS131.5 A26 2014   377.143'5—dc22
                                                                            2014004537

For Jeff

My Son
My Only Son
With My Love

Contents

Introduction 1

1 · War of Brothers 7

2 · God and State 39

3 · Conscience and Country 77

4 · Pariah Nation 105

Conclusion: Settling the Future 139

Acknowledgments 155

Bibliographical Essay 157

Index 169

About the Author 177

JEWISH STATE

PARIAH NATION

Introduction

Disputes over legitimacy and challenges to authority are deeply embedded in ancient Jewish history and texts no less than in the modern State of Israel. When the Israelites, newly liberated from slavery in Egypt, approached the Red Sea with Pharaoh's legions in close pursuit they implored Moses to return them to bondage rather than consign them to imminent death. No sooner had Moses ascended Mt. Sinai to receive the Ten Commandments than his rebellious people molded a golden calf to worship. After tribal leaders returned from scouting the promised land of Canaan, not even their report of its abundant "milk and honey" could dissuade faithless Israelites from loudly proclaiming their yearning for the security of Egyptian servitude over the promise of freedom in their own land.

Their litany of complaints erupted into open rebellion. Korah, from the priestly Levite family, led two hundred and fifty tribal chieftains ("men of repute," according to the biblical text) in a revolt against the rule of Moses and Aaron and their claim of divine sanction. "You have gone too far," Korah rebuked Moses, demanding to know why they exalted themselves "above the Lord's congregation." Challenging the legitimacy of Aaron's priestly leadership, Korah complained that nepotism, not popular will, was its true source. Was it not enough, added his fellow rebels Dathan and Abiram with bitter irony, "that you brought us from a land flowing with milk and honey to have us die in the wilderness, that you would also lord it over us?"

Did Korah lead a rebellion against autocratic and nepotistic rule— or a mutiny of faithless and jealous dissenters? Was he a democrat or a demagogue, a disgruntled Levite jealous of Aaron's superior status or a lawless renegade? Did Korah and his followers deserve their swift punishment of death for challenging divine authority? History has been a consistent judge. In his *Antiquities of the Jews*, Josephus concluded that Korah's rebellion was "a sedition, for which we know no parallel whether among Greeks or barbarians." Bible scholar James L. Kugel agrees: Korah, challenging divine authority and the leadership of Moses and Aaron, was "a truly dangerous figure."

Josephus, to be sure, was no stranger to seditious behavior. Commander of besieged Jewish fighters in the Galilee fortress of Jotapata, he had deserted his soldiers to seek safe refuge in a cave, claiming divine approval for his treasonous action. After manipulating the drawing of lots with his fellow renegades to save his own life, he surrendered to Vespasian, hailing the Roman commander as "Caesar and emperor." Duly rewarded for his apostasy, Josephus became a patrician Roman scribe who brilliantly recounted the failed rebellion of his people, whose cause he had betrayed. He placed full blame for the catastrophe on the Jewish Zealots, who "trampled upon all the laws of man and laughed at the laws of God." For Josephus, the ultimate source of legitimate authority was power, which the conquering Roman legions decisively possessed.

After the fall of Jerusalem in 70 C.E., ruling authority passed from kings to rabbis, who became the law men of Judaism, teaching Jews to "love the Lord thy God," to "walk in his ways," and to "keep his commandments." Replacing political power with religious piety, rabbis located themselves in the line of legitimate succession as interpreters of divine law. The Torah might have originated in Heaven, but its explication became an earthly responsibility. Prohibiting resort to gentile courts whenever possible, rabbis creatively asserted their own legal authority. Oral rulings were eventually compiled in the legal code known as the Talmud, which the rabbis interpreted "to bring the whole of life into conformity with the will of God." The Torah became "a tree of life," deeply rooted in the past but carefully nurtured to permit new growth as changing circumstances required.

The variegated Jewish legal system, regulating everything from human theft to oxen that gored, combined "legal" principles (regarding trespass, damages and other crimes and misdemeanors) with "religious" instructions (for culinary and holy day observance) and "ethical" admonitions (for compassionate treatment of widows, orphans, and strangers). It was, Bible scholar Nahum Sarna has written, an "interweaving of the spiritual, the cultic, the moral, and legal" that distinguished Jewish law under a God who instructed his chosen people: "You shall . . . keep all my statutes, and all my judgments, and do them." God commanded, rabbis interpreted divine command, and Jews were instructed to obey.

But the absence of Jewish political sovereignty imposed stringent limits on the scope of rabbinical legal authority. The terms of accommodation were expressed in the guiding principle of *dina d'malkhuta dina* (the law of the state is the law). Retaining power over internal Jewish affairs involving community, family, and ritual issues, rabbis necessarily deferred to governing authorities on matters of state and conflicts between Jews and Gentiles. Over time, as state power expanded, rabbinical authority receded. The title of the *Shulhan Arukh* ("set table"), the authoritative sixteenth-century code compiled by Rabbi Joseph Caro, implied that legal creativity was largely relegated to the past. Yet Torah remained the living law in widely scattered communities of religiously observant Jews. Despite their loss of a national home and shared exilic history, they bound themselves to their sacred law tradition and were deferential to its rabbinical interpreters.

By the nineteenth century the terms of emancipation and the obligations of national citizenship required Jews, especially in Western Europe, to pledge their allegiance to the nation-state and to its laws. Rabbinical interpretation, largely confined to textual exegesis, was circumscribed by limited enforcement power and the expanding scope of state authority. Before the century ended, the first Zionist settlements had aroused the concern, suspicion, and eventual wrath of the entrenched Orthodox rabbinate. Its leaders perceived the determined young political activists who arrived in Palestine from Russia as *apikoros*, or heretics, whose impatience for national restoration challenged the divine timetable for redemption. Nor did assertive Zionist pioneers display much respect for ultra-Orthodox Jews, praying for divine salvation and dependant for their sustenance on donations from the diaspora. Their mutual antipathy endures in Israel more than a century later.

Jewish statehood was restored in 1948 amid a violent and tragic struggle over legitimacy—not between rabbis and secular authorities but among Zionists. A month after independence was declared, Prime Minister David Ben-Gurion, fearing a right-wing *putsch*, ordered Israeli soldiers to attack fellow Jews on board the *Altalena* and sink the Irgun ship that had arrived from Europe with desperately needed military supplies for the war against invading Arab armies. Fought with guns and cannons on the Mediterranean coast, the *Altalena* tragedy climaxed fifteen years of bitter internecine warfare that had plagued the Yishuv, the Jewish community in Palestine.

In the newborn State of Israel, the law of the Jewish state was the law. But the rabbinate quickly learned to wield power within the secular political system. In the *quid pro quo* of political bargaining, rabbis became shrewd, if often infuriating, political partners whose support helped to sustain the ruling Labor party in power for nearly thirty years and the right-wing Likud party thereafter. But secular-religious conflict remained a defining attribute of Jewish statehood. Israelis seemed to have inherited the biblical struggles between brothers—Cain and Abel, Isaac and Ishmael, Jacob and Esau—over the legitimacy of their birthrights.

In the decade that spanned Israel's victory in the Six-Day War and Menachem Begin's election as Israel's first right-wing prime minister, the contours of secular-religious conflict began to shift. The triumphant return of religious Zionist settlers to Gush Etzion and Hebron, where Jewish communities had been brutally destroyed during the pre-state years, reframed the struggle over legitimacy. Who decides where, in their promised land, Jews may live: settlers or the government; religious or secular Zionists; rabbis or politicians?

Israel's invasion of Lebanon in 1982, launched against Yasser Arafat's PLO for cross-border terrorist attacks that had claimed a high toll of civilian lives, polarized the nation and reframed its legitimacy struggles. As Israeli military casualties mounted, civilian protest rallies were accompanied by the first significant eruption of military disobedience in Israeli history. In unprecedented numbers soldiers challenged the authority of the Israel Defense Forces (IDF), the most powerful unifying institution in the nation.

Refusal to serve in Lebanon was followed by refusal to serve in Judea and Samaria (the West Bank)—and, for increasing numbers of young Israelis, refusal to serve anywhere in what they labeled the "occupying army" of the IDF. Once again soldiers confronted the tormenting questions that had erupted during the bloody confrontation over the *Altalena*: Must orders always be obeyed? When does individual conscience override military commands? Can a Jewish and democratic state devise terms of legitimacy for its fighting forces that reconcile competing sources of authority?

Ever since 1975, when the United Nations declared Zionism to be "a form of racism," Israel has confronted an escalating international challenge to its legitimacy. The UN often seems most united when its constituent members and collateral organizations castigate Israel for its illegal "occupation" of "Palestinian" land. In political, academic, media, and cultural circles, Israel has been demonized as a "racist," "apartheid," even "Nazi," state. It is the pariah nation that much of the world loves to hate. Unique in history for its unprecedented restoration of national sovereignty in its ancient homeland, Israel has inherited the stigma of anti-Semitism that stalked the Jewish people in exile for two thousand years.

Each of these legitimacy struggles—between left and right, secular and religious, soldiers and state, and for international acceptance—is explored in the chapters that follow. To be sure, Israel is hardly unique among nations in experiencing domestic turbulence over the sources of legitimate authority. England, France, Russia and China, among others, have suffered divisive revolutionary convulsions over the legitimacy of governing institutions and their rulers. Six decades after the founding of their nation, Americans waged a brutal four-year civil war to finally resolve the seemingly intractable issues of national and state power, freedom and slavery—and the ultimate question of governance, who decides?

Yet Israel remains a historic anomaly. No other people has reconstituted national sovereignty after nearly two thousand years of dispersion, persecution and attempted annihilation. The establishment and preservation of a democratic Jewish state, in a region where authoritarian Muslim nations and autonomous terrorist organizations vow to destroy it, is no less remarkable. Even with their state, Jews remain "a people that dwells alone" in an enduringly hostile world. Israel's internal and external struggles over legitimacy remain a defining feature of its history, its national life and, in all likelihood, its future.

1 War of Brothers

The perilous journey to Jewish statehood during the years of the British Mandate provoked fierce internal Zionist conflict over divergent strategies for securing national independence. The pioneering Zionist dream of a socialist utopia, with kibbutzim as the model for Jewish national renewal, was challenged by the Revisionist vision of a militantly nationalistic middle-class society grounded in entrepreneurial opportunity. Their respective political leaders David Ben-Gurion and Vladimir "Ze'ev" Jabotinsky might have agreed upon the goal of Jewish statehood but they disagreed sharply over the means for achieving it, its identity, and its defining ideological and geographical boundaries.

Ben-Gurion decried the "perverted national fanaticism" of Revisionism, with its "deceitful and foolish trumpet-calls of victory" that "becloud the moral purity of our national movement and distort the redemptive and humanitarian content of the Zionist idea." Even after devastating Arab riots erupted in 1929, when more than one hundred Jews were murdered and the ancient community of Hebron was brutally destroyed, Ben-Gurion was willing to accept temporary Zionist-Arab federation rather than independent Jewish statehood. But for Jabotinsky, "an iron wall," impervious to Arab enmity, was necessary to protect Zionist settlement and prepare for national sovereignty. As early as 1923 he perceived that "there is not even the slightest hope of ever obtaining the agreement of the Arabs of the Land of Israel to 'Palestine' becoming a country with a Jewish majority."

In the hothouse of Zionist politics in Palestine, set against Adolf Hitler's rise to power in Germany, it did not take long before these ideological polarities framed and then fractured the Jewish community. In June 1933, a murder on the beach north of Tel Aviv ignited bitter hostility between Zionist political rivals that would reach its tragic climax fifteen years later, only weeks after independence, when the Irgun ship *Altalena* arrived on the coast of Israel.

Chaim Arlosoroff, a rising leader in the Mapai party that dominated the governing Labor Zionist political coalition, had moved to Palestine a decade earlier after receiving his doctorate at the University of Berlin. To his astonishment, he encountered what he described as a "massive nation" of Arabs. This perception indelibly molded his vision of the Zionist future: "We have only one way: the road of peace; only one national policy: a policy of mutual understanding." To facilitate Arab-Jewish "coexistence," he strongly advocated "narrowing down the geographical area" of Zionist autonomy in Palestine. After the 1929 riots, he began to meet with Arab moderates in an attempt to develop a bi-national alternative to Jewish statehood.

In June 1933, Arlosoroff traveled to Germany as the representative of the Jewish Agency to negotiate an agreement with the new Nazi regime, which would permit German Jews to immigrate to Palestine with some financial assets. Their substantial remaining resources would be transferred to the German government for the purchase and shipment of raw materials, chemicals, fertilizer, and iron to Palestine. The result, Arlosoroff believed, would be mutually beneficial to German Jews, Nazis and Palestinian Zionists. The safe departure of wealthy Jews from Germany would be assured; the Third Reich, already confronting a worldwide trade boycott by Jewish organizations, would enjoy a profitable market for exports to Palestine; and the Zionist economy would benefit from the flow of Jewish capital and German goods (purchased with Jewish money). Responding in a "top secret" memo to sharp criticism of his negotiations with the Nazi regime, Arlosoroff castigated the misguided "sentimentality" of his critics.

As word of the transfer agreement spread, Arlosoroff was berated in Revisionist circles. Abba Achimeir, leader of Brit Habirionim (a right-wing faction that adopted the name, if not the tactics, of the first century Zealots), accused him of "putting a knife in the back of the Jewish people while attempting to stretch out the hand of friendship to the Hitler government." The nation's honor, he editorialized in his newspaper *Hazit Haam*, had "been sold to Hitler for a whore's wages." In a pamphlet entitled "Manifesto of the Sicarii," Achimeir warned that those who colluded with the "Roman enemy" might once again meet their fate at the hands of Jewish assassins. Brit Habirionim denounced Arlosoroff's transfer agreement with Nazis as a "pact with the devil."

Two days after Arlosoroff returned from Germany to his Tel Aviv home, *Hazit Haam* sharply criticized the alliance between the Labor Zionist Mapai party and Hitler: "There will be no forgiveness for those who have for greed sold out the honor of their people to madmen and anti-Semites." The Jewish people, it proclaimed ominously, knew how to respond to "betrayers of the nation."

That Friday evening, after dinner, Arlosoroff and his wife Sima strolled along the north Tel Aviv beach. She noticed two men following them, but her husband reassured her that they were Jews. Near a Muslim cemetery on the outskirts of the city, they were stopped. One man shined a flashlight in Arlosoroff's face and asked, in fractured Hebrew, for the correct time. The other shot him with a Browning automatic pistol. Both assailants fled. Sima screamed: "Jews shot him." Her husband responded: "No, Sima, no." Several hours later, before Arlosoroff died in Hadassah Hospital, he repeated to a visitor that his assassins were not Jews.

His murder triggered the question that has never been conclusively answered: Who killed Arlosoroff? Was it a Revisionist, an Arab nationalist, a British agent? Police arrested two Arabs who confessed to the murder. But from a photograph (and, perhaps, under police pressure), his widow identified Avraham Stavsky, an activist in the Revisionist Zionist youth organization Betar, as the man who held the flashlight, and Tzvi Rosenblatt, another Polish Revisionist, as Arlosoroff's assassin. Amid a wave of vitriolic political accusations and recriminations, police arrested both men along with journalist Abba Ahimeir, claiming that he was the mastermind of the assassination plot.

The Arlosoroff criminal investigation quickly became a legal travesty, laced with allegations of purchased confessions, false witnesses, and manufactured evidence. The Arabs who had confessed to the killing recanted. Ahimeir and Rosenblatt, tried for murder by a court comprising two British judges (one of whom was Jewish) and an Arab, were acquitted. Stavsky's conviction and death sentence were overturned on appeal for insufficient evidence.

Although culpability for Arlosoroff's murder was never established, Labor party politicians remained convinced of right-wing guilt. Its leaders and faithful journalist allies launched what Hebrew University political scientist Ehud Sprinzak describes as "an unprecedented delegitimation of the Revisionist movement . . . as fascist and terrorist." Ben-Gurion, leader of the party that had sent Arlosoroff to negotiate with Nazi Germany, blamed "*biryonim* [zealots] thirsty for our blood." Referring to Jabotinsky as "Vladimir Hitler," he demanded that the Yishuv be cleansed of the "malignant leprosy" infecting Arlosoroff's enemies. Chaim Weizmann, president of the World Zionist Organization, identified Revisionism with "Hitlerism . . . in its worst possible form."

The transfer agreement negotiated by Arlosoroff was an excruciating moral bargain that proved too painful for open discussion among Zionists for years afterward. On the Right, collaboration with the Nazi government was a heinous act; on the Left, the murder of Arlosoroff exposed its political opponents as fascists and terrorists. For some Jews, the Arlosoroff murder, and the highly politicized procedures and trials that followed in its aftermath, evoked memories of the civil war that had destroyed national sovereignty nineteen centuries earlier.

The Arab revolt that began in 1936, spreading terrorist violence throughout Palestine, reignited the smoldering hostility between rival Zionist factions. The Haganah defense force was committed to a policy of *havlaga* (restraint), which did not satisfy more militant Zionists. Revisionist leaders demanded *ayin tachat ayin* (the biblical admonition of "an eye for an eye"). Unconcerned with presenting a benign face to ruling British authorities, the right-wing Irgun, which had split off from the Haganah, fought Arab terror with Jewish terror. It attacked Arab buses and cars and placed lethal explosives in Arab neighborhoods.

British conciliation toward local Arab leaders, precisely as the noose of annihilation was tightening around European Jews, triggered Irgun retaliation. Redirecting its violent attacks from Arab to British targets, it bombed military bases and killed army officers. Whether this was anti-British "terrorism," as left-wing Zionists labeled it, or justified retaliation against a policy that would doom the Jews of Europe no less than the prospect of Jewish statehood, the toxic mix of British appeasement, Irgun militancy, and Haganah restraint drove another deep wedge into the Zionist movement.

In 1944 (four years after Jabotinsky's death), Menachem Begin became the new leader of the Irgun. He had risen through Revisionist ranks in Poland, endured imprisonment in Siberian labor camps, and served in the Polish Free Army in Palestine. Begin, like his mentor Jabotinsky, was infuriated by Ben-Gurion's policy of cooperation—or, as some alleged, collaboration—with Mandatory authorities. While Nazis slaughtered Jews by the millions in Europe, the British government strictly adhered to its restrictive immigration policy for Palestine. Begin issued a "Declaration of Revolt." Provoked beyond endurance by Ben-Gurion's deference to Great Britain, he decided that the time had come "to break through the gates from within" and fight for independence. "Our people is at war with this regime—war to the end."

But Ben-Gurion remained steadfastly convinced that cooperation with the British government would be more effective and cost fewer Jewish lives. It would also build necessary international support for Jewish statehood once the war in Europe ended. He wanted to persuade the British and other Western governments that Palestinian Jews, unlike their Arab neighbors, were "a civilized community and a reliable ally." Urged by some Irgun officers to retaliate against their Zionist opponents, Begin responded: "I will never lend a hand to a war of brothers." He focused his attention on the British, convinced that they would not leave until they were driven out. Attacks against the centers of Mandatory power in Palestine were, therefore, necessary and must continue.

But the tenuous alliance between the Zionist left and right began to unravel amid internal tension between the Haganah and the Palmach, its elite fighting force, and between the Irgun and its breakaway Lehi faction. Haganah commander Eliahu Golomb declared publicly: "The dissident organizations are causing untold damage to Zionist diplomacy. . . . If there is no alternative, we will have to fight against these crazy and damaging actions."

Soon afterward, Ben-Gurion sent an emissary, Dr. Moshe Sneh—Haganah commander and member of the Jewish Agency—to try to persuade Begin to moderate his militancy. Recognizing Ben-Gurion as the leader of the Yishuv, Begin said that he would accept his command only "when he begins the war against the [British] government." At a second meeting several weeks later, Sneh emphatically reminded Begin that the Provisional Government was the democratically elected leadership and demanded the cessation of military action. Begin was warned that the government was prepared to end Irgun operations "at all costs."

Begin was not deterred from independent military action. The Irgun underground, he wrote in his memoir (*The Revolt*), "arose to overthrow and replace a [British] regime. We used physical force because we were faced by physical force." But, he firmly insisted, there would be no civil war among Jews: "we did not teach the Irgun fighters to hate our political opponents. . . . As to who would ultimately rule the State . . .— that was unimportant." Ben-Gurion, determined to build the foundation for statehood without fighting the British, rejected "mad actions" that could destroy Zionism from within. But "if there is to be no alternative," he warned, "we shall face force with force."

One month later, two agents of the splinter group Lehi, enraged by British rule in Palestine and determined to avenge the murder of their leader Avraham Stern by British police two years earlier, assassinated Minister of State Lord Moyne in Cairo. Labor party leaders, unwilling to provoke conflict with the British and eager not to be equated with Lehi, condemned the murder and pursued what Ben-Gurion called "controlled" cooperation with British authorities. The choice, he asserted, was between "Zionist political struggle" and "terrorism." Chaim Weizmann, a loyal defender of British policy in Palestine, hastened to assure Prime Minister Winston Churchill, who had railed after Moyne's assassination against "a new set of [Jewish] gangsters worthy of Nazi Germany," that Palestinian Jewry "will go the utmost limit of its power to cut out this evil from its midst."

Taking a harder line, Ben-Gurion lacerated Jewish "criminals who endanger our future." He urged the Yishuv "to cast out all members of this underground gang" and pledged Labor Zionist cooperation with British authorities in "disgorging" terror. Golomb described a struggle between "Zionist democracy" and "Jewish Naziism." The *Histadrut*, the Zionist Labor federation, approved a policy of collaboration with British authorities in order to stifle the Irgun. But within the Jewish Agency there were dissenters from the turn toward punitive retaliation against fellow Jews. Rabbi Fishman-Maimon of the religious Mizrahi party, and Yitzhak Gruenbaum, of the General Zionist party, resigned from the executive committee in protest. Gruenbaum labeled collaboration with the British against fellow Zionists "the greatest tragedy" for the Zionist movement.

Determined to suppress political opposition, Ben-Gurion launched the notorious *"Saison,"* the hunting season, to pursue and arrest Irgun leaders. It was necessary to act, he asserted, "not just to talk." The Season triggered what Begin described as "an all out crusade by Haganah and the Jewish Agency for our destruction." As Jews turned against Jews, during a time (as Sprinzak concludes) of "unprecedented Jewish collaboration with the British against other Jews," angry words provoked hostile acts. But Begin reiterated to his Irgun followers: "There shall not be a war of brothers."

Nearly two hundred Palmach soldiers spearheaded the fight against Irgun dissidents, whose leaders were abducted and incarcerated in kibbutzim and nearby mountain caves. There they were interrogated, and occasionally tortured, before being turned over to British authorities who deported 251 Irgun fighters to Eritrea. The Jewish Agency intelligence service and the Haganah cooperated as informants for the Palestinian police and British Secret Service against their right-wing opponents. The names of hundreds of Irgun members, Weizmann informed Churchill, were transmitted to British authorities. Determined to fight the British, not other Jews, the Irgun refrained from retaliation. "Not civil war," Begin insisted. "Not that at any price."

From November 1944 until the following March, "hunting brothers" remained Labor Zionist policy. Begin, disguised as an Orthodox rabbi named Israel Sassover, went into hiding in a quiet residential neighborhood in Tel Aviv. He instructed his loyal fighters that regardless of the "terrible crime" inflicted against them by their Labor Zionist opponents, they must not retaliate. They obeyed their leader.

But in a proclamation drafted by Begin for public posting, the Irgun warned: "We Shall Repay You, Cain." In raging fury, it declared: "You rampage, Cain, ... not to war for freedom, but for war of brother against brother." While Jews were being slaughtered by the Nazis, and Palestine was closed to desperate Jewish refugees by the British government, "you chose yourself an ally, Cain: the oppressive regime in the homeland." Begin's bitter indictment followed: "You incite, inform, betray, abduct, and hand men over, Cain." Eventually, he warned, "Cain" would be judged with "German murderers" and English "betrayers."

The Season proved to be "a dismal triumph" for Ben-Gurion. The collaboration of his government with British police and soldiers against the Irgun, Sprinzak writes, "left a deep scar in the Israeli collective memory," covering a wound that never fully healed. Irgun restraint during the Season, he concluded, represented "one of Menachem Begin's finest moments."

By the end of World War II, as the unimaginable horrors of the Holocaust were revealed, shared anger over draconian British immigration restrictions in place ever since the 1939 White Paper reunited Palestinian Jews across their political divide. A United Resistance Movement was formed, comprising the Haganah, Irgun, and Lehi. But their brief period of unity lasted only until July 1946, when the Irgun in its most spectacular attack against the Mandatory government blew up a wing of the King David Hotel in Jerusalem, headquarters of the British administration in Palestine. Despite advance warnings to evacuate the building, which went unheeded by British authorities, nearly one hundred civilians—mostly British, but also Arabs and Jews—were killed.

Although Haganah commander Moshe Sneh had participated in the planning and ordered the attack, the Haganah, uninformed of its precise timing, immediately condemned it. British outrage impelled Ben-Gurion to disband the United Resistance Movement. His loathing of Begin, and the "terrorist mindset" of his Irgun "thugs and terrorists," rekindled internal Zionist acrimony. The Irgun was dispatched into political and moral exile, beyond the pale of Zionist legitimacy.

Yet for a brief moment in May 1948, when the Jewish nation proclaimed its independence in its ancient homeland, partisan discord yielded to national reconciliation. Religious and secular disagreements over the Jewish identity of a Jewish state had surfaced during the drafting process. Labor party preferences for territorial compromise clashed with right-wing yearning for "the greater land of Israel" within biblical borders. But in the founding text of the old-new nation, potentially divisive differences were carefully camouflaged with ambiguity.

Ben-Gurion, citing the American Declaration of Independence as a precedent for territorial vagueness, wrote: "A nation declaring its independence does not have to define its boundaries. We should say nothing about them because we don't know what they will be." The surging hostility of Israel's Arab neighbors, who rejected the United Nations partition agreement and were poised to annihilate a Jewish state within any borders, meant that boundaries would be decided by war, not by eloquent declarations.

The next evening, Menachem Begin delivered a radio address to the nation in which he exulted in "the first Hebrew revolt since the Hasmonean [Maccabean] insurrection that has ended in victory." Begin acknowledged: "One phase of the battle for . . . the return of the whole people of Israel to its homeland, for the restoration of the whole Land of Israel to its God-covenanted owners, has ended." But, he insisted, it was "only one phase." The "truncation of the homeland," he declared, "is illegal. It will never be recognized."

Speaking to the *Histadrut* three days later, Ben-Gurion conceded: "Our land was reduced, Jerusalem was made an international city . . . and our borders are bad from a political and military standpoint." But, he proudly asserted, "there has never been a greater achievement than this." Indeed, the Jewish people once again had their own state, if only within a sliver of their promised land. Years of struggle and sorrow, frustration and achievement, against the horrific backdrop of the annihilation of European Jewry, had finally been crowned with the restoration of Jewish statehood after nearly 1,900 years of exile.

Military supplies were desperately needed for survival. Yitzhak Ben-Ami, a leader of the Hebrew Committee for National Liberation, one of several Revisionist groups established to rally American support for the Jewish national cause, had met with Begin in Palestine to plan additional shipments of refugees and weapons. Upon his return to the United States Ben-Ami was contacted by Avraham Stavsky, the Revisionist activist who had been sentenced to death and then exonerated for the murder of Arlosoroff. They negotiated the purchase of a 4,000-ton, diesel-powered LST-138 that had participated in the D-Day invasion four years earlier to transport fighters and munitions to the nascent Jewish state.

Rescued from the mothballed American fleet on the Hudson River near West Point, the ship was moved to Gravesend in Brooklyn and named *Altalena*, once Jabotinsky's pen name (meaning "see-saw" in Italian). "We needed a name," explained Eliahu Lankin, commander of the Irgun in the diaspora, "that would be understood by the friends of Zion while remaining obscure to the rest of the world." Stavsky recruited Monroe Fein, a 25-year-old Navy veteran from Chicago who answered a local newspaper advertisement, to serve as captain. Fein had commanded a similar ship in the Pacific. He was, Lankin wrote, "an excellent seaman, intrepid, and . . . a Jewish patriot."

For nearly a year, while its sponsors struggled to obtain the necessary funding for the journey to Palestine, the *Altalena* marked time with a series of inconsequential voyages. It hauled potatoes from New Brunswick to Virginia and sailed to Florida for lumber. During the winter of 1947-48 it made stops in Cuba, Italy, France and Morocco before returning to Europe to await authorization for the departure to Palestine.

On May 15th, the day after Israel declared its independence, Begin delivered a radio address to the new nation. "Within the boundaries of the Hebrew independent state," he declared, "there is no need for a Hebrew underground. In the State of Israel, we shall be soldiers and builders. We shall respect its Government, for it is our Government." Outside the boundaries of the state, however, where "the homeland is not yet liberated," the Irgun would continue its military struggle. That meant Jerusalem, designated by the UN as an international city. As Shmuel Katz, a member of the Irgun high command and a close adviser to Begin, wrote: "We never forgot Jerusalem, where the Israeli government refused to claim sovereignty."

At midnight, Begin and three members of the Irgun high command—Yaakov Meridor, Chaim Landau and Katz—met with Yisrael Galili, former head of the Haganah who had recently become Ben-Gurion's Deputy Defense Minister. Galili was accompanied by Levi Eshkol from the Ministry of Defense. Begin informed them that the Irgun had purchased an American naval ship. Once bureaucratic problems in France were resolved, it would bring to Israel hundreds of volunteers for the army and substantial supplies of weapons. Ben-Gurion's representatives did not object.

The next day Ben-Gurion, serving simultaneously as Prime Minister and Defense Minister in the Provisional Government, informed its members that due to the shortage of rifles only 40 percent of Jewish military recruits could be armed. The situation, he warned, was "extremely serious." On May 26th, the government established the Israel Defense Forces as the army of the State of Israel and prohibited the "continued existence of any other armed force." The Irgun promptly announced that it would cease military operations inside the recognized borders of the new state.

One week later, Begin again met with government and military officers, including Galili and Yigael Yadin, head of military operations, to coordinate the integration of Irgun military units into the new Israeli army. Its battalions would join the Israel Defense Forces, while remaining unified under their own commanders. It would turn over its military supplies to the IDF and refrain from separate weapons purchases. Nothing was explicitly stated about Jerusalem, where the Israeli government would not exercise sovereignty. Begin assumed the freedom of Irgun military units (along with Lehi and Palmach fighters) to continue to engage in battle there, beyond the partition borders. The agreement was signed on June 3, 1948.

Since February the *Altalena* had been sailing between Marseilles and Casablanca, awaiting the opportunity—contingent on funding, availability of weapons, the coordinated arrival of passengers and crew, and permission from the French government—to depart for Palestine. In Marseilles, diplomatic officials from various countries closely monitored its activities. The American Consul General notified the Secretary of State that "a converted Liberty ship flying the Panamanian flag" had arrived from Genoa.

The local Panamanian consul boarded the ship and found it in "a lamentable state of sanitation, 'the dirtiest he had ever seen.'" Detecting no signs of adequate equipment for loading or handling cargo, he notified local police that it was "suspicious" and informed Captain Fein not to "attempt to engage in any improper activities if he expected to sail the vessel from this port." The consul, his American counterpart reported, "had in mind the Palestine situation." Haganah agents also came on board to explore possibilities for supplementing the shipment with weapons for their own military forces. Negotiations were halted, Fein recalled, after they received orders from Israel "to have nothing to do with the *Altalena*."

The Irgun commander in Europe responsible for coordinating the *Altalena* expedition was Eliahu Lankin. Born in Russia, he grew up in China and came to Palestine in 1933. Active in the Irgun, he was arrested by the British in 1944 and sent to a detention camp in Eritrea, from which he escaped. Based in Paris after the war, he scouted Europe for military supplies to sustain the struggle for Jewish independence.

The departure of the ship depended, in the end, on permission from the government of France. "In reality," Lankin subsequently conceded, "we had nothing to offer the French in return for their arms." But the Irgun could provide assurance that "these arms would be used to liberate our country from the tyranny of British rule and to defend ourselves from the invading Arab armies. If the fulfillment of this aim also harmed the prestige of France's traditional enemy [England], then we could only be grateful for this confluence of goals." In the end, that convergence of interests proved decisive.

On May 29th the *Altalena* moved from Marseilles to nearby Port-du-Bouc. One week later, the French Minister of Armed Forces as instructed by the Foreign Minister's office signed a secret agreement with the Irgun. France would deliver the requested munitions, valued at more than 150 million francs. Described by a critical French official as a "war operation" conducted "outside any regular procedure," the agreement was vaguely identified as a decision of the Government "for reasons of foreign policy."

French army trucks, driven by soldiers under the command of French army officers and loaded with military supplies, arrived in Port-du-Bouc. A Haganah representative in Paris informed Ben-Gurion by cable that the *Altalena* would be transporting immigrants and weapons. The arsenal included 300 Bren guns, 50 German Spender guns, 500 anti-tank guns, 1,000 grenades and 5 million rounds of ammunition. "It was my understanding," Captain Fein recalled, "that all preparations were being made with the full knowledge and acquiescence of the Israel government." Just before departure, Fein subsequently reported, "a messenger returned from Palestine" with communication procedures and landing instructions. He understood this to mean that the arrival of the *Altalena* "had been completely agreed to and approved by the government" of Israel.

At twilight on June 11th, just before the beginning of the Jewish Sabbath and a United Nations ceasefire, the *Altalena* pulled away from the same port where the refugee ship *Exodus* had departed eleven months earlier. Nearly a thousand people on board sang *Hatikvah*. At midnight Irgun leaders heard a BBC broadcast that Israel and warring Arab states had accepted the ceasefire. Under its terms, the importation of arms and men of military age was prohibited for one month. The BBC also reported that an Irgun ship, transporting military supplies and hundreds of fighting men, had sailed from Port-du-Bouc. The American Consul in Marseilles sent an "Urgent" cable to the State Department reporting the departure of a "Jewish immigrant ship" for Palestine with "800 Jewish volunteers and a shipment of arms."

The BBC broadcast caught Irgun leaders on board by surprise. "We had not expected this international announcement of our secret mission," Lankin conceded. "Now with the world apprised of our movements, the probability of an attack stared us brutally in the face." But no one imagined that the attack would come from the government and army of the State of Israel.

In Tel Aviv, Menachem Begin heard a repeat of the BBC broadcast and decided to stop the ship, at least temporarily, while the truce remained in force. His aide Zipporah Levy repeatedly radioed his orders to the *Altalena*: "Keep away—await instructions." Begin, she remembered, "was very calm but determined to stop them." But no one aboard the *Altalena*, cut off by faulty radio connections from their command in Israel and support staff in Paris, could hear the urgent message.

Dismissing the potential hazards of the mission, Irgun leaders were determined to complete it. "We regarded the war in Israel as a life-and-death struggle," Lankin wrote, and the military supplies on the *Altalena* "could change the course of the war." In anticipation of a British naval attack on the ship, machine guns were mounted on deck. American and British soldiers with World War II experience, led by a commando who had served in France and a former marine who had fought in the Pacific, underwent rigorous daily training to form the nucleus of a special fighting unit should there be an emergency landing in "hostile territory." With the possibility of an extended journey to wait out the truce, food and water were carefully rationed.

That night Fein, Stavsky and Lankin gathered in the radio room to resume attempts to contact their commanders in Israel. "We had almost given up when, through the static, we heard a young woman's voice calling our code names." It was Begin's personal secretary, Yael, repeating a message in English: "Listen to me: Keep away! Keep away!" But no further radio contact was possible. Begin wired Irgun headquarters in Paris: "She can't come home now." To Lankin, the Irgun commander on board, "it was almost unbearable to contemplate the thought of the *Altalena*'s precious cargo never reaching the shores of Israel. I told Fein to continue en route to Israel with all possible speed."

Even before leaving Port-du-Bouc the *Altalena* had been closely monitored by Israeli intelligence agents. They knew the contents of its cargo, its departure date and its destination in Israel. Nonetheless, news of its leaving aroused mounting suspicion in government and military circles. Isar Harel, director of the Haganah intelligence service that carefully monitored its journey, suspected that its weapons would be used for Irgun purposes contrary to government policy. Palmach Colonel Meir Pa'il was dismayed that although the government itself was continuing to import weapons covertly in violation of the cease-fire, the Irgun was engaging in a flamboyant public display of disobedience.

On June 15th, Begin met once again with Deputy Defense Minister Galili to update the government on the *Altalena*. The purpose of the meeting, according to Begin, was to provide representatives of the Defense Ministry with "all the information about the *Altalena* and to request the government's decision as to whether the ship should or should not arrive during the ceasefire." An aide presented "the details about the *Altalena*, its people and equipment." Begin remained willing "that the government decide and tell us whether the *Altalena* should proceed and arrive in Israel, or whether we should send it back." His proposal that its weapons and munitions be stored in Irgun warehouses, under joint supervision with the IDF, was rejected. Galili promised to respond further after consultation with his superiors, meaning, of course, Ben-Gurion.

The next morning, Galili telephoned Begin: "We agree to the arrival of the vessel. As quickly as possible." To avoid UN aerial surveillance the ship was instructed to land at Kfar Vitkin, a moshav near Netanya, eighteen miles north of Tel Aviv. Lankin was delighted with the news. Kfar Vitkin, after all, was a Haganah stronghold: "If Begin was ordering us to anchor at Kfar Vitkin—the lion's den of the Irgun's political adversaries in Israel—then an agreement must have been negotiated between us." It was, for Lankin, "a clear sign of cooperation in the *Altalena*'s landing—a sign of internal harmony, of brotherhood." For Begin, "worry was replaced by joy."

On June 16th, Ben-Gurion mentioned the *Altalena* in his diary for the first time: "Tomorrow or the next day their ship is due to arrive." He noted, in detail, its military contents, concluding: "They should not be turned back. They should be sent to an unknown beach." The government plan, according to Haganah intelligence chief Harel, was to equip Irgun units to fight anywhere beyond Israeli rule. That meant Jerusalem.

But there remained an ominously unresolved problem: the distribution of weapons and munitions. Ben-Gurion understood the June 3rd meeting to have assured that the Irgun would place "all its weapons and military equipment at the disposal of the High Command of the Israel Defense Forces." Begin, consistent with his own understanding of the agreement, had continued to insist that twenty percent of the weapons would be allocated for the Irgun fighting forces in Jerusalem. He wanted the remainder to go to Irgun units in the Israel Defense Forces or be stored in their own armories.

Galili, according to Shmuel Katz, a member of the Irgun High Command, "indicated that the request for Jerusalem would be considered favorably." (According to Ben-Gurion's diary, however, "Yisrael [Galili] told me that IZL, contrary to his instructions, decided to send weapons to Jerusalem.") Galili did not agree that the remaining eighty percent of the weapons would be distributed directly to Irgun battalions in the IDF. Their understanding, Galili insisted, stipulated that the Irgun must turn over all military equipment and weapons to the Israel Defense Forces "without any conditions."

There was disagreement among Begin's advisers, some of whom, Hillel Kook most emphatically, rejected any precedent for distributing weapons in the army according to political quotas. After the group reached consensus, Begin telephoned Galili to report their revised position: "We insist on one condition only—20% of the arms should go to the Irgun in Jerusalem. The rest goes to the I.D.F. units according to general staff decisions." Galili agreed, but rejected Begin's insistence that the remainder go solely to Irgun units in the Israel Defense Forces.

Under pressure from Katz, who opposed discrimination either for or against the Irgun, Begin again telephoned Galili and agreed that the remainder would go to the army. But no agreement was reached as to where the arms would be stored and under whose control. Despite Begin's concessions, Galili advised Ben-Gurion that "a new and dangerous situation has arisen: a demand for a kind of private army, with private weapons, for certain units in the army." Ben-Gurion was fiercely determined that Zionist factionalism must yield to a unitary government and military under his exclusive command. He would not tolerate the existence of "private armies"—neither on the right or left.

Within the fledgling Jewish state a fierce struggle was simmering over political, no less than geographical, boundaries. For fifteen years, ever since the Arlosoroff murder, left and right had clashed over the meaning and future of Zionism and the source of political authority and legitimacy in the nascent state. After barely one month of national sovereignty, their struggle was about to reach its tragic climax on the beaches of Kfar Vitkin and Tel Aviv.

Shortly before sunset on June 19th, *Altalena* passengers and crew caught their first glimpse of the coast of Israel. "Our Zionist volunteers from all over the world," Lankin remembered, "soldiers, exiles, concentration camp survivors, people who had lost so much and had so much to gain—all clung to the deck railings and strained their eyes.... We had reached the Promised Land." The ship sailed along the coast searching for the twin red signal lights that marked its destination. It finally arrived at the Kfar Vitkin beach after midnight, but high waves prevented landing. It was instructed to pull back out to sea and return the next evening.

That night Ben-Gurion called the Cabinet into emergency session. There were reports that Irgun soldiers were leaving their IDF units to assist in the unloading of weapons on the beach. Foreign Minister Moshe Shertok warned the ministers: "We may now be facing a blatant, public violation of the truce by Jews, without our being personally responsible for it. I am speaking here of an Etzel [Irgun] operation." Ben-Gurion restated the June 3rd agreement under which the Irgun had promised "to put all its weapons and military equipment at the disposal of the High Command of the Israel Defense Forces" and "cease operations within the State of Israel and all areas under the jurisdiction of the Government of Israel."

Ben-Gurion was adamant: "There are not going to be two armies. And Mr. Begin will not do whatever he feels like. We must decide whether to hand over power to Begin or tell him to cease his separatist activities. If he does not give in, we shall open fire." The Cabinet unanimously agreed, providing Ben-Gurion with the legitimate authority he needed: "The Government charges the Defense Minister with taking action in accordance with the laws of the land." Ben-Gurion noted bluntly: "Taking action means shooting."

After sailing west for eight hours the *Altalena* turned back toward Israel. During the aborted landing the night before, Captain Fein had discovered that that an underwater shelf prevented the ship from reaching shore. He halted the *Altalena* forty meters from the end of a small pier extending from the beach. It was 9 p.m. on Sunday, June 20.

Menachem Begin came from shore by motorboat to greet the new arrivals, who responded with "an ear-splitting cheer." They "milled around him, drunk with excitement." Irgun fighters "touched him, they shook his hand, they called out thank you, congratulations and endearments." Landing the *Altalena*, wrote Shmuel Katz, "seemed a fitting last act" for the Irgun. For Begin, "it was a great and historic occasion," symbolically ending his long struggle as an underground renegade.

Within two hours, as Irgun fighters departed in units, nearly all the passengers had disembarked. From the beach they were transported to a camp in nearby Netanya where they could rest briefly before their induction into the army. Then the arduous task of unloading cargo began. Several dozen men remained behind to bring the crates of weapons to shore in a launch, two lifeboats, and small craft provided by local volunteers. Some Palmach men arrived, ostensibly to help, but after boarding and inspecting the ship they departed and were not seen again. On the beach, an observer recalled, "khaki-clad men ran about shouting orders; groups marched in all directions; motors revved up."

But amid the euphoria there were ominous signs. Earlier that night Captain Fein had noticed "two unidentified ships" a mile offshore, recognized at daybreak as Israeli navy corvettes. Israeli naval commander Paul Shulman (a United States Navy veteran who had served as a deck hand on board the *Exodus*) ordered the corvettes to approach the *Altalena* and monitor the debarkation and unloading, which proceeded "slowly and in a disorderly manner." He observed "about a hundred armed IZL men" on the beach, "but not at the ready. . . . They were not arranged for defense. They worked slowly, not in a hurry or *schvitz* [sweat]." The Irgun men, Shulman noted, "nicely welcomed the people in our boat."

Reports filtered in that Irgun soldiers who had left their IDF units to help with the unloading had been stopped and detained on the road from Netanya. Israeli soldiers under the command of Moshe Dayan had begun to surround the debarkation area. Begin's chief of operations, Amihai Paglin, advised him to return the weapons to the ship, which should pull back to sea until the truce ended. Begin would not consider the suggestion. He seemed unruffled, assuring Lankin that "an arrangement" with the government was imminent.

In a military staff meeting attended by Chief of Operations Yadin, army officers were briefed by Galili. According to Dan Even, commander of the Alexandroni Brigade on the beach at Kfar Vitkin, Galili reported the impending arrival of "a boat filled with arms and ammunition." Galili acknowledged: "We knew the arms were due to arrive and reached an agreement whereby we and they were to unload the arms together." But following Galili's briefing, and with Yadin's authorization, Even prepared for the possibility of military action.

The next morning the Government Press Office announced: "The Government regards this attempt by an independent group to bring in arms, particularly during the truce period, as a grave violation of Israel's laws and of her international obligations, as well as an infringement of the clear agreement reached recently with the heads of Etzel . . . [who] were to accept the authority of the State." The government and military command "are determined to stamp out immediately this traitorous attempt to deny the authority of the State of Israel and of its representatives."

When last-minute attempts to reach agreement failed, Galili drafted an ultimatum for Commander Even to deliver to Begin. It ordered "confiscation of all weapons and war materials," to be turned over to the State of Israel and placed with Even for safekeeping. Shortly before noon on June 21st, Even delivered the message to Irgun leaders on the Kfar Vitkin beach. If military supplies were not relinquished, he warned, "I will immediately use all the means at my disposal to implement the order. . . . You have ten minutes in which to reply." The purpose of the operation, Even instructed his officers, "is to force the Irgun to turn over to the Army the weapons that arrived on the LST." Ben-Gurion demanded: "Either they accept orders and carry them out, or [we] shoot." Rejecting further negotiations, he insisted: "The time for agreements has passed . . . [and] force must be applied without hesitation." In his own handwriting, Ben-Gurion added: "*Immediately.*"

On board the *Altalena*, Lankin was "stunned" by the ultimatum. Begin tried to reassure him that Meridor would meet with Even to reach an understanding to prevent bloodshed. A United Nations plane flew low overhead; the Israeli navy corvettes moved into position to block passage to the west; word arrived that Israeli soldiers had surrounded the beachhead. Kfar Vitkin had been completely sealed off by Commander Even's soldiers.

At a nearby military airport orders were received to prepare several planes for a possible bombing run over the *Altalena*. One of the pilots, Boris Senior, had served in the British Royal Air Force during World War II. After the war ended and he learned about the Holocaust he joined the Irgun, immigrated to Palestine, and enlisted in the air force. Ordered to take off and bomb the *Altalena*, he angrily refused: "I will never be capable of bombing my Jewish brethren." When other pilots also decided not to participate, the mission was aborted.

Late that afternoon, Begin summoned several dozen Irgun men on the beach into formation to apprise them of negotiations with the IDF. He walked inside their open rectangle and began to speak. Suddenly IDF soldiers raked the beach with machine-gun bullets and mortar shells. Within moments, Yitzhak Ben-Ami recalled, "we were in a state of uncontrolled siege." Yaakov Meridor, Begin's second in command, ordered: "Don't shoot back." An Irgun fighter realized: "I couldn't shoot. My brother was on the other side." "We were confused and ashamed at the same time," another remembered, "instead of welcoming us they were killing and wounding many of our men whose only purpose was to help."

With darkness falling, Ben-Ami and a friend from their Betar youth movement days took refuge in a sandy foxhole. Ben-Ami asked if he had read Josephus. "Do you remember the description of the final days in the defense of Jerusalem . . . [when] the Judeans continued to massacre each other . . . Doesn't this look like the Third destruction of the Temple?" Ben-Ami recalled: "Thus I spent my first night on the soil of free Israel, dodging the bullets of my brothers."

In the wheelhouse of the *Altalena*, Julian Berenson, a 43-year-old American navy veteran, lifted his rifle "to shoot . . . those who were shooting at us. But then I thought: Who am I, going to shoot and kill Jews! And I put my rifle down." Some IDF soldiers refused to obey orders. Yeshayahu Yarimi protested: "I'm here to fight the enemy. I won't fight another Jew." He instructed the soldiers in his squad: "Do what your conscience tells you." Yarimi was one of eight soldiers to be court-martialed for their disobedience that day. Six Irgun men and two IDF soldiers died in the fighting at Kfar Vitkin. The years of animosity between Zionist political enemies had finally, and catastrophically, exploded in violence.

As chaos erupted on the beach, Captain Fein suspected "a sneak Arab attack." He restarted the engines, intending to head out to sea to protect the ship. But the Irgun high command—Begin, Stavsky, Lankin, and Merlin—had decided to board the *Altalena* and sail south to Tel Aviv. Begin wanted an opportunity to communicate directly with the government and, according to Shmuel Katz, "put an end to what [he] still hoped was a perilous misunderstanding somewhere." The Irgun could also expect stronger public support in Tel Aviv than Kfar Vitkin. ("Whatever plots were brewing in Ben-Gurion's mind," Ben-Ami wrote, "could not be carried out in Tel-Aviv, in full view of thousands of people.") When the launch carrying the Irgun leaders came under machine-gun fire from the navy corvettes Fein maneuvered the *Altalena* to provide a shield, enabling them to board safely.

Commander Even informed the government that the Irgun had surrendered and agreed to turn over all weapons on shore to the IDF. Under army supervision, armored vehicles left the beach packed with English rifles, Bren guns and ammunition. An Israeli army communique reported that the Kfar Vitkin beach had been "seized by the dissidents" (who, in fact, had been instructed by the government to land there). As an IDF army unit approached them, it continued, "the Irgun opened fire using machine-guns, anti-tank weapons and one mortar" (an "attack" uncorroborated by any other source). The army's objective had been "to force unconditional surrender" and compel the Irgun to relinquish weapons and vehicles and abide by military orders. Ben-Gurion wrote in his diary: "IZL Day. What was destined to happen—finally happened." He enumerated the military supplies that were seized at Kfar Vitkin: 2,080,000 English cartridges, 1,473 English rifles, 30 to 40 Bren guns, 5 English piats, 3,300 English piat shells, and 60 boxes filled with other weapons. The crisis seemed to have abated.

Trailed down the coast by navy vessels, there were intermittent gunfire exchanges as the *Altalena* maneuvered to prevent another ship from slipping between it and the shore. Shortly after midnight on June 21 the *Altalena* ran aground, 150 meters off the Tel Aviv beach at the end of Frishman Street, opposite Palmach headquarters in the Ritz Hotel. Captain Fein remembered: "We hit the beach at top speed and settled down to await daylight and further developments."

There was a flurry of attempts to resolve the crisis without renewed violence. Several local village mayors approached Ben-Gurion, who spent the night at army headquarters in Ramat Gan outside Tel Aviv, to demand a ceasefire. Unknown to the Prime Minister, Interior Minister Gruenbaum had met with Avraham Stavsky to discuss the distribution of weapons from the *Altalena*. Gruenbaum's independent action infuriated other ministers. "The main question here," Shertok had insisted at the Cabinet meeting the day before, "is the sovereignty of the State of Israel. . . . We must use every means at our disposal, including military force, to make Etzel accept Government policy." To Labor Minister Mordechai Bentov there was "no alternative: either the Government acts as a government should, or it will be clear to the entire world that it is helpless. We cannot retreat."

Ben-Gurion reiterated: "The State's authority is the main principle." The lines were clearly drawn, he insisted: "There can be no State without an army under the control of the Government." The arrival of the *Altalena* off the Tel Aviv shore, and reports received by Deputy Chief of Staff Zvi Ayalon that Irgun soldiers who had abandoned their posts were arriving in Tel Aviv with "plans to attack IDF headquarters," stoked fears of an insurrection.

Thirty minutes after the *Altalena* beached, Yadin conferred with Galili before reporting to Ben-Gurion. Hearing his report, Ben-Gurion decided that force was inevitable. At an urgent 4 a.m. meeting, Chief of Naval Operations Shmuel Yanai assured Ben-Gurion that the *Altalena* could be disabled without gunfire by using smoke grenades and boarding the ship from nearby navy vessels. But the Prime Minister, Yanai recalled, was "pacing nervously from side to side, talking and yelling." He was "upset and angry. . . . He shouted at everyone." Yanai concluded: "His aim was . . . to destroy the munitions on the *Altalena*" as the only way to prevent civil war. Ben-Gurion demanded that "the ship be turned over to the Government immediately, and if necessary use force to back up that demand."

Unwilling to negotiate further with the Irgun, Ben-Gurion insisted upon compelling "the enemy . . . to unconditional surrender, by all the means and methods available." After considering various alternatives, including permitting the *Altalena* to sail peacefully away, the Cabinet decided by a 7-2 vote "to demand that the ship be turned over to the State."

Ben-Gurion ordered Commander Yadin to act in accordance with the Cabinet decision. The General Staff issued orders, signed by Yadin, to the Kiryati Brigade, the Artillery Corps, the Navy, and Air Force, "to bring the enemy on the ship docked at Tel Aviv harbor to surrender by all means at our disposal. . . . Be ready for the beginning of the operation and opening of fire, according to my order and in line with the instructions of the government of Israel." There would be "warning fire"; then a demand for "unconditional surrender"; finally, if necessary, "a continued operation until it reaches a conclusion."

At a press conference, Foreign Minister Shertok announced: "The Government is resolved to maintain its sovereignty and its ability to fulfill its international obligations. It will not permit undisciplined armed groups to foster political and military anarchy. The Etzel ship must be turned over to the Government immediately and unconditionally." Nothing, he insisted, was more important than "upholding State authority." Galili, who had represented the government in negotiations with Begin since mid-May, added (erroneously): "the I.Z.L. has broken the agreement. They did not inform us of the date of the boat's arrival nor where it was going to anchor." (He either did not know, or ignored, Ben-Gurion's explicit instructions for the Kfar Vitkin landing.) With the State "engaged in civil war," Galili asserted, the government had "no choice but to resort to force."

But there were problems with the government plan. Just as pilots had refused to bomb the *Altalena* at Kfar Vitkin, Haganah commander Michael Ben-Gal expressed doubts that he could "rouse his men to the action" ordered by the government. The High Command turned instead to the Palmach, certain that its "ideological animus toward the dissenters" would overcome any constraints. Yigal Allon, the Palmach commander who had played a significant role in combating the Irgun during the Season, was instructed by the General Staff to launch operation "Purge" against IZL "forces" comprising several dozen men (including Begin) still on board the *Altalena*.

Ben-Gurion told him, Allon recounted, "Yigal, we are facing an open rebellion.... The entire future of this country is in the balance." In a dramatic tone, he demanded: "Get Begin!" Yadin added: "You might have to kill Jews." Allon suggested that a cannon be deployed; if the Irgun did not surrender, it would be fired. Yadin and Ben-Gurion agreed. Allon was convinced (according to biographer Anita Shapira) "that he was fighting against the forces of fascism threatening to take over the state." The Kiryati brigade was supplied with a battery of 65-mm cannons.

At 8:30 that morning a 26-year-old Palmach officer, Yitzhak Rabin, arrived at Palmach headquarters at the Ritz Hotel. He was looking for his girl friend Leah, who worked for the information department. Informed by Allon that Irgun men from the *Altalena* were "trying to take control of the beach and unload the arms," Rabin was appointed commander of the Palmach headquarters building. "Rumor follows rumor," he remembered: "The IZL wants to take over all of Tel Aviv . . . no, even that is not enough . . . it intends to forcibly take control of the new state." Outside Palmach headquarters, "confusion reigns. No one knew what to expect."

In mid-morning, a launch was lowered from the ship carrying a dozen men, 30 rifles, 6 submachine guns and one anti-tank bazooka. From the *Altalena* bridge Joe Kohn observed "truck-loads of soldiers taking up positions on houses and high ground above the beach." As the launch approached shore, two machine-gun crews were ordered to fire; they refused. Their commander, Moshe Keren, was ordered to shoot at his insubordinate soldiers. He replied: "Not that." His superior officer arrived to command the crews to open fire; again they refused. Elsewhere on the beach flurries of gunfire targeted the new Irgun arrivals. The launch, quickly unloaded by Irgun men on shore, returned to the ship.

After a piat shell exploded below Palmach headquarters (Rabin recalled in a 1983 interview), "we arrive[d] at the conclusion that there is no choice but to wipe them out from our midst. . . ." Rabin and another officer went to the roof and threw grenades at "the separatist forces" on the beach. Rabin remembered: "Irgun people got hurt. One of their units raised a white flag. They requested a pause to evacuate the wounded. We called for ambulances." While the battle raged, hundreds of Israelis gathered near the beach to watch Jews attacking Jews.

When the launch left the *Altalena* at 11:30 to return to shore, "all hell broke loose." Bursts of gunfire from IDF positions on the beach, and from overlooking buildings, strafed the shore and the ship. "We were suddenly in the midst of war," Lankin realized, "yet it was not Arabs or British firing upon us, spilling our blood, but our fellow Jews." Two *Altalena* crew members were killed and Irgun leader Avraham Stavsky was mortally wounded. He died, Eri Jabotinsky wrote bitterly, on the same beach where Arlosoroff was murdered—"and at the hands of the same man, Ben-Gurion, who had unsuccessfully tried to hang him then."

To Arbel Zerubavel, Yigal Allon's intelligence officer, it was clearly "a rebellion against the State of Israel," requiring that the "dissidents" be "wiped out." Zerubavel had "no hesitation" about firing, nor did he have "even a shadow of regret." Allon, he remembered, acted without "any hesitation about *milchemet achim* [war of brothers]." But Palmach soldier Amnon Dror recalled: "Firing on each other: it seemed illogical, unbelievable. I had many doubts, when I pointed the gun at the approaching boat filled with Jews." But he overcame them: "You tell yourself, you are guarding Israeli democracy. And with this belief, you shoot."

Some soldiers in the Kiryati Brigade, "unable to face the difficult necessity to prevent the acts of the IZL," left their weapons behind and departed from the beach. In the Mahal regiment of foreign volunteers David Migdal witnessed "Jews killing other Jews" and refused to participate. Given the choice by their commander to obey orders or go to jail, Mahal soldiers carried their weapons without ammunition. Irgun member Abba Groznick remembered: "If Begin had told us to fight we would have, but he did not want war between brothers and we accepted his leadership." Irgun fighters did not return fire.

The government convened an emergency meeting shortly after noon to deal with the crisis. Ben-Gurion was sharply challenged by right-wing and religious party members, led by Interior Minister Gruenbaum, who accused Galili of reporting falsely and Ben-Gurion of obstructing efforts to end the crisis without violence. Gruenbaum insisted: "We must negotiate . . . the 800 immigrants who came on the ship have already been removed and dispersed." But Agriculture Minister Aharon Zizling responded: "We are facing an open rebellion. . . . A political coup is being deliberately aimed against the army command." Ben-Gurion warned: "This is an attempt to destroy the army. This is an attempt to kill the state." There would be "no negotiations—but only surrender of the ship to the Government and acceptance of all army orders." By a 7-2 vote, the Irgun was instructed to surrender the *Altalena*.

On the beach Rabin managed to reach an agreement with Irgun fighters to stop the shooting before it provoked "a mutual massacre." Negotiations foundered over the government demand for an unconditional Irgun surrender and relinquishment of all weapons to the IDF. But by early afternoon a tenuous cease-fire was in place. At 4 p.m., Ben-Gurion ordered Yadin (who subsequently claimed that he only intended "warning shots") to resume firing.

"All of a sudden," recalled a Haganah soldier, "we heard a shot from the north. . . . It was a cannon." The crew commander, Hilary Dilesky, was a South African volunteer who had arrived in Israel only two months earlier. There were four cannons in his battery; his was chosen to fire the first shot. Receiving his orders, he recalled, "I suddenly was struck with a heavy, deep feeling that I didn't want to shoot."

Dilesky approached a group of high-ranking officers to speak to his corps commander. He said, in English for he could not yet speak Hebrew: "I hadn't come to Israel to fight Jews." The commander shouted that his job was to obey orders. It was, Dilesky recalled nearly fifty years later, "a fateful moment" when he realized that "following orders was the right thing to do." But, he added, "My heart was broken when we began firing. This has been a burden all my life, and still is."

In rapid succession, three cannon shells passed near the *Altalena*, exploding harmlessly in the sea. Captain Fein conferred with Begin, advising him that with a direct hit, "the ship, the cargo and possibly a good many lives would be lost." Before Begin could renew radio contact with Irgun headquarters on shore, the cannon fire resumed. Fein ordered the Star of David lowered and raised a white flag of surrender. Moments later, a cannon shell slammed into the *Altalena*, igniting a blazing fire in the cargo hold. Crewmen raced below to open the hose valves but they were unable to extinguish it. "Smoke billowed from all the portholes and ventilators," Lankin remembered; "the deck was enveloped in a thick black pall." Fein ordered everyone to abandon ship.

On board the nearby *Wedgwood*, navy doctor Shalom Weiss saw the white flag waving from the *Altalena*. But shooting from the beach continued: "Rifle and machine-gun fire kept hitting living targets." On the navy ship *Eilat*, crew member Eli Warshavsky watched "escaping men shot in the water." From the beach Azriel Carlebach, editor of the daily newspaper *Ma'ariv*, witnessed "Jewish young men . . . with steel helmets on their heads and machine guns in their hand, ready to fire. . . . In the sea, on the mast of the ship, and on its deck, Jews stand, waving a white flag, and shouting: 'Don't fire!'" But as men jumped overboard, Joe Kohn observed from the *Altalena* bridge that "continuous small arms fire from shore . . . was directed at everyone in the water." A 17-year-old Haganah soldier never forgot that "there were people on our side who waited until they saw heads above water, and then they fired at them."

Uri Yarom, a young Palmach soldier (who would command Israel's first helicopter squadron), was stunned by what he witnessed: "The wounded were being lowered off the boat. From the shore people started swimming toward them to offer help, but from the hotel and nearby houses indiscriminate shots were aimed at the helpless wounded and those who swam to rescue them!" He long remembered the fighter wearing a *Hashomer Hatzair* (Socialist Zionist) uniform "who directed the snipers to their targets and pointed to each head that bobbed above the water's surface. . . . Before my eyes was waged a war between brothers. Jews are shooting Jews—in order to kill!" A French volunteer swimming ashore was hit by gunfire and drowned. Israel Gorelnik, a 20-year-old Palmach soldier, was assigned the "very difficult" task of guarding Irgun fighters who arrived amid the gunfire. They asked him: "What are you doing to us?"

It was chaotic and traumatic: "screams in the water pierced the air, bullets were spraying the decks and whistling everywhere." Irgun men on the beach, Rabin recalled, were in "total hysteria," shouting "Begin is on the ship." Palmach soldiers, excited at the prospect of finally eliminating their political nemesis, opened fire "as if from a feeling of wanting to kill Begin." The Irgun leader remained on board, supervising the lowering of the wounded, including the dying Stavsky, into small kayaks that were frantically rowed out from shore. Begin was among the last to leave, followed by Lankin and Fein who jumped into the sea just before a series of violent explosions engulfed the *Altalena* in flames. "In the final salvo," Lankin wrote, "millions of bullets from the crates exploded, a dream gone up in smoke and fire."

That day in Tel Aviv, ten men from the *Altalena* and one IDF soldier were killed in the fighting. It was, Rabin remembered, "a terrible day, a black day." But he remained convinced that Ben-Gurion had made the "brave decision to forcibly put an end to a situation of two Jewish armies where one decides to provide itself with weapons."

Lankin subsequently reflected: "Perhaps this was naïve on our part. We truly believed that the political differences between us would be ironed out later.... I felt deeply ashamed that while fighting for its very life against the Arabs, Israel still could not make peace within its own family." Fein, interviewed several days later by an Associated Press reporter, stated firmly: "the Government knew the ship was coming.... It was the Government who designated Kfar Vitkin as the place on the coast where we were to land and unload."

Tel Aviv, a city in turmoil, was placed under curfew. "Palestine's roads," wrote journalist Arthur Koestler, who had arrived in Israel three weeks earlier, were "bristling with armed patrols." The *Palestine Post* reported "sten-gun patrols at every corner." Yigael Yadin, who described the Irgun men on board the *Altalena* as "enemies," commanded "Operation Purification" to cleanse the nation of Irgun contamination. Under wartime emergency regulations authorizing extra-legal action, he ordered raids on Irgun bases and the homes of its activists. IDF assault units attacked Irgun headquarters in Tel Aviv, where two hundred commanders and soldiers were arrested and their weapons confiscated. Once again, as on the beaches of Kfar Vitkin and Tel Aviv, there was no resistance. Five senior Irgun commanders, Lankin, Meridor, Hillel Kook, Moshe Hason and Bezalel Amitzur, were held in detention for two months.

At a Cabinet meeting, Ben-Gurion encountered sharp criticism of government decisions. To the four religious Zionist ministers, the sinking of the ship was both undemocratic and illegal. Rabbi Fishman-Maimon and Moshe Shapira from the Mizrahi party demanded the immediate release of Irgun prisoners. Interior Minister Gruenbaum proposed a judicial inquiry accompanied by the establishment of a committee to determine how best to maintain law and order, preserve the unity of the Israel Defense Forces, and accelerate the pardoning of prisoners "to avoid civil war." Once his proposal was accepted, Ministers Fishman-Maimon and Shapira resigned, while Gruenbaum and Peretz Bernstein remained to challenge Ben-Gurion's actions.

At a meeting of the Provisional State Council, with all thirty-seven members present, Ben-Gurion summarized the "rebellion." He praised Commander Even for acting "with a maximum of efficiency and a minimum of bloodshed." The terms of surrender accepted by the Irgun at Kfar Vitkin had required the cessation of all "hostile acts" and surrender of all weapons and military equipment. "This appeared to be the end of the Etzel revolt," Ben-Gurion concluded. But the *Altalena* had "slipped away."

Arriving in Tel Aviv, "it refused to comply with our orders to leave the city and turn over its cargo of weapons to the authorities. The Government had previously decided that if this was not done, force would be used against the vessel, and so it was." Describing the episode as "an armed uprising" fed by "the chicanery of the dissidents," Ben-Gurion warned: "The arrogant action of armed gangs inside the country gravely endangers our ability to defend our future and the future of the entire Jewish people." The army and the nation, he insisted, must "uproot this evil."

By a vote of 24-4, the Council adopted a resolution expressing "its support of the actions of the Government aimed at preventing Etzel from bringing in weapons without Government permission."

Two days later, senior military officers took an oath of allegiance to the State of Israel. At the conclusion of the ceremony, Ben-Gurion declared: "The Oath that you have just taken links you with the Hebrew commanders from the days of Joshua, the fighting and liberating Judges, the Kings of Israel and Judea, Nehemia, the Maccabees, the heroes of the war against the Romans in the days of the Second Temple. . . ." Jewish national independence had finally been restored. But the groundless hatred between Jews that had undermined Jewish sovereignty in the first century hovered menacingly over the fledgling State of Israel.

An anguished Begin was the first to speak publicly after the devastating attack, delivering an emotional (critics claimed hysterical) radio address to the nation from Irgun headquarters. The arrival of the *Altalena*, he insisted, was not "an act of provocation." Representatives of the Provisional Government had known about it for "at least four days" before the ship reached Kfar Vitkin. "To our great joy official and precise consent" had been granted; "the entire discussion was only concerning the allocation of the arms." Begin asked: "For years [the Irgun] had dreamed of these arms. . . . How could we not give [them] to our fighters in the army?" To be sure, there was "bitterness . . . deep within us" from the "dark and bitter days and nights when our men were tortured, beaten and given up to the British intelligence." But Irgun fighters had nonetheless joined the Israel Defense Forces with the assurance that they would be "under your command and fight the common foe at your command."

When his men came under fire at Kfar Vitkin, Begin explained, he had decided to sail to Tel Aviv to resolve the "snag in relations." But there, too, "fire was directed against Jews and they kept firing." Even the Arab Legion in the Old City of Jerusalem, he recounted scathingly, had respected a truce to remove wounded Jews. "Hebrew fighters killed," he lamented, "to make the man [Ben-Gurion] who has ever surrendered to the foreigner appear firm towards Jews." Although the government of Israel had honored truces demanded by the British, "here it was different. Here their force was directed against Jews and they kept firing without stop." Even with the *Altalena* ablaze, "they were firing at wounded men in the water . . . at the command of the head of your government."

With rising emotion that climaxed in choking rage and weeping, Begin asked: "What did the government hope to achieve by shelling the ship? Why was the cease-fire broken? Are not these arms needed by us all? Why did they not come to negotiate with us? They, who at the slightest beck and call run to negotiate with [British Foreign Minister] Bevin? . . . Why did they behave in such a barbaric manner?" By sinking the *Altalena,* he claimed, the government had "lost its legitimacy." Accusing Ben-Gurion of a "crime," Begin nonetheless implored his loyal Irgun followers: "Raise not your hand against your brother. Not even today. . . . Simple Jews who give their all for their nation, we shall continue to love Israel and fight for it."

In his speech to the Provisional Council the next day, Ben-Gurion strongly asserted his own version of what had happened, and why. Vigorously defending his actions, he condemned "an attempt, pregnant with calamity, by the Irgun Zvai Leumi to wound the unity and sovereignty of the State, its military power and its international status." With the establishment of the Israel Defense Forces (at a time when the Haganah, Palmach, Irgun, and Lehi still retained their separate identities as fighting units), "the formation or maintenance of any armed forces" other than by the new army had been explicitly forbidden. Ben-Gurion emphasized the necessity of "a united army, loyal to one Government" for resistance against the foreign enemies that Israel confronted.

The government, he asserted, had made "concessions" to the Irgun by permitting its fighters to join the IDF in separate units that would enable them to preserve their distinctive identity. In return, however, the Irgun was required to "cease to exist as a military unit," surrender its weapons, and terminate its independent efforts to procure military supplies. But "the Irgun and its Command continued to operate; arms and equipment were still obtained independently, and the sources thereof denied to the Army." That, Ben-Gurion claimed, was "the dark background... of the grievous doings" at Kfar Vitkin and Tel Aviv.

The Prime Minister vigorously defended his decision "to break the dissident organization" with military force. By bringing the *Altalena*, a "mutinous craft," to Israel the Irgun had disregarded its own commitments and defied the "statutes" of the nation (although it had received Ben-Gurion's explicit approval for landing the *Altalena* at Kfar Vitkin). "No State can countenance private citizens or organizations thus importing... even the tiniest armory, much less the wholesale consignment of rifles and machine-guns that the Irgun tried to land this time." Such "indiscipline and faithlessness," Ben-Gurion asserted, "is a frightful threat to the State and might set the fuse for a disastrous civil war." Once the Irgun refused to yield control of the ship to the government, "my duty was clear. The safety of the State must be preserved, the law carried out—and I knew that only by force could it be done."

"Was it not enough to undergo the murderous ordeal of Arab hatred," Ben-Gurion asked, "that this bitter aftertaste of blood should be proffered us by fellow-Jews?" With Israel confronting a fight for survival, "armed revolt... spells ruin of the Yishuv's strength to defend itself and its future." The existence of "rebel gangs" could not be tolerated. Had the weapons on board the *Altalena* "fallen into the hands of terrorists... they might have wrecked the State and the freedom of its Yishuv."

Indeed, Ben-Gurion warned, had the Irgun retained the weapons that were on board the *Altalena* it could have persisted in "domestic terrorism, attacking and even killing, as they killed before...." The state would not tolerate a "gang of terrorists," functioning as "a private army with private arms." An "armed minority" had usurped the monopoly of the state on the legitimate exercise of force; its continued existence assured further bloodshed. "More than once has the Irgun spilled Jewish blood, and the blood of others; these things must not happen again."

Given the evident dangers, including "a truce infringed, our sovereignty risked," Ben-Gurion insisted that "to burn this ship was the most loyal service we could render the Yishuv." He did not mention, either publicly or in meetings with his ministers, that his navy commander had offered alternatives to violence for disabling the *Altalena*. Instead, in his concluding peroration he exulted: "Blessed be the cannon that sunk that ship. [It] is worthy of being mounted in the new Temple when it is built." It became known, almost immediately, as "*ha-totach ha-kadosh*" ("the holy cannon").

Triumphantly asserting state power and, implicitly, his own Ben-Gurion not only challenged the actions of his political opponents but their legitimacy. The Irgun was an untrustworthy and defiant "gang of terrorists." It had "usurped" power that belonged to the state and, by extension, to Ben-Gurion as its leader. It had been prepared to plunge the new nation into a civil war while incurring the wrath of external authorities (once the British, now the United Nations) to advance its own partisan interests. He warned against a society "in which there is no single authority, no single arsenal, no single discipline." The State, he asserted, had been "forced" to attack in self-preservation. "It was better that the ship was burned."

The *Altalena* confrontation climaxed two decades of intense acrimony between the political left and right that began with Jabotinsky's Revisionist challenge to Labor Zionism. It spiraled into slander and political trials after the Arlosoroff murder, erupted during the hunting "Season" at the end of World War II, and reached its violent culmination on the beaches of Kfar Vitkin and Tel Aviv six weeks after independence.

Perhaps Begin had clung too long to his naïve faith that fifteen years of bitter internecine ideological and political conflict, and the legacy of suspicion between the government and the Irgun, could have been surmounted if only he was given the opportunity to leave the ship in Tel Aviv to resolve the "snag in relations." His craving for Irgun legitimacy, and for government recognition of its contributions to the struggle for independence, may have blinded him to Ben-Gurion's determination to resist any challenge, real or imagined, to his own authority.

Demanding the concentration of power and authority in his hands, Ben-Gurion rarely displayed tolerance for political opposition, whether inside his own Mapai party or to his government. His animus toward Begin was personal no less than political; he despised his Irgun challenger as an emotional rabble-rouser seeking and prepared to seize by force the power that Ben-Gurion was determined to monopolize. The precariousness of the new state, in conjunction with Ben-Gurion's determination to concentrate power in his own hands, framed his decision to use military force against his political opponent.

Begin could not imagine that Ben-Gurion, who viewed him as an enemy of the state, would resort to force to settle their disagreements (although past experience might have suggested otherwise). Commanding his Irgun fighters not to return fire, he believed that Ben-Gurion was bound by the same constraint. For Begin, the *Altalena* offered the final opportunity for his followers to shed their status as political pariahs. Tarnished by the King David Hotel bombing and the massacre of Arab villagers in Deir Yassin, he could hope to wipe the moral ledger clean by contributing arms and fighters to the cause of victory. It especially infuriated him that Ben-Gurion, so deferential toward the British government even as it repudiated Mandatory obligations, persistently displayed his enmity toward the Irgun with arrests, betrayal, exile and, finally, gunfire.

Both leaders, it turned out, tragically misread the motivations and intentions of their political opponents. The *Altalena* confrontation, for Ben-Gurion, was a struggle over political authority and power. Begin's yearning for the Irgun to be recognized for its participation in the fight for independence, and its determination to continue the desperate struggle for the Old City of Jerusalem, was perceived by Ben-Gurion as an attempt to launch a *putsch* to overthrow the government, *his* government. The authority of the state, Ben-Gurion had insisted on the eve of battle, "is the main principle." Nothing, Foreign Minister Shertok echoed, was more important than "upholding State authority."

To government ministers, following Ben-Gurion's lead, the Irgun was not the opposition; it was the "enemy." In the end, rival political ideologies overrode the shared goal of national independence. The consequences for loyal soldiers and fighters, on both sides of the political divide, were devastating. The Irgun, at Begin's command, withheld fire against their Jewish "brothers." Some Haganah and Palmach soldiers disobeyed orders and refused to bomb the *Altalena* or shoot crew members as they swam ashore. Their palpable anguish suggests that they could not bear the nightmare of participation in another Jewish civil war.

"Among us," Ben-Gurion subsequently conceded, "the disputes are not like those of more-or-less normal people, but like those of zealots." It was a rare moment of self-insight. By then, in a final spasm of zeal, and apprehension lest the burnt hull of the *Altalena* become an Irgun memorial site, he ordered the navy to tow it out to sea and sink it.

Within weeks of proclaiming independence, the clash of personalities and politics brought Israel to the brink of civil war. Begin may have craved recognition and respect too much, while Ben-Gurion surely had an excessive need for deference to his forceful will. So Begin, who would never engage in battle against fellow Jews, imagined that Ben-Gurion was bound by the same constraint. But he was not. Ben-Gurion justified his own willingness to use force against his political opponents by contriving their willingness to use force against him to seize the power that he was determined to monopolize.

In one of the worst self-inflicted tragedies of Jewish history, the war for Jewish national restoration had fractured at a critical moment into a bloody battle over political legitimacy. Any state, sociologist Max Weber wrote, must claim a monopoly on "the legitimate use of physical force." But a crucial component of legitimacy, Middle East scholar Bernard Lewis suggests, is the presence of a political leader who "does not need to use excessive force or brutality to maintain himself in power." In June 1948 these competing imperatives exploded into violent conflict. With statehood finally secured, the struggle over legitimacy morphed into a perpetually nagging conflict over the identity of Israel: could the Jewish people become, as its Proclamation of Independence anticipated, "a nation, like all other nations, in its own sovereign state," to be welcomed into "the family of nations"?

2 GOD AND STATE

In the lands of their dispersion, Jews could not replicate the political and religious institutions that had sustained a sovereign Jewish polity in their own ancient homeland. They learned how to survive defeat and exile as a "text-centered" people, governed by rabbinical interpretation of the Torah and Talmud. The boundaries of Jewish political autonomy were determined by Gentile rulers, but a significant measure of communal independence and cohesion survived the loss of national sovereignty.

The religious foundation of Jewish life, resting on God, Torah and commandments, was eventually challenged from within. In the nineteenth century, newly emancipated European Jews rejected rabbinical authority and ghetto confinement to become citizens of the modern nation state. Responding to their apostasy, traditional rabbis and their loyal followers, identified as *haredim* (who trembled at the word of God), decried the subversive freedom of secular modernity that was embraced by *epikoros* (heretics) who denied the divine authority of Torah.

Before the end of the century, memories of ancient sovereignty and modern examples of successful European nationalist movements inspired handfuls of Eastern European Jews to dream of returning to their own promised land. A tiny cohort of Zionists arrived in Ottoman Palestine, where communities of pious Jews were embedded in the holy cities of Jerusalem, Hebron, Safed, and Tiberias. The newcomers looked elsewhere, seeding barren land with agricultural settlements that became the foundation for the eventual restoration of national sovereignty.

Zionism challenged the religion of Judaism that had sustained Jews during nineteen centuries of exile. A group of German rabbis, who became known as the *Protestrabbiner*, responded with a sharp critique of Jewish nationalism. Not only was Zionism, they asserted, "antagonistic to the messianic promises of Judaism, as contained in the Holy Writ and in later religious sources," but it also undermined the obligation imposed upon Jews "to serve the country to which they belong with the utmost devotion." Rabbi Zadok HaCohen Rabinowitz, the Hasidic spiritual leader, warned that if Zionists (whom he labeled "inciters and seducers") should gain power, "they will seek to remove from the hearts of Israel belief in God and in the truth of the Torah."

A Jewish state built by socialist revolutionaries, warned ultra-Orthodox rabbis in Jerusalem, would merely preserve "the exile of Israel in the Holy Land." They wanted nothing to do with Zionist heretics who represented "the evil urge [*yetzer harah*] of the Jewish people." Rabbis were prepared to defer the millennial yearning for the return to Zion and Jerusalem to the messianic era. Exile would end and redemption would follow when God willed it, not when Zionists built a state. A distinguished rabbi lamented: "How can I bear that something be called 'the State of Israel' without the Torah and commandments (heaven forbid)?" But assertive young Zionist pioneers were determined to build self-sufficient communities from which a Jewish state would emerge long before the arrival of the Messiah.

A seemingly irreconcilable conflict between religious tradition and secular modernity loomed over the Yishuv. Zionists rejected the rabbinical authority that had preserved Jewish life in exile, yet they could hardly escape Jewish history, symbols, or texts. A secular national rebellion against religious Orthodoxy, Zionism was nonetheless inspired by a religious tradition that embraced the land promised by God to the Jewish people. Orthodoxy and Zionism might represent polar approaches to Jewish life in modernity, but with the emergence of a Jewish national movement neither secular Zionism nor religious Orthodoxy, then or since, could define itself without confronting its Jewish Other.

Theodor Herzl's encounter with anti-Semitism during the scandalous Dreyfus trial in France, the first nation to have emancipated Jews, set his Zionist course in the 1890s. He dreamed of a modern state that blended Jewish nationalism with European liberal values. Herzl's primary source of inspiration, revealed in his books *Der Judenstaat* [The Jewish State] (1896) and *Altneuland* [The Old New Land] (1902), was the enlightened West, with "ideas which are the common stock of the whole civilized world." Religion was anathema: "We do not mean to found a theocracy," he insisted, "but a tolerant modern state" in which "our clergy" would not have "even the slightest chance to assert their whims. We shall keep our priests within the confines of their temples."

Herzl was even willing to locate the "aristocratic republic" of his dreams far from Zion, in Argentina or Uganda.

Before the first Zionist Congress convened in Basel in August 1897, Herzl's trusted associate Max Nordau asserted: "Zionism has nothing to do with theology." But when David Wolffsohn, a Lithuanian Zionist who attended the Basel conference, displayed a *tallit* (prayer shawl) with its traditional blue stripes now framing the Star of David, delegates enthusiastically embraced it as the national flag of the nascent Zionist movement. For most Zionists, however, religion was an obstacle to be overcome on the journey to statehood. Chaim Weizmann, who would become Israel's first president forty-five years later, wrote to Herzl in 1903: "The young make their first step a search for freedom from everything Jewish." Only through Zionism, liberated from religion, could Jewish youth be "saved." Jewish culture, he insisted, "should no longer be confused with Jewish religious worship." Religious Judaism was what Zionists left behind in Europe on their journey to the Promised Land and eventual Jewish statehood. "If there is anything in Judaism that has become intolerable and incomprehensible to the best of Jewish youth," Weizmann claimed, "it is the pressure to equate its essence with the religious formalism of the Orthodox."

But the religious tradition was tenacious and, at times, even flexible. Following Herzl's dramatic call for a Jewish state, a new Orthodox organization named *Mizrahi* (spiritual center) emerged to endorse the Zionist dream and infuse it with religious content. Its leaders advocated "the Land of Israel for the People of Israel in accordance with the Torah of Israel," an appeal that would resonate among religious Zionists decades later after the Six-Day War. Although the ultra-Orthodox rabbinate adamantly rejected this subversive blend of religion and nationalism, the integration of Judaism and Zionism remained at least a dormant possibility, even if neither religious Jews nor secular Zionists were yet prepared to embrace it.

David Ben-Gurion, the fiery socialist who would become the founding father of Jewish statehood, had learned love of Torah (and Hebrew) as a young boy from his maternal grandfather, a rabbi. His mother dreamed that David would follow in her father's religious footsteps. Indeed, for a time, the young boy studied Talmud in *cheder*. But his father, a founding leader of *Hibbat Zion* (Love of Zion) in the Russian city of Plonsk, was his primary source of inspiration. After his bar mitzvah, David and his friends established a Zionist youth group; then, as an engineering student in Warsaw, he joined the Jewish Social-Democratic Party (Poale Zion) and became a union organizer and Marxist revolutionary.

Determined to implement his political principles in Palestine, Ben-Gurion arrived there in 1906 at the age of twenty. As attentive a student of the Bible as he remained throughout his life, Ben-Gurion viewed Zionism as "a revolutionary movement"—"a revolt against a tradition of many centuries, helplessly longing for redemption." Under his leadership, socialism and Zionism were fused into the inseparable components of Jewish national rebirth, a secular rebellion against religious Orthodoxy and its political passivity. Yet when Ben-Gurion was asked about the source of Zionism while testifying before the British Peel Commission in 1936, he instantly responded: "The Bible is our mandate." Even this resolutely secular Zionist would not repudiate Jewish sacred memory.

The Labor Zionists, who dominated politics during the pre-state years and for three decades following independence, remained at best ambivalent, and often hostile, toward the religion of Judaism. Orthodox Jews—perceived as "poor, uneducated, superstitious, cowardly"—epitomized what secular Zionists found repulsive about Jewish life in the diaspora. To be sure, they borrowed from the religious tradition to suit their own need for continuity with the Jewish past. The Bible became a source of history, if not divine revelation. Prophetic pleas for justice were eagerly embraced as a valid social agenda for modernity. Even in secular kibbutzim, traditional Jewish holidays, especially Passover with its ennobling story of the struggle for freedom from Egyptian slavery and the harvest festivals of Shavuot and Sukkoth, were enthusiastically celebrated. Ancient religious images—the Star of David (from whose house the Messiah would arise) and the menorah (from the sanctuary in Solomon's Temple)—were recast as iconic Zionist symbols.

But nationalism, not religion, provided the framework for Zionist legitimacy. Ben-Gurion's political rival in Palestine after World War I, Vladimir ("Ze'ev") Jabotinky, was born in Odessa to cosmopolitan parents who were completely detached from the Jewish religious tradition. Like Herzl, Jabotinsky was "the rationalist and secular-minded" child of nineteenth century European liberalism. But after the horrible Kishinev pogrom (1903), when dozens of Jews were murdered and hundreds injured in what was then the capital of the Bessarabia province of the Russian Empire, he became a Zionist, organizing Jewish self-defense units and subsequently fighting in the British Jewish Legion during World War I.

A member of the executive council of the Zionist Organization in Palestine, Jabotinsky broke with mainstream Zionism to establish the right-wing Revisionist movement. Suspicious of the "childish humanism" to be found in the Bible, he castigated Orthodoxy for its narrow-mindedness, telling his son that he saw "no holiness in the Jewish ritual." Jabotinsky believed that "justice exists only for those whose fists and stubbornness make it possible for them to realize it."

The most creative—and, to his disciples, revered—advocate of the synthesis of Judaism and Zionism was Abraham Isaac Kook, Ashkenazi Chief Rabbi of Mandatory Palestine from 1921 until his death in 1935. Rabbi Kook came slowly to accept the idea of secular nationalism. "The wicked among our own people, who cast off the yoke of the Torah, we must hate and spurn," he wrote early in the century. He insisted that Zionism as mere nationalism, without Judaism, was "a sterile notion," indeed an "abomination."

Over time, however, Rabbi Kook's antipathy moderated. "One cannot altogether dismiss the success of the Zionists," he conceded. Disapproving of their eagerness to jettison the religious core of Judaism, he nonetheless supported their nation-building efforts, recognizing that "the hope for the return to the Holy Land is the continuing source of the distinctive nature of Judaism." He wondered: "Who can discern the mysterious workings of God, to fathom why there should be among those who serve this cause people who are so thoroughly tainted with heresy?"

Rabbi Kook (not unlike Ben-Gurion) came to believe that "the source of Zionism is the most supreme source of holiness, the Bible." The ideology of Zionism and the prospect of Jewish statehood were "sacred expressions of messianic redemption." There must be fusion, he asserted, between the people of Israel, the Land of Israel and the Torah of Israel. Sharply criticized by a rabbi in Safed for becoming "a Zionist in his old age" who was "ready to sacrifice his soul for the settlement of Jews in Eretz Israel," Rabbi Kook insisted that "Whoever . . . speaks in defense of Jews even when they do not fulfill God's will is praiseworthy."

Few ultra-Orthodox Jews or resolutely secular Zionists were persuaded by Rabbi Kook's attempts at religious and national synthesis. The Orthodox rabbinate would not defer to Zionist atheists in Tel Aviv; nor would secular Zionists recognize rabbinical authority. Conflict between Jewish religious tradition and Zionist revolutionary principles seemed irreparable. But the Holocaust horrifically demonstrated that without national sovereignty Jews—whether secular or religious—were helpless before their enemies. With the decimation of Eastern European Jewry and the destruction of its centers of prayer and study, rabbinical challenges to Zionist supremacy receded. From Jewish tragedy, as Ben-Gurion had predicted, would arise Zionist opportunity.

The Israeli Proclamation of Independence expressed—with careful ambiguity where necessary—a resolute effort to bridge the wide chasm separating secular Zionism and religious Judaism. Its opening words recognized that "the Land of Israel was the birthplace of the Jewish people," where they had created "a culture of national and universal significance." It was "the self-evident right of the Jewish people to be a nation, like all other nations, in its own sovereign state." The State of Israel "will be based on the precepts of liberty, justice and peace taught by the Hebrew Prophets." But there was no hint of prophetic insistence on fidelity to Torah.

The concluding peroration, carefully drafted and parsed, offered a framework for secular-religious reconciliation: "Placing our trust in the Rock of Israel [*Tsur Yisrael*] we set our hand and testimony to this Declaration, here on the soil of the homeland, in the city of Tel-Aviv, on this day, the eve of the Sabbath, 5 Iyar, 5708, 14 May, 1948." That single sentence (as literary scholar Harold Fisch perceptively observed) encapsulated the latent ambiguities of Jewish statehood at the moment when ancient memories, religious devotion, and Zionist yearning converged in a national solution to the Jewish problem.

The "Rock of Israel" might refer to God, or to the collective national will. (Religious Zionists had preferred "the Lord of Israel"; secular Zionists opposed the reference altogether.) The word *betachon,* inserted immediately preceding that ambiguous locution, could mean "security" (military) or "faith" (religious). The borders of the new state were left undefined; only Tel Aviv was explicitly included within them. The timeless promise to remember Jerusalem ("If I forget you, O Jerusalem," Jews had faithfully recited ever since the Babylonian exile, "let my right hand forget her cunning") was temporarily forgotten. Designated by the United Nations for international status, Jerusalem lay outside the narrowly partitioned borders of the new state.

Double dating the Proclamation implied that Israel was bound by a dual calendar that absorbed traditional Jewish and modern Western

(Christian) time. So, too, its reference to "the eve of the Sabbath" might refer to the late Friday afternoon when the Proclamation was actually signed or represent, symbolically, a harbinger of Jewish redemption. With the signing concluded just before the beginning of the Sabbath, Ben-Gurion graciously invited Rabbi Yehuda Leb Fishman, the oldest member of the Proclamation drafting committee, to recite the traditional *Shehehiyanu* prayer of thanksgiving (during which Ben-Gurion remained bare-headed). But before the first session of the Knesset convened, he went to a Jerusalem synagogue to recite his own prayer of thanksgiving. For the first time in forty years, Ben-Gurion recorded in his diary, he had attended a synagogue service in the Land of Israel.

The Proclamation of Independence framed rather than resolved the ambiguities and challenges of Jewish statehood. Ben-Gurion, in his own words, was "determined that Israel should be a secular state, ruled by a secular government and not a religious authority." Indeed, he conceded: "I want the state to hold religion in the palm of its hand." The Proclamation praised the Jews who had "reclaimed the wilderness, revived their language, built cities and villages, and established a vigorous and ever-growing community." It pledged to "uphold the full social and political equality of all its citizens, without distinction of race, creed or sex." There was no mention of religious Orthodoxy. Left unresolved was whether the State of Israel could be both democratic and Jewish. That question, writes Tel Aviv University law professor Leora Bilsky, "has haunted Israeli society ever since the establishment of the state." It would become the defining conundrum of Jewish statehood.

Although the Proclamation pledged a national constitution within four months, its continuing absence sixty-five years later (and into the foreseeable future) reflects the tangled secular-religious politics of legitimacy in the Jewish state. Paradoxically, its very absence became (and remains) a requirement for national unity. "There is no need in Israel for a man-made constitution," insisted Agudat Yisrael rabbi Meir David Levinstein, "If it contradicts the Torah of Israel, it is a revolt against the Almighty; if it is identical with the Torah, it is superfluous." A rabbinical colleague warned that a constitution would create "a Galut [exile] in the midst of Jews, after the Galut we have known in the midst of Gentiles."

To ultra-Orthodox Jews, Zionists were "heretics and unbelievers" whose disregard for *halakha* (Jewish law) belied their claim to legitimacy. At the extreme, Satmar Rabbi Joel Teitelbaum, who opposed the very existence of a secular Jewish state, denigrated Zionism as the "anti-messianic work of Satan." To Rabbi Amram Blau, leader of the tiny rejectionist Naturei Karta movement, Zionists were "wicked, unbelieving, ignorant, utterly irresponsible heretics."

Seeking to bridge the chasm, Rabbi Yehuda Leib Maimon, the first Minister of Religious Affairs, advised secular Israelis that "the State of Israel cannot exist without the Torah of Israel," while reminding Orthodox Jews that "it is impossible for the Torah to exist fully without a State of Israel." As independence neared, the Jewish Agency Executive, the ruling body of the Yishuv, approached Agudat Yisrael (founded in 1912 to unite Orthodox opponents of Zionism) to seek its support for statehood with assurances that the existing terms of accommodation between Orthodoxy and Zionism from the pre-state period would be preserved. The guiding principle was "to prevent the division of the Jewish nation into two nations."

The Status Quo agreement, whose provisions were outlined in a 1947 letter from Ben-Gurion to Agudat Yisrael rabbis, affirmed religion as a core component of public life in Israel. It specified that the government, and all national institutions, would respect the Sabbath and Jewish holy days, when public services would be closed. The religious requirements of dietary observance (*kashrut*) would be observed in all public institutions, including government facilities and the Israel Defense Forces. The Orthodox rabbinate would be granted complete authority over marriage, divorce, and burial. Orthodox religious schools, like secular schools, would receive government subsidies. Orthodox yeshiva students would be exempted from the military service that was compulsory for secular Israelis. Preservation of the Status Quo agreement, wrote S. Zalman Abramov in his aptly titled *Perpetual Dilemma*, was "the price paid for the avoidance of a Kulturkampf."

Ben-Gurion was attentive to the religious tradition but he refused to be held captive to it. In his famous meeting with Rabbi Abraham Isaiah Karelitz (known as the *Hazon Ish*), the leader of the ultra-Orthodox community, the issue of supremacy and deference arose. The rabbi cited the Talmudic story of two wagons, one empty and the other full, approaching each other on a narrow road. Which one was entitled to the right of way? According to the Talmud, the empty (secular) wagon must yield to the wagon loaded with Jewish law and learning.

Ben-Gurion was not persuaded. Israel, he insisted, must be a "nation of law," but not religious law. "Our state is not a theocracy," conceded Rabbi Yehuda Leib Fishman, but it must be faithful "to the tradition of our fathers and to the unique nature of Jewish history." Rabbi Meir Bar-Ilan, another prominent religious Zionist leader, was more insistent: "With the return to our land there is an obligation to revive Jewish law and not to go astray after other gods." Whether rabbis or judges possessed the final authority to interpret law in a Jewish state remained unresolved. But there would not be a national constitution, then or since, lest the inherent tensions between secular Israelis and religious Jews over its defining principles tear the nation apart.

Ben-Gurion tried to reassure Orthodox Cabinet ministers that there would be no "antireligious coercion or provocation." Nor, however, would the government turn Israel into "a theocratic state" by imposing "the Law" on its citizens. Believing that "the State of Israel and the Jewish People share a common destiny," he conceded: "We oughtn't separate religion from the state." Religious freedom, no less than freedom from religion, was required. The irrepressible tension between religiously observant Jews and secular Israelis, veering from conciliation and accommodation to hostility and crisis, would continue to complicate the emergence of a unifying national identity.

In a concession with enduring ramifications, as yet unresolved, Ben-Gurion agreed to exemptions from military service for *haredi* men who studied in *yeshivot* (approximately four hundred at the time). They fulfilled the Hazon Ish's preference for a "society of scholars" who devoted their lives to full-time study. That compromise endured for decades until the number of exemptions, reaching into the tens of thousands, provoked an increasingly bitter (and continuing) struggle over ultra-Orthodox entitlement to exemption from military service.

Zionism may have climaxed in the transformation of Jews into "a nation like all other nations." But national unity required a measure of accommodation to Orthodox sensibilities and religious symbols even if legitimacy—the right to rule—ultimately depended upon democratic elections, not divine revelation. Since under no circumstances would Ben-Gurion build a ruling political coalition with Menachem Begin's despised Herut party, support from Orthodox religious parties became a necessary component of Labor party governance and remained so for nearly thirty years.

With the arrival of waves of Mizrahi immigrants from Middle Eastern and North African communities, Jewish identity in the Jewish state became bitterly contentious. The traditional religious practices of Yemenite Jews, who were consigned to immigrant absorption camps, struck secular Zionist officials as too "primitive" for their successful integration into Israeli society. Nahum Levin, who exercised authority over education in the immigrant camps, warned that they were inundated with yeshiva students who "represent the power of darkness" that jeopardized "the future image of the State of Israel."

The camps were bitterly described as the "occupied territory" of Ben-Gurion's ruling Mapai party; government officials were accused of committing "cultural and religious genocide." Rumors circulated that Yemenite boys were forced to cut their *peyot* because, they were told, "you don't need side-locks in Israel." A member of the Knesset from the religious Mizrahi party warned that a "bloody civil war" could erupt if "religious and cultural murder" persisted.

Within a year after the proclamation of Israel's statehood "the power struggle for the future soul of the state," as journalist Tom Segev described the virulent secular-religious conflict, erupted in the streets of Jerusalem. Residents of the ultra-Orthodox enclave of Mea Shearim were infuriated to discover that nearby cinemas were selling tickets and showing films before the Sabbath ended. Angry demonstrations in downtown Jerusalem led to violent clashes with police. The "cinema riots" were part of the "battle for the Sabbath" as *haredi* Jews protested, occasionally violently, against secular Israelis who "desecrated" the day of rest. "For us," explained Rabbi Itzhak Meir Levin, leader of Agudat Yisrael and a member of the Knesset, "the Sabbath stands for the very existence of the Jewish people, and its violation means the end of the state and the destruction of the nation."

The defining paradox of Jewish statehood endured: Zionism represented a national rebellion against religious Judaism. The terms of peaceful coexistence between Israeli "sabras" and *haredi* Jews proved to be elusive. Over the years the flashpoints of conflict would include butcher shops selling pork, construction of a municipal pool where men and women could swim together, El Al flights on Shabbat, conscription of women into military service, archeological excavations that might desecrate ancient Jewish burial sites, and Shabbat traffic on roads abutting religious neighborhoods. As in the cinema riots, ultra-Orthodox fury periodically erupted into mass protests and even violence when *haredi* space confronted the threat of secular intrusion.

In the new Jewish state even defining "Jew" was problematic. Under the Law of Return, enacted by the Knesset in 1950, "every Jew" had the right to immigrate to Israel. But who was a Jew? Eight years later a Carmelite monk known as Brother Daniel applied for an immigrant certificate. Born in Poland to Jewish parents as Oswald Rufeisen, he had been active in a Zionist youth group. Imprisoned by the Nazis, he escaped and obtained a certificate as a German Christian, further endangering his life by assisting Jews to flee to safety. Taking refuge in a convent, Rufeisen converted to Christianity.

Brother Daniel based his application for Israeli *oleh* (immigrant) status on "my belonging to the Jewish people, to which I continue to belong, although I embraced the Catholic faith in 1942, and joined a monastic order in 1945." His application was rejected under Interior Ministry guidelines that "anyone declaring in good faith that he is a Jew, and does not profess any other religion, shall be registered as a Jew." Ironically, both Brother Daniel's lawyer and the State Attorney cited rabbinical authority to support their divergent opinions. According to the Babylonian Talmud, his attorney claimed, "a Jew, even if he has sinned, remains a Jew." But a convert, the State Attorney responded, was at best only a partial Jew who was not entitled to full *halakhic* rights.

The Supreme Court was pulled between Israeli and Jewish legal principles. (According to the traditional religious definition, a Jew was someone born to a Jewish mother or converted according to *halakha*). The Justices relied upon rabbinic authority to rule that Brother Daniel, born to a Jewish mother, was indeed Jewish according to Jewish law. But under the Law of Return (if not in rabbinical courts), "Jew" had a secular meaning "as it is understood by the ordinary plain and simple Jew." As one Justice noted, "A Jew who does not believe in religion, any religion, . . . is still a Jew. Can it be that [Brother Daniel], who has embraced another creed, but has remained attached to the Jewish people, is not a Jew?"

But, another Justice responded, "a Jew who has become a Christian is not called a Jew." While a Jew living in Israel was "bound by an umbilical cord to historical Judaism," Brother Daniel, a Christian who had rejected his Jewish national past, was "a brother far distant" who "will not be part of the Jewish world." Relying upon "the intuitive perceptions of the Jewish community at large," the Court ruled that Brother Daniel could not claim automatic citizenship as a Jew under the Law of Return but he could obtain citizenship through the naturalization process. In the end, *halakhic* principle yielded to government definition.

But the problem of Jewish identity in the Jewish state remained vexing. In the wake of the Brother Daniel decision an Interior Ministry directive stipulated that "any person declaring in good faith that he is a Jew shall be registered as a Jew." If both parents "declare that the child is Jewish, the declaration shall be regarded as though it were the legal declaration of the child itself"—even if the mother was not a Jew. But the National Religious Party, staunchly opposing that expansive definition, provoked a Cabinet crisis. At Ben-Gurion's insistence, a special committee was authorized to consult with "Jewish sages in Israel and abroad" for guidance about the Jewish identity of children from mixed marriages.

Respected author S.Y. Agnon, who claimed to have "nothing to add or to subtract" from the words of the ancient Sages, counseled Ben-Gurion "to refrain from concerning yourself with matters of religion, whether for good or ill." But the prime minister wrote to forty-seven "wise men," including ultra-Orthodox, modern Orthodox, and "free thinkers" in Israel and the diaspora, to seek their opinion on a *halakhic* and public issue of defining importance for the Jewish state.

Rabbi Yehuda Leib Maimon, a member of the first Knesset and former Minister of Religious Affairs, bluntly dissociated himself from the "intellectuals" to whom Ben-Gurion had addressed the letter (including Supreme Court Justice Felix Frankfurter and philosopher Isaiah Berlin): "I do not trust their intellect." He reminded the prime minister that "The question 'Who is a Jew?' has been answered for thousands of years . . . according to our eternal Torah and tradition."

Five members of the Rabbinical Court in London warned of the "inseparable schism in the nation that would necessarily result from any deviation in the laws of the State of Israel from the time-honored precepts of *halakha* in matters of personal status, descent and family." Rabbi Zecharya HaCohen in Yemen cautioned that "in every generation, there are means of temptation, and in our time there are but a few who resist." To Hebrew University Bible scholar Yehezkel Kaufmann, a secular state of Israel did not alter the definition of a Jew as a "religious term." Indeed, asserted Army Chief Rabbi Shlomo Goren, "it is impossible to separate or divide between Jewish nationality and religion."

Renowned Lubavitch Rabbi Menachem Mendel Schneerson asserted that a Jew "is only a person who was born to a Jewish mother," or converted under "the precise procedure . . . according to tradition, as detailed in the *Shulkhan Arukh*." Rabbi Joseph Dov Soloveitchik, the leader of American Orthodoxy, insisted that "the mother determines the sanctity of the child and his membership in the Jewish people." Evidently concerned that an alternative definition might be chosen, he pointedly asked: "Will the State of Israel be constructed upon the destruction of all that is holy to Israel?"

Given the weight of rabbinical opinion, and more urgent political issues to resolve, the government was not prepared to redefine "Jew" contrary to *halakha*. In 1960, the Interior Minister issued a directive that only a person born of a Jewish mother could be registered as a Jew. But the vexing issue of Jewish identity would not disappear. Benjamin Shalit, a former career naval officer whose non-Jewish wife had registered as British under the "Nation/Ethnic" category, and no faith under "Religion," challenged that policy. Shalit wanted their son to be registered as professing no religion, yet "Jewish" according to nationality. When the Interior Ministry refused, Shalit appealed to the Supreme Court.

In a 5-4 ruling covering two hundred pages, the Justices expressed their sharp divisions over retention of the traditional *halakhic* definition, deference to personal choice of identity, the authority of the registry to disregard it, and whether the Court, rather than the Knesset, should decide such a fundamental (and volatile) issue. Once again, as in the Brother Daniel case, the ruling government coalition was in danger of dissolving under pressure from the religious parties. A bare majority of the Justices overturned the 1960 directive, ordering the registration of young Shalit (and his sister) as belonging to no religion.

When the issue came before the Knesset early in 1970, it provoked vigorous debate and impassioned public demonstrations. A bill was introduced defining "Jew" as "a person born to a Jewish mother, or who was converted to Judaism, and who is not a member of another religion." But there was no mention of *halakha*, the traditional standard for conversion. Orthodox opponents, rejecting any diminution of their traditional authority, warned of an irreparable schism. Secularists defending the legitimacy of their own Judaism opposed legislation that might cripple aliya from abroad by excluding non-Orthodox diaspora converts. New legislation preserved the *halakhic* definition of "Jew," while omitting any mention of *halakhic* criteria for conversion.

That, of course, inevitably raised the question of who was a "convert"? Because the validity of conversion turned on whether an Orthodox rabbinical court had performed it, the Orthodox rabbinate in Israel did not recognize non-Orthodox conversions abroad. But could Israel decide who was a Jew in the diaspora, where most conversions were not performed by Orthodox rabbis? Not only might this disagreement rupture relations between Israel and diaspora Jews; it had the potential to severely limit Jewish immigration. In the end the Jewish state, where Orthodoxy alone enjoyed official religious legitimacy, decided not to decide who was a Jew outside its borders. But for those wishing to marry in Israel the Orthodox rabbinate retained the power to apply the *halakhic* definition.

So it was, during the first two decades of statehood, that the terms of precarious reconciliation between antiquity and modernity, Judaism and Zionism, and religion and state, were (if often acrimoniously) defined and refined. The result was a form of dual legitimacy in which secular Israelis and religious Jews retained control over their separate personal and jurisdictional spheres within the guiding principles of the Status Quo agreement.

The Armistice lines of 1949 had imposed a different set of boundary issues. National borders had long been a source of contention among Zionists. Jabotinsky's Revisionist movement had insisted on a Jewish state within the original boundaries of Mandatory Palestine, on "both banks of the Jordan." But his successor Menachem Begin redefined the "whole Land of Israel" west of the Jordan River only. From the 1930s on, Ben-Gurion was prepared to secure a state within any borders, no matter how narrowly partitioned.

The Armistice agreement had separated the State of Israel from Judea and Samaria, a large portion of the biblical homeland of the ancient Israelite tribes and the Davidic kingdom. It became known as Jordan's West Bank. The Jewish Quarter in the Old City of Jerusalem, inhabited for centuries by a pious community clustered near the Western Wall, the holiest site in Judaism, had been evacuated and destroyed during the fighting in 1948. Thereafter Jordan prohibited Jews from entering the Old City to worship at the Wall. The venerable Jewish cemetery on the Mount of Olives was desecrated and inaccessible.

Other ancient holy sites—*Me'arat HaMachpelah* in Hebron, the burial caves of the patriarchs and matriarchs of the Jewish people, Rachel's tomb outside Bethlehem, and Joseph's Tomb in Nablus (biblical Shechem)—were located in territory forbidden to Jews by its Jordanian occupiers. Arab intransigence toward the existence of a Jewish state within any borders remained undiminished. Surrounded by enemies sworn to its destruction, Israel endured for nineteen years within precarious and porous boundaries, barely nine miles wide at their narrowest point just north of Tel Aviv. Temporary seemed destined to become permanent.

On Independence Day in May 1967, Rabbi Tzvi Yehuda Kook addressed his former students at their annual reunion at the Mercaz Ha-Rav, the Jerusalem yeshiva named after his father. Following his father's death he had struggled to transform the yeshiva into a spiritual center for religious Zionist renewal. But its embrace of Zionism marginalized it within the Orthodox community, while its Orthodoxy isolated it from the secular Zionist mainstream.

The annual Independence Day celebration normally was a festive reunion, with enthusiastic singing and dancing. This time, however, Rabbi Kook suddenly departed from tradition to recount his despair, nineteen years earlier, at the moment when the Jewish state was born. "I was torn to pieces," he recalled emotionally. "I could not celebrate." The State of Israel had been separated from the biblical Land of Israel. Suddenly, a visitor recalled, Rabbi Kook's soft voice "rose to crescendo, bewailing the partition of historic Eretz Israel."

Reciting the names of inaccessible biblical sites and cities Rabbi Kook cried out: "They have divided my land. Where is our Hebron? Have we forgotten it? And where is our Shechem? And our Jericho—will we forget them?" His impassioned lament stunned students and graduates in the audience. "He spoke like a man whose soul was torn asunder," one recalled. "No one in the country spoke like this," another realized. "They thought the Land of Israel ended where the State of Israel ended." Rabbi Kook's heartfelt cry "echoed in us, as if . . . the spirit of prophecy had descended upon him."

One month later, with Egypt, Syria and Jordan poised to attack, premonitions of imminent national annihilation—another Holocaust—swept through Israel. Bomb shelters were built and graves were dug in public parks. On June 5, 1967, the first day of what would become known as the Six-Day War, IDF Chief Rabbi Goren began his broadcast to the nation with the *Sh'ma*, reminding Israelis of "the Lord our God" and concluding with the plea from Psalm 118: "O Lord, save us! O Lord, send us success."

His prayer was answered almost instantly. Early that morning a preemptive Israeli attack destroyed the Egyptian air force; the next day King Hussein's army was in flight across the Jordan River. Paratroop Brigade Commander "Motta" Gur led the military assault into the Old City of Jerusalem. Reaching the Western Wall, he touched "the wall of prayer, the wall of tears," declaring, "We are dreaming." Within six days the State of Israel was reconnected to the biblical homeland of the Jewish people and to the ancient sites of its religion and nationhood.

No one felt its powerful impact more deeply than victorious Israeli soldiers who unexpectedly encountered Jewish history, before their eyes and within themselves. After exultant paratroopers entered the Old City through the Mughrabi (Lion's) Gate, crossed the Temple Mount and descended to the Western Wall, Rabbi Goren arrived with a Torah scroll. He recited the mourner's *Kaddish* for fallen soldiers, followed by the *Shehehiyanu* prayer. Then he joyously blew his shofar. Euphoric soldiers, suddenly experiencing the convergence of their Israeli and Jewish identities, spontaneously burst into song, prayer and tears.

A soldier stepped up to kiss the Wall: "The touch of my lips opened the gates of my emotions and the tears burst forth. A Jewish soldier in the State of Israel is kissing history with his lips." An Orthodox paratrooper wrote: "I believe that the hand of God was in my participation in the battle for the liberation and reunion of Jerusalem. . . . I felt as if I had been granted the great privilege of acting as an agent of God, of Jewish history." Even a kibbutznik from the left-wing *Hashomer Hatzair* movement expressed his feelings in biblical verse: "Let us go into the house of the Lord, Our feet shall stand within Thy Gates, O Jerusalem" (*Ps.* 122:1-2). Defense Minister Moshe Dayan arrived at the Wall to place a note between the stones, as had been Jewish custom for centuries before 1948. He proclaimed: "We have reunited the city, the capital of Israel, never to part with it again." IDF Commander Yitzhak Rabin praised the soldiers whose sacrifices "have brought about redemption."

No less astonishing than the military victory was the religious resonance of the Six-Day War, named by the staunchly secular Rabin to echo the biblical days of creation. A true sabra, an unsentimental man who rarely showed emotion in public, Rabin could not conceal the spiritual meaning of the war for the soldiers who fought and survived to savor their victory. Their "sense of standing at the very heart of Jewish history," he acknowledged upon receiving an honorary degree at the newly restored Hebrew University on Mt. Scopus, had released "springs of feeling and spiritual discovery." The paratroopers who conquered the Western Wall, he recalled, "leaned on its stones and wept." Their sudden surge of emotion, "powerful enough to break through their habits of reticence, revealed as though by a flash of lightning truths that were deeply hidden."

Rabin did not identify those truths, but jubilant Israelis experienced them in the weeks following the war when, by the tens of thousands, they flocked to Jerusalem and Hebron. Two months later, in a ceremony at the ancient Jewish cemetery on the Mount of Olives, Dayan—born in Degania, the first Zionist kibbutz—captured the ecstatic moment, not of military conquest but of sacred homecoming: "We have returned to all that is holy in our land. . . . We have returned to the cradle of our people, to the inheritance of the Patriarchs. . . . We have returned to the Mountain [Temple Mount], to Hebron and to Nablus. We will not be parted from the holy places." After an exultant tour of the Temple Mount, Rachel's Tomb, and Machpelah, Ben-Gurion met with Cabinet members to insist: "On Jerusalem we must not budge. We have to quickly establish a large settlement there. The same with Hebron."

The Six-Day War was not only a stunning military victory. No one better captured its deep spiritual meaning than literary scholar Harold Fisch, who described it in *The Zionist Revolution* as "a truly religious moment, the experience of miracle, of sudden illumination. . . . We were suddenly living in the fullness of our own covenant history." Israelis "who had never known they were Jews suddenly awoke to their inheritance." The Israeli claim to land, for the first time explicitly, rested upon the Bible as the deed of title, originating in God's promise to Abraham: "To your people I will give this land" (*Gen.* 12:7). In June 1967, state, religion, and territory suddenly converged. From Hebron in the south to Shechem in the north and Jericho to the east, the modern State of Israel had suddenly become contiguous with the lost territory of its ancient homeland.

It was a transformative historical moment; even secular Israelis were deeply moved by this astonishing confluence of past and present, Judaism and Zionism. In an illuminating collection of postwar conversations with soldiers from *kibbutzim* (published in English as *The Seventh Day*), the religious meaning of return was revealed. "When we heard of the conquest of Jerusalem," a *kibbutznik* recounted, "there wasn't a single one who didn't weep, including me. Then, for the first time, I felt not the 'Israelness' but the Jewishness of the nation." "Even though I'm not religious," another *kibbutznik* recalled, "the Wall meant an awful lot to me. . . . It symbolizes everything." Another soldier was deeply moved when he suddenly realized that "the whole of the Promised Land is ours." A religious soldier observed that his secular friends, "kibbutz-educated towards an attitude of scorn for traditional religious values, [were] now overwhelmed by a feeling of holiness, and as elated and moved as I was."

But for some soldiers, the joy of victory was tempered by their unexpected encounter with the biblical landscape, which left them unmoved. "I had no sensation of returning home," recounted one kibbutznik. "Holy or not," another soldier remembered, the return to Jerusalem "left me cold." Kibbutznik paratrooper Haimito Moscowitz arrived at the Western Wall after engaging in brutal house-to-house fighting outside the Old City. "I saw that there were some soldiers crying at the Wall. Religious ones. They were praying. I was very angry. I felt nothing. I thought, because of this so many people had to die? Then to hell with all the religious people. I wanted them all to die."

The editors omitted expressions of political and religious elation that challenged their own secular liberal principles. The statement of a former Palmach commander was deleted after he described the return to Judea and Samaria as the fulfillment of what his Zionist father and grandfather had done before him when settling the land. It was not a comparison that the editors were eager to affirm. Interviews with soldiers from Rabbi Kook's Mercaz HaRav yeshiva were excluded because they did not share the "unease over victory and occupation" that the editors wished to emphasize. Their surging religious nationalism would not be permitted to overshadow the ambivalence of sensitive secular kibbutzniks.

One of the interviewers, an aspiring young writer from kibbutz Hulda named Amos Oz, subsequently expressed his regret at the triumph of "yeshiva students" over kibbutzniks in 1967. The "values, ideals, conscience, world view" of secular Zionism, he lamented, were now being challenged by "victory and miracles, Redemption and the coming of the Messiah," and by the "nationalistic-religious fantasy" of Israelis whose exuberant blend of Zionism and Judaism Oz deplored.

But the Six-Day War, journalist Amos Elon recognized, "suddenly confronted Israel with its history"—its Jewish history. Bravely fought by soldiers from kibbutzim, the exemplary repository of Labor Zionist values, their victory galvanized religious Zionists, who would seize their unanticipated opportunity to redefine Zionism as the religious expression of Jewish nationalism. Consequently, the war reframed the Israeli struggle over legitimacy within deeply divisive disagreements about religion, geography, history, and the meaning of Zionism that have yet to be resolved.

The government immediately acted to demolish the ramshackle Mughrabi neighborhood, built by Muslims adjacent to the Western Wall to impede Jewish access, and to rebuild the Jewish Quarter, whose residents had been driven out by Jordanian soldiers nineteen years earlier. With a broad national consensus for Israeli sovereignty in Jerusalem, East Jerusalem was annexed. After nearly two decades as a partitioned city divided by barbed wire Jerusalem was united under Jewish sovereignty, with its neighborhoods, markets and holy sites accessible to all, for the first time in two thousand years.

Hebron, where King David had ruled before relocating his throne to Jerusalem to unite his kingdom, was more problematic. Barred by Muslims ever since the thirteenth century from entering the Machpelah enclosure, which was converted into a mosque, a small and fractured Jewish community with Sephardi roots in Turkey and Mesopotamia and Ashkenazi origins in Eastern Europe had struggled to survive spiritually and economically. By the end of the nineteenth century, infused with the arrival of newcomers and support from Jewish philanthropists abroad, the Hebron Jewish community was revitalized. New synagogues, yeshivas and a medical clinic testified to its spiritual and material growth.

But in 1929, amid a wave of Arab rioting, murder and plunder that swept through Palestine, the community was decimated. In a horrific outburst of Arab fury, Hebron Jews were raped, mutilated and tortured; sixty-seven men, women, and children were mercilessly slaughtered. After British soldiers evacuated nearly five hundred wounded and traumatized survivors the most ancient Jewish community in the Land of Israel ceased to exist. To secular Zionists, however, Hebron was merely one more "city of slaughter" whose religious Jews were too timid to fight back. Jews who had "gone to the slaughter like sheep" were castigated as "a disgrace to Zionism." For nearly forty years Hebron remained *Judenrein*. Few Zionists lamented its loss.

The euphoria of tens of thousands of Israelis arriving in Hebron in June 1967 to explore their long forbidden city and pray at ancient holy sites was incomprehensible to some secular Zionists. Revered archeologist Yigael Yadin, whose widely popular Masada excavations had unabashedly celebrated the killing (by their own compatriots) and suicide of nine hundred Jewish Zealots to avoid Roman capture, denounced as "idolatrous" the worship of national and religious relics. Jews who imagined that they were praying at the tombs of their patriarchs and matriarchs in Hebron, Yadin said dismissively, were more likely idolaters at the graves of Arab sheiks.

But a handful of religious Zionists, graduates of Rabbi Kook's yeshiva, were determined to rebuild the destroyed Jewish communities in Hebron and nearby Gush Etzion and, in the process, to fuse Zionist nationalism and religious Judaism. For Hanan Porat, who had grown up in Gush Etzion, a mixed cluster of secular and religious kibbutzim south of Jerusalem, the opportunity to link "theology, historical experience, and political activity" was galvanizing. Porat belonged to a cohort of Gush Etzion survivors who remembered how marauding Arabs had "cut our roots brutally," slaughtering more than 200 kibbutzniks who fought desperately to their tragic end the day before Israel declared independence. Annually thereafter, on Israel's Memorial Day commemorating the fall of Gush Etzion, the child survivors would gather at the southern edge of Jerusalem to gaze sorrowfully at the solitary tree in the distance that marked the site of their destroyed and inaccessible community.

Several months after the war, as the Labor government authorized new military security settlements on the Golan Heights and in the Jordan Valley, Porat vigorously lobbied Knesset members for the restoration of his boyhood home. News of his efforts reached Moshe Levinger, another Mercaz HaRav graduate. Following military service, Levinger had combined rabbinical duties with shepherding on a kibbutz near the Golan Heights. There he came to appreciate the Zionist determination to settle the land, which blended with his religious convictions. Porat and Levinger, joined by Elyakim Haetzni, a maverick lawyer who had fled Germany with his family in 1938 and was severely wounded during the Independence War, planned the return to Hebron. Haetzni insisted that for Jews "nationality and religion are one . . . inseparable." That insight would redefine the struggle over Zionist legitimacy, until the Six-Day War defined exclusively in secular terms.

For the Passover holiday in April 1968, Levinger rented the Park Hotel in Hebron. Thirty families attended the Seder. After their festive meal the joyous participants danced and sang *v'shavu banim l'gvulam* (God's promise that "your children shall return to their borders"). Jeremiah's prophecy remained inspirational: "You shall yet plant vineyards upon the mountains of Samaria; . . . the voice of joy, and the voice of gladness" will once again be heard "in the cities of Judea" (*Jer.* 31:17, 21; 33:10-11). From Sde Boker in the Negev came word from Ben-Gurion:

"We will make a great and awful mistake if we fail to settle Hebron, neighbor and predecessor of Jerusalem."

The holiday ended but the Park Hotel visitors refused to leave. After six weeks of negotiation Defense Minister Dayan approved their relocation from the center of Hebron to an army base overlooking the city. Two years later, in response to their growing numbers, the government authorized the construction of "upper Hebron," to be named Kiryat Arba (the biblical name of Hebron). It offered a temporary solution, but the settlers remained determined to restore the ancient Jewish community in the old Jewish Quarter in the center of the city.

Ever since its late nineteenth century origins Zionism had meant settling the coastal plain of Palestine and the Galilee, not the hills of Judea and Samaria. The holy cities of Jerusalem and Hebron were beyond the boundaries of commitment for secular Zionists who wanted to build kibbutzim and make the land fertile, not worship at religious shrines. But after the Six-Day War it was difficult for the Labor government to deny the fundamental Zionist principle of settling the Land of Israel, even if the settlers were religious Jews. The definition of Zionist legitimacy had been transformed by the triumphant return to the biblical homeland.

As the old Sabra ideal of "settlement, militarism, and activism" was infused with religious faith, secular Zionists became apprehensive that modern "enlightened" Israel was being overrun by the forces of zealotry, irrationality and religious obscurantism. What religious settlers perceived as the necessary revitalization of Zionism their critics decried as a "religious raid into the heart of secular Israel." Who, in the end, was empowered to define Zionist legitimacy (and Israeli national boundaries) — secular Zionists, whose predecessors had settled the land and built a nation; or religious Zionists, who were determined to emulate that settlement model throughout biblical Judea and Samaria?

The opportunity for settlement never would have arisen but for unyielding Arab resistance after the Six-Day War to the very existence of Israel. Although Foreign Minister Abba Eban promised that Israel would be "unbelievably generous" in defining peace terms, where "everything is negotiable," Arab leaders at the Khartoum summit conference in late August pledged: "No peace with Israel, No negotiations with Israel, No recognition of Israel." Eban memorably concluded that Arabs "never miss an opportunity to miss an opportunity."

For the next six years the Labor government paid slight attention to settlement building. With the exception of security outposts scattered along the Jordan River and the Golan Heights, the return to Gush Etzion and development of Kiryat Arba defined settlement limits. But the shock of the Yom Kippur War, which caught Israel unprepared and hastened the end of Labor Party rule, prompted a group of Rabbi Kook's disciples to form Gush Emunim ("Bloc of the Faithful"). Its Manifesto called for a "reawakening among the Jewish people for the fulfillment of the Zionist vision in its full scope. . . . The sources of that vision are the Jewish tradition and roots."

Gush Emunim became the spearhead of religious Zionist settlement. Determined to "rejuvenate" Zionism at a time when the pioneering spirit seemed less inspirational to Israelis than Western values of materialistic striving and individual self-gratification, Gush activists saw themselves as the heirs of authentic Zionism and inheritors of God's covenantal promise of the land to Abraham. Zionism and Torah—not Western consumerism or dreams of normalization—provided their sources of inspiration. "A government that prevents settlements," they pointedly asserted, "undercuts its own legitimacy."

Gush Emunim launched a "religious raid into the heart of secular Israel." Its goal was the convergence of the State of Israel with the Land of Israel. "The Jewish people," the settlers' governing council insisted, "are not a foreign occupier in their own land." Gush Emunim not only challenged the territorial boundaries of Israel but also, as Hebrew University sociologist Gideon Aran observed, "the boundaries of Judaism." It constituted "an authentic and original attempt to revitalize traditional Judaism" by embracing Zionist tactics and goals.

As international pressure mounted on Israel to relinquish the West Bank, Gush Emunim leaders decided to act. Rabbi Kook urged his followers to "forcefully and boldly . . . remind the government and people of the State of Israel that no concession of our land will be permitted." To their revered rabbi, relinquishing any part of the Land of Israel was a "sin." Territorial compromise, he admonished Defense Minister Shimon Peres, would be "inane folly" likely to ignite "an internal war regarding Judea and Samaria, and everyone will rise up against this government." He reiterated the ruling of Nachmanides, the esteemed thirteenth century Spanish rabbi and philosopher, that there is a religious duty to occupy the Land of Israel, "and not to let it [pass] to the rule of other nations."

God and State · 61

In June 1974, one hundred Gush Emunim activists set out to establish the first settlement in the heart of Samaria, near Nablus. Named Elon Moreh, it marked the place where, according to the Book of Genesis, God had promised Abraham that his descendants would inherit the land. The evening after a new government led by Yitzhak Rabin received narrow Knesset approval, the Elon Moreh settlers reached their destination—without government authorization but validated, in their eyes, by Jewish history and Zionist settlement in the Land of Israel. They were the newest pioneers, following in the footsteps of their Labor Zionist predecessors who had sprinkled the land with watchtower-and-stockade settlements to protect the borders of the nascent state.

The next day Rabbi Kook and military hero Ariel Sharon joined them. A clash loomed between "our obligation toward the Land of Israel" (proclaimed in the Gush Emunim Manifesto) and the rule of Israeli law as determined by the (Labor) government. Some government ministers cited the *Altalena* precedent to justify the vigorous assertion of state authority. That night soldiers tore down the fence that barricaded the settlers. Sharon shouted at them to refuse orders, explaining to a hesitant soldier: "This is an immoral order. I wouldn't follow an order like that."

The settlers were dispersed but the scenario was repeated a year later at nearby Sebastia. Gush Emunim rallied three thousand supporters to establish a new settlement there with a flier that declared: "Remember! We are following the path, rich in deeds, of the fathers of the Zionist movement." Religious Zionists arrived during Hanukkah to live in tents and study in a makeshift yeshiva. When a rabbi from the Bnei Akiva religious youth movement brought a Torah scroll, hundreds of young men linked arms to dance joyously around him, while singing "The Land of Israel belongs to the People of Israel." Driving from Jerusalem to witness the escalating confrontation between settlers and the government, Haim Gouri recalled the words of fellow poet Nathan Alterman: "anyone who gives up Samaria will have to change the prayer book, because the history of nations has never heard of a nation giving up its homeland."

Defense Minister Peres arrived to deliver a government ultimatum: "clear the area within one day, [or] the government will force you out." Rabbi Levinger tore his shirt in the traditional ritual of mourning; settlers chanted from the Book of Lamentations, recounting the destruction of ancient Jerusalem. Ministers from the National Religious Party, in which Gush Emunim was embedded, supported the settlers; ministers on the left demanded government action to evacuate them. Prime Minister Rabin decided to dispatch the army to evict them, by force if necessary.

But Chief of Staff Mordechai Gur told Rabin that five thousand soldiers would be needed for the mission to succeed. "The chief of staff," Rabin subsequently wrote, "did not bother to hide that he was not excited to carry out the action . . . my impression was that he would order the IDF to remove the settlers only against his own will." Rabin, who had commanded Palmach fighters on the Tel Aviv beach to open fire on the *Altalena*, was "choked with rage" at Gur's hesitation. His government squelched repeated attempts to establish the settlement before finally permitting the unrelenting Gush Emunim activists to live in Camp Kedum, a nearby army base, while negotiations over their future site continued.

The election of Menachem Begin as prime minister in 1977 transformed Israeli politics. Begin was a conspicuous exception to the secularism of the pioneering generation of Zionist leaders. Descended on his mother's side from a line of distinguished rabbis, he had received a religious Zionist education in Brest-Litovsk, a city filled with synagogues, Zionist youth movements, and a rich Jewish culture. But he never forgot the persecution of Jews and his father's struggle "to defend Jewish honour."

A political outcast after the violent confrontation over the *Altalena*, Begin wandered in the Israeli political wilderness. Ben-Gurion would not even acknowledge him by name in Knesset debates (recognizing Begin only as "the gentleman next to Mr. Bader"). On the election night when he finally became prime minister, Begin wore a *kipa* and recited Psalms as he faced exultant supporters. After he was asked to form a new government he visited Rabbi Kook to receive his blessing before going to pray at the Western Wall.

Upon assuming his official duties, Begin confessed: "I have the feeling of the *chazzan* on the High Holy Days when he stands before the Holy Ark and he appeals to the Almighty in the name of the whole congregation, and he says to God, 'I have come to plead before you on behalf of your people, Israel, who have made me their messenger, even though I am unworthy of the task. Therefore, I beseech you, O Lord, make my mission successful.'" Emotionally and rhetorically, Begin became Israel's first (and, until now, only) prime minister to frame his politics within Jewish religious language.

Shortly after his election Begin visited Elon Moreh. Holding a Torah scroll, he promised the ecstatic settlers: "Soon there will be many more Elon Morehs." When the Supreme Court ruled that they illegally inhabited private land owned by local Arabs, they relocated to land recognized by the Court as state land. The new settlements of Kedumim and Ofra were established nearby. The seeds of religious Zionist settlement were beginning to germinate.

Gush Emunim activists were relentless. But it was not merely a matter of establishing new settlements, the hallmark of generations of Zionist pioneers. After nearly three decades of Labor Party rule, and the near disaster of the Yom Kippur War, settlers confronted secular Israelis with an unprecedented religious Zionist challenge. "No government," Rabbi Levinger insisted, throwing down the gauntlet of legitimacy, "has the authority or right to say that a Jew cannot live in all of the parts of the Land of Israel."

Settlement leaders did not conceal their discomfort with democratic principles, especially when Jewish rights to the land were at stake. Lawyer Elyakim Haetzni, one of the founding fathers of the Hebron community, declared: "Even if 100 percent of the Jewish inhabitants of Israel should vote for its separation from the Land of Israel, that 'hundred percent consensus' would not have any more validity than the 'hundred percent consensus' that prevailed within the people of Israel when it danced around the golden calf." Any Israeli government that ceded portions of the biblical homeland, settlers claimed, sacrificed its legitimate authority. The Covenant between God and the Jewish people, Hanan Porat insisted, was decisive. According to Rabbi Tzvi Yehuda Kook: "We are commanded both to possess and to settle. . . . We cannot evade this commandment." Even David Ben-Gurion had affirmed to British Mandatory authorities: "The Bible is our mandate."

Settlement leaders were stunned when Prime Minister Begin, negotiating a peace treaty with Egypt, agreed to the removal of Jewish settlers from Sinai and Palestinian autonomy in the West Bank. The forcible eviction of settlers from their homes in Yamit by Israeli soldiers set an ominous precedent for Judea and Samaria. Kiryat Arba leaders decided to force the issue and return to Hebron. Ten women accompanied by thirty-five children were transported at 4 a.m. to the rear of Beit Hadassah, the old medical clinic in the center of the Jewish Quarter. They climbed ladders, cut window wires and entered the abandoned building. Enthusiastic singing by the excited children brought an Israeli soldier from his nearby guard post to investigate. When he asked how they had entered the building a four-year-old girl responded, "Jacob, our forefather, built us a ladder and we came in." The struggle over legitimacy was joined, and settlements were—and have remained ever since—at the crux of the conflict.

With the surge of religious Zionist settlement, vigorously encouraged by Begin's Minister of Agriculture Ariel Sharon, the settler population doubled (to 40,000). In 1984, an appropriate year for fictional dystopia, novelist Benjamin Tammuz warned that "messianic religious fanaticism" now ruled over Israel, while the left-wing newspaper *Al-HaMishmar* anticipated "Dark Medieval Fascism." A new generation of Israelis, wrote journalist Doron Rosenblum, watched while its homeland was "pulled out from under its feet." Within five more years the number of settlers had nearly redoubled.

The narrow election victory of Yitzhak Rabin in 1992, followed a year later by the Oslo Accords, posed a serious threat to the future of settlements. An unprecedented wave of Palestinian terror attacks and murders, especially in and near Hebron, evoked memories of the horrific destruction of its Jewish community in 1929. Military warnings of an impending attack alerted Baruch Goldstein of Kiryat Arba, the resident medical doctor who worked around the clock treating victims of Palestinian terrorism. In an attempt to prevent what he feared would be another massacre of Hebron Jews, Goldstein preemptively murdered twenty-nine Muslims and wounded more than one hundred worshippers inside the Machpelah mosque.

Prime Minister Rabin, who had previously denounced Jewish settlers as "a cancer in the body of Israeli democracy," responded to Goldstein's horrific attack by declaring his intention to expel Jews from the Tel Rumeida neighborhood of Hebron (the probable site of the ancient biblical city). His decision triggered a firestorm of rabbinical fury—and a major legitimacy crisis as rabbis challenged the authority of the government to remove Hebron Jews from their homes.

Rabbi Goren lacerated Rabin's "criminal initiative" to evacuate settlers. "According to the *Halakha*," he declared, "the meaning of the destruction of Hebron, God forbid, . . . is like the killing of people." For that reason, "we have to give our life in the struggle against this vicious plan of the government of Israel, which relies on the Arabs for its majority, and be ready to die rather than allow the destruction of Hebron." Other prominent rabbis in the religious Zionist movement, with a loyal following among yeshiva graduates serving in the IDF, added their voices in support. Addressing soldiers directly, they not only advised that the Tel Rumeida evacuation orders constituted illegal expulsions from Jewish property; taking an unprecedented step, they urged disobedience of any order to evacuate settlers from their homes.

By then the Rabin government, having lost the support of the religious Shas party for its willingness to relinquish Israel's biblical patrimony, depended on the votes of five Israeli Arab Knesset members for its razor-thin ruling majority. Defending their unprecedented power, Rabin claimed that challenges to the legitimacy of his government represented racist attacks against Israeli democracy. His refusal to call new elections enraged the National Religious Party, whose leaders vigorously defended the right of Jewish settlement and demanded a public referendum as the only democratic way to resolve the conflict.

As protest mounted, rabbis absolved soldiers from any obligation to obey government evacuation orders. Right-wing opponents of the Oslo Accords displayed posters depicting Rabin wearing an SS uniform or an Arab keffiyeh, symbolically delegitimizing his government for its alliance with enemies of the Jewish people. Elyakim Haetzni asserted that "an IDF soldier, though Jewish, who would pull us, our wives, our children and grandchildren from our home and make us refugees will, in our view, be conducting a pogrom. We shall look upon him as a violent thug acting like a Cossack."

Under mounting rabbinical pressure, with diminished public support for the Oslo Accords as Palestinian terrorism increased, Rabin backed away from the decision to evacuate Tel Rumeida. The Council of the Chief Rabbinate expressed relief to remove from its agenda "the question of military orders to evacuate settlers or settlements—which are against the *Halakha*." Settlements had become the flashpoint of increasingly acrimonious religious and secular Zionist conflict over competing sources of legitimacy in the Jewish state.

One year later, following implementation of the Gaza-Jericho autonomy plan and the return of PLO leader Yasser Arafat from Tunisian exile, the Eretz Israel Rabbinical Union, representing one thousand rabbis, condemned "the so-called peace agreement, made by a government supported by a tiny majority with a critical Arab Knesset vote." Anyone "who can stop this 'agreement' and does not do so, breaks the rule 'you shall not stand idle when there is danger to your brother.'"

Once again in 1995, as in 1948, Israelis were in open conflict over the irrepressible conundrum of legitimacy: who decides? This time, however, it was not the political left and right that were locked in combat; now rabbis were challenging the authority of elected officials to relinquish portions of the historic Land of Israel. "Never before," concluded Ehud Sprinzak, "had such an intense delegitimation campaign been conducted in Israel."

As the struggle intensified, it provoked sharp challenges to the ruling authority of the Rabin government, lacking (for the first time in Israel's history) a Jewish majority in the Knesset. If Israel was a democratic state, a state of all its citizens, that should not have mattered. But, if it was a Jewish state, it could hardly have mattered more, as religious Zionist and rabbinical opposition to Rabin's Oslo commitments demonstrated. And if Israel was both democratic and Jewish, where was the line to be drawn over the legitimacy of sacrificing "land for peace"—and who would draw it?

Following a wave of Palestinian suicide bombings that killed nearly one hundred Israelis, prominent rabbis from the Rabbinical Council of Jewish Settlements considered whether to bring government leaders to trial for violating the *halakhic* principles of *din rodef* and *din moser*. Under Jewish law a *rodef*, who was prepared to murder or abet the killing of another Jew, could be put to death without trial to protect Jewish life. A *moser* was a Jew who could justifiably be killed for relinquishing Jewish property to a Gentile.

Could the government, the rabbis asked, "be regarded as accomplices to acts of murder committed by terrorists?" If so, should its leaders "be tried according to the *Halakha*?" Which court should issue a verdict—"an ordinary secular court" or "a court of justice"? Should government ministers be warned that they might face "the *Halakhic* ruling of *din moser*, as ones who surrender the life and property of Jews to the Gentiles?" These ominous questions, which framed the debate in religious circles over the Oslo plan to relinquish portions of the Land of Israel, hovered over the Rabin government.

With the signing of the Oslo II Accord in September 1995, Palestinian autonomy was extended over West Bank Arab cities and villages. The heightened danger to Jewish settlers once Israeli army units were withdrawn provoked another sharp response from rabbinical authorities. Asserting "a permanent military camp is a Jewish settlement in the full sense of the term," they cited "a Torah prohibition to evacuate IDF bases and transfer the place to the Gentiles." They implored the government "to avoid putting soldiers through a decision involving a choice between the army's orders and loyalty to their ethical convictions."

Rabin was infuriated by rabbinical intrusion into matters of governance: "It is unheard of that the democratically elected government will be forced by rabbis, using the *Halakha*, to instruct soldiers to disobey orders. There has never been anything like this in Israel's past history." Rabin seemed to be approaching an *Altalena* reprise, when the government of Israel might once again reach the brink of civil war over perceived challenges to its right to rule.

The Oslo Accords aroused the fury of right-wing Zionists—who were hardly confined to settlements—toward the government. Among them was Yigal Amir, a twenty-five-year-old former yeshiva student and Golani Brigade soldier, who was enrolled as a law student at Bar Ilan University. After assassinating Prime Minister Rabin he explained: "If not for a *Halakhic* ruling of *din rodef*, made against Rabin by a few rabbis I knew about, it would have been very difficult for me to murder." Although Amir was a resident of the Tel Aviv suburb of Herzlyia, settlers were widely castigated after Rabin's assassination for creating the political climate in which such a heinous act could occur. But to National Religious Party leader Zevulon Hammer, this response signaled an attempt "to delegitimize the whole religious camp."

Amir's trial exposed the unresolved conundrum of separate Israeli and *halakhic* legal systems. During his pre-trial interrogation, Amir had referred to Rabin as "a Jew who murdered fourteen Jews that were aboard the ship *Altalena*," bearing responsibility "for his persecution of everything sacred to Judaism." Citing *halakhic* justification for his action, Amir's reliance on the *din rodef* principle implicitly challenged the legitimacy of the court that placed him on trial. As legal scholar Leora Bilsky observed, he posed the ultimate question of legitimacy: "what is the hierarchy of secular law and Jewish law in the State of Israel?"

In his trial, Amir insisted that Israel's continued existence as a Jewish state required the supremacy of *halakha* over civil law. He claimed *halakhic* authority to justify his killing of the prime minister. But he did not persuade the court whose legitimacy he implicitly challenged. Presiding Judge Edmond Levy, himself a religious Jew, rejected Amir's claim of justification under *din rodef*. His reliance upon *halakhic* principle, Judge Levy asserted, was "a cynical and blatant exploitation of the *halakha* for aims that are foreign to Judaism." Jewish law, the judge instructed Amir, was subordinate to the law of the state.

Judge Levy offered an illuminating rebuttal—on religious grounds—to Amir's challenge. Mixing sacred and secular references, he ruled that without the authority of the Sanhedrin, the supreme Jewish court of antiquity, rabbis could no longer apply the principle of *din rodef* to rule on *halakhic* issues. The Court condemned "the sin of senseless hatred" (the religious principle of *sinat hinam*), insisting that there was "no greater desecration of God" than Amir's action, based upon his attempt "to find in the Torah facets it does not have in order to justify his terrible deed." Amir had claimed: "There is a commandment more important than 'thou shalt not kill'—that to 'save a life' . . . even when one kills in war." But the Court pointedly referred to "the revelation of Mt. Sinai—'thou shalt not kill.'" That commandment, it added, "should beat in the heart of every civilized person and all the more so in the heart of a Jew who has taken upon himself voluntarily to observe the 613 precepts of Jewish law."

The Rabin murder and Amir's trial, Professor Bilsky concludes, exposed "the fragile coexistence of Israel's two fundamental values as a "Jewish and democratic state." Amir's murderous act and his claim of self-defense attempted to erase "the fault line between the Jewish religion and democratic law." But the Court ruled: "the aura the defendant wishes to wrap himself in, as one who has sacrificed himself on the altar of his faith, is false." Amir and "those of his ilk," Judge Levy added, were "the nightmare of any seeker of democracy." Although Amir, noted Judge Oded Mudrick, was "a person whose biography . . . seemed to reflect the ideals on which the Zionist movement had been established," nonetheless "the sign of Cain will stand out eternally on the defendant's forehead."

Amid these dramatic—and traumatic—conflicts over legitimacy a quiet judicial revolution was transforming Israeli law. In the absence of a constitution, thwarted by religious opposition since the establishment of the state, the Knesset had enacted a series of "Basic Laws" authorizing its own powers and those of the president, the military, and the judiciary. Additional Basic Laws secured state land authority and, after 1967, Jerusalem as the capital of Israel. Knesset member Amnon Rubinstein aptly described these laws as "the half-legitimate heirs to the defunct constitution."

Basic Law proposals for the protection of human rights were repeatedly introduced. But the religious parties, whose support invariably was essential to preserve coalition governments, firmly opposed legislation that might limit the powers of the rabbinate. Rubinstein, leader of the left-wing Meretz party, persisted. He introduced the Basic Law on Human Dignity and Liberty, which survived extensive negotiation and compromise with religious party leaders to become law in 1992. It guaranteed protection of fundamental human rights that expressed "the values of the State of Israel as a Jewish and democratic state": "life, body and dignity," property, privacy, confidentiality, and freedom to leave and enter the country.

But, as Rubinstein conceded, there was "a price to be paid" for even so limited an enumeration of human rights. Rabbinical courts retained exclusive jurisdiction regarding marriage and divorce. A provision for "freedom of movement" within the country was deleted to assure that no vehicular traffic could pass through Orthodox neighborhoods on the Sabbath. An explicit reference to equality was removed lest it elevate non-Orthodox religious communities and their rabbis to Orthodox status. A proposal to guarantee freedom of speech was omitted so as not to protect pornography or blasphemy.

Although these Basic Laws made no mention of judicial review, the Supreme Court under Chief Justice Aharon Barak (1995-2006) grasped the opportunity to expand the scope of its own authority. Admiring the power exercised by American courts, Barak asserted: "Everything is justiciable." He insisted: "The term 'Jewish and democratic' does not contain a contradiction, but rather a completion, a complementing." The state institution that must uphold "our values as a Jewish, democratic state" is the judiciary—"primarily the Supreme Court."

Barak presided over what he proudly identified as a "constitutional revolution," applying judicial activism in the service of "universal" (i.e. Western liberal) values. He referred to prior judicial deference to rabbinical rulings as "casual utterances" that were "fundamentally in error." In a case involving contested jurisdiction over divorce proceedings, the Court overruled the decision of a rabbinical court, long vested with final authority over family issues. That led to his denunciation by the Orthodox community as "persecutor of the Jews" and provoked a huge public demonstration against the Court. Its organizer, a *haredi* Knesset member, warned that continued judicial intervention would incite "war." A rabbi castigated judges and left-wing Jews "who prefer human rights and humanism for our enemies to the security of the state and its citizens." A rally spokesman predicted: "We will undermine the legitimacy of the Supreme Court," while a protester held a sign reading "The Torah of Israel cannot be judged."

The Status Quo agreement showed signs of fraying. Compromises with ultra-Orthodox rabbis that had been essential for Israeli unity during the early years of statehood, when national survival was precarious, seemed increasingly burdensome fifty years later. In the interim, Israeli society had been transformed by an individualistic ethos of freedom of choice based on Western—especially American—liberal norms. Strict state control over the economy had yielded to stunningly successful private initiative and innovation in business and technology. Especially among Ashkenazi Israelis, the old collectivist Zionist ethos of austerity and sacrifice for the state had become less appealing than personal freedom. Secular Israelis began to enjoy the opportunities and pleasures of a vibrant consumer culture—even on the Sabbath when malls, restaurants and cinemas enticed affluent young patrons. By the 1990s, historian Dov Waxman observes, Israeli popular culture was "increasingly universalist and Jewishly neutral."

Demographic changes further undermined the old Zionist culture. During the 1990s, the arrival of one million Russian immigrants, most of whom were secular and many of whom were not Jewish, reduced the scope of rabbinical authority. Western newcomers, especially from the United States, brought with them Conservative and Reform Judaism—whose legitimacy was not recognized by the Orthodox rabbinate in Israel, which still claimed exclusive jurisdiction over marriage and divorce and, since 1967, control over public space at holy sites. The surging appeal of pluralism, tolerance and freedom of choice, reinforced by judicial rulings protective of individual rights, confronted the *haredi* community with an unprecedented challenge to its autonomy and authority in both the private and public spheres.

Military exemptions for yeshiva students had long been a flashpoint of secular-religious acrimony. Mindful of the decimation of Orthodox communities during the Holocaust, certain that ultra-Orthodoxy could not survive in a modern Jewish state, and for the sake of secular-religious reconciliation, Ben-Gurion had accepted the indefinite postponement of military service for *haredi* men. Those for whom "the study of Torah is their profession," whose days as yeshiva students would become a lifetime of dedication to religious texts, would not be required to serve in the Israel Defense Forces.

Insisting upon "a united army," Ben-Gurion shrewdly used the IDF as "the catalyst for social cohesion" that was essential for national stability and security, while assuring religious party leaders that military officers would be educated "to understand and respect the religious soldier." Military Chief Rabbi Shlomo Goren tried to instill "a sense of shared identity, shared values and shared purpose" among secular and religious soldiers by weaving Jewish teachings and rituals into military life. The laws of *kashrut* and *Shabbat* observance would be respected. Soldiers were obligated to attend the *kiddush* ceremony that welcomed the Sabbath. New inductees received their own Bible and every military base was required to have a synagogue. The first *hesder* yeshiva, integrating Torah study with military service in a five-year program following high-school graduation, opened in 1953. Modeled on the Zionist Nahal program that combined soldiering with farming on kibbutzim and agricultural settlements, *hesder* yeshivas instructed their students that military service was a religious imperative no less than a civic obligation.

But the insistence by *haredi* rabbis upon the necessity of uninterrupted, virtually lifelong, Torah study for the preservation of Judaism eventually undermined the viability of the Status Quo Agreement. By the turn of the century nearly 50,000 yeshiva students received financial subsidies from the state whose citizenship responsibilities they evaded with their avoidance of military service. With rabbinical cooperation, the IDF initiated a program to gradually integrate some ultra-Orthodox young men into its ranks. A special unit (*Nahal Haredi*) was established to encourage religiously observant volunteers to perform military duties within a framework of strict *halakhic* observance. Only men could serve in the battalion, where the laws of *kashrut* were strictly observed. Rabbis insisted that there be no close interaction with female soldiers. Within little more than a decade, the *Nahal Haredi* unit expanded from thirty to nearly one thousand soldiers. Its motto came from Torah: "And your camp must be holy" (*Deut.* 23:14).

In 2002, the Knesset enacted the Tal Law to codify the continuing exemption from military service for thousands of yeshiva students engaged in full-time religious study. The Supreme Court warned that the law was discriminatory but permitted the exemptions to remain in place until its mandated expiration a decade later. Amid the search for an alternative, ultra-Orthodox rabbinical opposition to required military service for yeshiva students remained adamantly unyielding. As one rabbi declared: "Anyone who understands that isolation from the culture of sinners is the foundation of our existence will struggle with all his strength against any process of integration with Israeli society." Law professor Yedidia Stern, appointed to a government committee charged with revising the law, observed: "two worldviews grapple in the center of the Israeli arena: religious and liberal." The terms of reconciliation were elusive.

In 2012, the Court ruled that the Tal Law was an illegal infringement on equality. Thousands of haredi men gathered outside a military recruitment office in Jerusalem to protest against the prospect of conscription. Warnings against the "licentious military" appeared on Jerusalem billboards. Haredi youngsters were taught "why the army institutions are not, and will never be, legitimate." One year later Prime Minister Netanyahu's ministerial legislative committee submitted a proposal to the Knesset that would exempt only 1,800 yeshiva students from military service, permitting others to study for three years until they were drafted at age twenty-one. It was, declared an Orthodox Knesset member, "a black day in the history of Jews in Israel." It spilled into violence when a haredi soldier, visiting relatives in Jerusalem's Mea Shearim neighborhood, was assaulted by dozens of ultra-Orthodox men. A mutually acceptable political solution for equal sharing of the burden of military service remains elusive.

Secular-religious conflict has also intensified with competing, and increasingly acrimonious, claims over control of public space. In 2011, an eight-year-old girl walking to school in Beit Shemesh, where ultra-Orthodox families had relocated from their overcrowded Jerusalem neighborhoods, was spat upon and verbally abused by haredi men for dressing, in their (presumably averted) eyes, immodestly. Outside a local synagogue, gender separation was rigidly enforced with different sidewalks for men and women. A violent clash erupted between young yeshiva students and police over the posting of signs warning "immodesty dressed women" not to enter their neighborhood. Beit Shemesh came to symbolize the seemingly intractable conflict between ultra-Orthodox *halakhic* restrictions and the personal freedom of choice demanded by the secular majority of Israeli citizens.

The growing haredi presence outside Jerusalem increased the need for inter-city public transportation. But rabbinical insistence upon gender-segregated buses became another source of bitter discord. It erupted into national awareness when a female soldier refused the demand of a yeshiva student (whose religious study exempted him from military service) to relocate to the rear of the bus. Verbally abused by other haredi male passengers, she filed sexual harassment charges. No less abhorrent to secular Israelis, a group of religious soldiers walked out of a military ceremony because their norms of public modesty were violated when female soldiers began to sing.

Sacred public space, especially adjacent to the Western Wall, became a repeated flashpoint of contention. Since the mid-1980s, an organization known as Women of the Wall struggled, in the words of its mission statement, "to achieve the social and legal recognition of our right, as women, to wear prayer shawls, pray, and read from the Torah collectively and out loud at the Western Wall." Their monthly public challenges defied the gendered guidelines set by the Ministry of Religious Authority, the government agency charged since 1967 with supervision of Jewish holy sites.

The controversy generated contradictory Supreme Court rulings. In 2002, the Court approved the right claimed by Women of the Wall to pray and read from Torah in the smaller women's section of the Western Wall plaza. Within a year, however, persistent ultra-Orthodox opposition prompted judicial reconsideration. In a 5-4 decision, the Court upheld the rabbinical prohibition on women wearing *tallitot* or *tefillin*, and reading Torah, in the gender divided plaza. But it instructed the government to provide a suitable alternative location for mixed gender prayer. The designated site, around the corner of the Western Wall, was located near an ancient gateway to the Temple Mount known since its mid-nineteenth century discovery as Robinson's Arch.

Women of the Wall, led by Anat Hoffman, challenged that proposal. Raised in Israel as a self-described "totally secular Jew," Hoffman had discovered liberal Judaism as a student at UCLA. Women of the Wall, she conceded, "did not evolve here in Israel, this is an import from abroad." But the Western Wall, she insisted, "is way too important to be left to the Israelis."

The ultra-Orthodox rabbinate in Israel does not look kindly upon foreign imports, especially when they threaten its norms of religious observance. Nor do liberal Jewish women appreciate challenges to their cherished principle of gender equality. Conflict erupted in October 2012 when Hoffman, arrested at the Wall for audibly reciting the *Sh'ma* prayer while wearing a *tallit*, claimed to have been humiliated and abused by the police during her overnight confinement. Her mistreatment went viral, prompting furious denunciations of haredi gender discrimination and the government of Israel for tolerating it.

The Jerusalem District Court ruled that women in prayer shawls praying audibly do not disturb the public order or violate "local custom." (Indeed, old photographs reveal men and women interspersed in prayer at the Wall—but the women did not wear *tallitot* or *tefillen*.) Hoffman, with characteristic flamboyance, exulted: "We are continuing in the path of the paratroopers who liberated the Kotel." Jewish Agency chairman Natan Sharansky, appointed by Prime Minister Netanyahu to develop a mutually acceptable compromise, proposed extending the Western Wall plaza around the corner to Robinson's Arch, with space provided there for egalitarian prayer.

Whether the gender-separated religious practices of Orthodox Jews and the gender equality demanded by liberal Jewish women can be reconciled remains undetermined—and unlikely. The potential for conflict loomed larger than the prospect of compromise. By mid-2013, Women at the Wall were vastly outnumbered in their monthly protests by thousands of religious girls brought in busloads by their rabbis to reclaim the holy site for Orthodoxy. Further complicating the territorial struggle, the religious affairs minister of the Palestinian Authority, which adamantly rejects Jewish authority over any part of the Old City, announced its unalterable opposition to any alterations to the Temple Mount area that would expand the space for Jewish worship, whether by ultra-Orthodox men or liberal Jewish women.

The "preferred status" granted to Orthodoxy in Israel, suggests legal scholar Gila Stopler, assures "a permanent tension between the state's commitment to liberal values . . . and its commitment to an Orthodox and even ultra-Orthodox version of Judaism." For the insular haredi minority, secular modernity poses a mortal danger to its understanding of Torah-based Judaism. But to the secular Israeli majority, haredim are an intrusive, intolerant, discriminatory and anti-democratic remnant of the Jewish religious culture that Zionism, infused with modern liberal principles, was intended to replace. Once again, the ultimate conundrum of legitimacy looms over Israel: who decides?

The contradictory values of a secular, pluralistic Zionist majority and a defiantly insular ultra-Orthodox minority have defied reconciliation ever since 1948. "Who is a Jew?" has been resolved, but the parameters of a "democratic and Jewish" nation remain contentious. Haredi Jews challenge the legitimacy and authority of the state while claiming entitlement to government benefits that sustain their insulation from the responsibilities of citizenship assumed by secular Israelis. The result, suggests Hebrew University sociologist Nachman Ben-Yehuda, is a "theocratic democracy" characterized by "ambiguity, delicate balances, and prolonged and continuous debates and negotiations" to preserve the precarious equilibrium that neither its critics nor beneficiaries enthusiastically embrace. In this "war within," as two Israeli journalists describe the conflict, no cease-fire is imminent.

Not even the unanticipated convergence of Zionism and Judaism following the Six-Day War, which ignited a surge of national exaltation and unity, could bridge the secular-religious chasm. Gush Emunim pioneers blended Zionist precedent with the authority of sacred texts to justify their settlement efforts. But to many secular Israelis, Jewish settlers remain misguided religious fanatics whose illegal occupation of "Palestinian" land strips Israel of its international legitimacy, undermines any possibility of Zionist normalization, and provokes an endless *kulturkampf*.

The synthesis of nationalism, liberalism and religion—securing, in contemporary parlance, a "democratic and Jewish" state—remains elusive. Whether these are complementary or contradictory values, destined to become a source of national unity or the provocation for interminable conflict, is impossible to predict. For now, it remains the unresolved dilemma of Jewish statehood and the source of its most persistently acrimonious struggles over the democratic and Jewish legitimacy of the nation. As Gershom Scholem, the renowned Hebrew University scholar of mysticism asked, "What are we first and foremost, Jews or Israelis?" His question has yet to be decisively answered.

3 Conscience and Country

The fusion of nationalism, religion and military power was deeply embedded in Jewish antiquity. The Hebrew Bible celebrated military leaders who obeyed divine command. Joshua, appointed by God to lead the Israelites into their promised land, was instructed to "be strong and very courageous" in his battles with the Canaanites and "to do according to all the Torah" (*Josh.* 1:6-7). The mighty warrior Gideon was divinely chosen to smite the Midianites and liberate the Israelites from foreign rule and idol-worship (*Judges* 5:11-16). Upon securing a united kingdom, David praised the Lord as "my rock, and my fortress, and my redeemer" (*Ps.* 18:3).

Perhaps most famously, *The First Book of Maccabees* recounts that Mattathias, rejecting the blasphemy and sacrilege demanded by King Antiochus, told the royal officers who came to Modi'in to enforce compliance: "I and my sons and my brethren walk in the covenant of our fathers. Heaven forbid that we should forsake the Law" (2:20-22). After slaying a Jew who was prepared to obey the royal decree of idolatry and the military officer who arrived to enforce it, Mattathias called out: "Let everyone that is zealous for the Law and that would maintain the covenant come forth after me" (2:27). During Hanukkah, Jews continue to celebrate the revolt of the Maccabees, an enduring reminder of rebellion against ruling authority in the name of divinely revealed law.

But with the Roman conquest in 73 CE and the defeat of the Bar Kokhba rebellion six decades later, Jewish sovereignty and the military power that had sustained it ceased to exist for nearly two millennia. Jews were compelled by their own powerlessness to heed the admonition of the prophet Zechariah: "Not by might nor by power but by my spirit, says the Lord Almighty" (*Zechariah* 4:6). Rabbis who interpreted *halakha* in the Jewish communities of exile honored the guiding principle that the law of the state was the law. Revising history to justify their political and military powerlessness, they recast King David from a bold warrior to a scholar instructing students. Bar Kokhba, no longer praised as a fighter for Jewish freedom, was denigrated as a "false messiah." In the absence of national sovereignty, rabbis transformed Hanukkah from a military uprising into the miracle of a tiny cruise of oil that burned for eight nights.

For the sake or, at least, hope of self-preservation and collective survival, non-belligerency defined the prolonged diaspora experience. Yet Maimonides, the renowned twelfth century rabbinical scholar and philosopher, acknowledged the possibility of war. He carefully instructed the fighter to "rely on the Hope and Redeemer of Israel," knowing that he "is waging war for the glorification of His Name and will place his soul in His hands." He cautioned the soldier who "ponders too much the dangers of war . . . for the people of Israel depend upon their army." And he carefully distinguished between obligatory wars for religious causes from all others, including defensive wars or even wars to conquer the Land of Israel. For nearly eight centuries, however, no Jewish army existed to implement Maimonides's principles.

In the pre-state era, Zionist pioneers defended themselves against Arab marauders, but the *Hashomer* (watchmen) were not inclined to cite religious sources to justify their retaliatory responses. After the outbreak of violent Arab rioting in 1920, the formation of the Haganah ("defense") expressed the ambivalence of Labor Zionist leaders regarding the use of force. Self-defense might be necessary, but the Yishuv was more focused on building a new society of Jewish farmers and workers than asserting military power. The prolonged Arab uprising that erupted in 1936 prompted sharp criticism of Haganah restraint from Revisionists, who formed their own aggressive fighting units, the Irgun and Lehi, to severely punish attacks against Jews.

The Israel Defense Forces, officially established two weeks after independence, absorbed the Irgun, Lehi, and elite Palmach units into a single army. But military disobedience erupted virtually simultaneously with the birth of the State of Israel. Haganah soldiers who refused to shoot their Jewish "brothers" during the *Altalena* confrontation obeyed their conscience, not their commanders. They acted according to their understanding of the obligation of a soldier to obey orders unless he received a command that he believed to be wrong.

During the early years of statehood, no experience was more formative for young Israeli men than their years in the Israel Defense Forces.

Understood to be a privilege no less than a legal obligation, military service became a fundamental national rite of passage from which only ultra-Orthodox Jews and Arab citizens were exempt. The obligation to serve was an honor that was deeply ingrained, virtually universal, and rarely challenged.

Five years after independence, eighteen-year-old Amnon Zichroni became Israel's first widely reported conscientious objector. Zichroni served briefly in an infantry unit but, claiming that he was a pacifist, he refused to carry weapons. Brought before a military tribunal, he was sentenced to seven months in prison. There he launched a three-week hunger strike until the Minister of Defense intervened to secure his release from the army. But Zichroni was the conspicuous exception. In a society in which "the omnipresence of war" defined daily reality, writes journalist Yoram Peri, there were "collectivist pressures pushing toward consensus, solidarity, and conformity." Consequently, selective conscientious objection had no status in Israeli law.

Yet even in wartime, as one horrific event demonstrated, there were boundaries to military action and obedience to orders had limits circumscribed by law. At the beginning of the Sinai war with Egypt in 1956, Arab villages near the Jordanian border were placed under strict curfew for security reasons; residents were warned that violators would be shot. A large group of villagers from Kafr Qasim, unaware that the curfew starting time had been advanced, belatedly returned from their fieldwork. In a tragic massacre, border police opened fire. Nearly fifty Arabs, including two-dozen teen-age and younger boys and girls, were killed.

Judge Binyamin Halevi, who presided over the military trial of the police and their officers, issued the memorable ruling that justified refusal to obey "manifestly unlawful" orders (a term drawn from the Military Justice Law of 1955). "The distinguishing mark of a manifestly unlawful order" (which every normal person would presumably recognize), he wrote, "is that above such an order should fly, like a black flag, a warning saying 'Prohibited!'" It became an enduring, if malleable, precedent for military disobedience in dire circumstances, when "the horrific results of blind obedience," as Judge Halevi asserted, must guide a soldier's decision whether to obey orders.

The Israel Defense Forces became the primary instrument of national cohesion. Three years of active duty, followed by two decades of military reserve obligations, bound Israelis to their country and to each other. The Six-Day War inspired an unprecedented commitment to military service by young religious men, who combined Torah study and military duty in the *hesder* program. During the Yom Kippur War they proved to be valiant fighters. Praised by commanding officers for their personal courage and inspirational model, they were mourned for the disproportionate battlefield losses that their bravery exacted.

But the IDF eventually confronted within its own ranks the consequences of an increasingly polarized nation. Unrelenting Arab hostility, foreshadowing seemingly endless conflict, began to erode the commitment of secular Israelis to military service. In 1970, one hundred graduating high-school students issued a "declaration of intent" to Prime Minister Golda Meir: "We are wondering why we should fight in a repeated war which holds no future." Two years later two reservists declined to serve in Judea and Samaria, declaring their willingness to undertake "more legitimate duties" within Israel's pre-1967 borders. Another reservist claimed that "policing occupied territory could not be regarded as 'defending my country.'" Posted in Sinai, where he witnessed Bedouin almond trees bulldozed for a new settlement, Peretz Kidron declined "as a matter of conscience and conviction" to report for duty.

Shortly before Egyptian President Anwar Sadat made his momentous visit to Israel in 1977 to launch peace negotiations, a group of high school students asked Prime Minister Begin: "How do you expect us to go to war when we are not sure whether the road that leads to war is just?" Four high-school members of a Trotskyite organization proclaimed their unwillingness to join an "occupation army." (One of them, Geora Neuman, spent eight months in prison.) Twenty-seven high-school seniors signed a letter to Defense Minister Ezer Weizman indicating their intention, inspired by "opposition to the occupation and suppression of the Palestinian people," to refuse to serve in Judea and Samaria.

Gad Elgazi, one of the signees, kept his word. Confined for 120 days, he remained adamant. Court-martialed and sentenced to one year in prison, Elgazi's persistent refusal was unprecedented. The Supreme Court rejected his appeal, ruling: "No military organization can tolerate the existence of a general principle according to which individual soldiers can dictate their place of service, be it for economic or social reasons, or for reasons of conscience."

The Camp David Accords with Egypt, requiring Israeli withdrawal from Sinai, stunned Gush Emunim settlement activists and supporters, who felt betrayed by the Begin government. Rabbi Yisrael Ariel urged settlers to "do battle in Yamit in order to save Judea and Samaria." Rabbi Kook once again opposed territorial compromise, but he backed away from encouraging disobedience to government evacuation orders. Although dismantling the Yamit settlement required the forcible military eviction of settlers from their homes, their dramatic last stand was largely symbolic. The value of Jewish solidarity, and the prospect of peace with Egypt, took priority over any impulse to disobey military commands.

But the Sinai evacuation posed a potential "existential conflict" over the ultimate sources of authority and legitimacy in Israel. Anticipating the possibility of future evacuations, the Chief Rabbinate declared that "according to our holy Torah and unequivocal and decisive halakhic rulings," no part of the historic Land of Israel could be relinquished. Gush Emunim rabbis asserted that any government declaration or action "that contests our hold on the Territories has no validity and is considered null and void."

Within a decade, the outburst of euphoria after the Six-Day War, which had briefly united secular and religious Israelis in celebrating the unification of the State of Israel with the Land of Israel, fragmented into acrimonious division and menacing confrontation. The Begin government's encouragement of settlement fueled dissent within the IDF. During the Begin-Sadat negotiations, nearly three hundred and fifty reserve officers and enlisted men signed an open letter to the Prime Minister expressing concern that "a government policy that leads to continued rule over one million Arabs is liable to change the Jewish democratic nature of the State." Publication of their letter sparked the formation of Peace Now, led by former members of IDF combat units who advocated Israeli withdrawal from Judea and Samaria.

By the early 1980's, Israel had endured years of PLO cross-border terrorist attacks from Lebanon and waves of missiles fired from the Bekaa Valley into northern Galilee communities. The attempted assassination of Ambassador Shlomo Argov in London prompted the decision by Begin and his Cabinet to expel Yasser Arafat and the PLO from southern Lebanon (as King Hussein had previously driven them from Jordan). But as the IDF pushed closer to Beirut, "Operation Peace for Galilee" became a quagmire. Israeli casualties quickly mounted and hundreds of soldiers were killed in the first ten days of fighting. Intended as a brief, geographically limited incursion, the invasion provoked massive Israeli civilian protest and unprecedented military disobedience.

When the IDF was commanded to advance beyond the original twenty-five mile invasion limit and place Beirut under siege, rumbles of dissent spread through the officer ranks. Colonel Eli Geva, the youngest IDF commander, refused the assignment to lead his elite tank brigade in an attack on West Beirut because he anticipated that it would expose his soldiers and Lebanese civilians to high risk of death. Informing brigade commanders that he was prepared "to sound the alarm" and "break the conspiracy of silence" over plans to invade the city to root out the PLO, he requested relief from his command to serve as an ordinary soldier. His refusal was described by journalists Ze'ev Schiff and Ehud Ya'ari in their history of the Lebanon war as "a radical step absolutely unprecedented in the history of the IDF." After meeting with the Chief of Staff, Defense Minister Sharon, and Prime Minister Begin, Geva was dismissed from military service.

Nearly one hundred and fifty soldiers refused to report to their units to fight in Lebanon. Several hundred reservists joined an organization called Yesh Gvul ("There is a Limit"). Formed before the war to oppose military service in Judea and Samaria, which it considered to be "occupied" territory, Yesh Gvul broadened its focus and underscored its left-wing political identity to include opposition to the Lebanon war. (A refusenik observed: "It was a source of joy for the Left that a visible action was being exercised while the Right held the power.") Within less than a year, Yesh Gvul had gathered nearly 1,500 signatures from reservists for a letter to Begin and Sharon that declared: "Instead of Peace for the Galilee, you brought us war without end. For this war, these lies, and this occupation there is no national consensus. Bring the soldiers home!" Ishai Menuchin, a reserve major and co-founder of Yesh Gvul, declared: "It never occurred to me that I might be used as a tool of occupation or be asked to fight in wars of choice, as opposed to wars of defense." He pledged his continued service in the Israel Defense Forces, but not in "the Israeli Occupation Force."

Until the Lebanon War, it had been virtually inconceivable that draft-eligible young men would refuse to serve in the IDF. Every previous war—in 1948, 1956, 1967 and 1973—was widely understood by Israelis to have been necessary and just, leaving no alternative. But the war in Lebanon was Israel's first televised war; it was fought on foreign soil where Palestinian fighters were indistinguishable from the Lebanese civilians among whom they were deeply embedded; and it was the first war waged by a right-wing government. Equating Lebanon with the

West Bank as territory unlawfully occupied by Israel, secular soldiers on the political left forged a sharp critique of the Begin government. They perceived it as a "political" war, not a "defensive" war to protect the existence of the nation.

As the national consensus on military service fractured, draft-eligible young men began to question whether their highest obligation was to their nation or to themselves, to the laws of the state or to the dictates of conscience. Increasingly, they reserved to themselves the right to decide whether to report for duty or obey orders. "I felt that my life was endangered for unjust causes," declared one refusenik, referring to the invasion of a sovereign state. Selective refusal, said another, applied "the code of civil disobedience, as forged by Gandhi and Martin Luther King, to that least likely of settings, the army."

Nearly three thousand reservists requested permission to fulfill their service "within the boundaries of the State of Israel, and not on Lebanese soil." The refuseniks, a survey by Haifa University scholar Ruth Linn revealed, were predominantly Ashkenazi university graduates in their thirties, with prior military service in Judea and Samaria. They believed that the Lebanon war lacked the necessary "no choice" justification for Israeli military action, while posing considerable risk of harm to innocent civilians (and, not incidentally, to themselves).

Menachem Begin's "war of choice," provoking sharp challenges to the legitimacy of the government that waged it, was sharply distinguished by its opponents from previous "wars of necessity." A proliferation of Holocaust and Nazi analogies revealed the intensity of domestic opposition to military service in an increasingly unpopular war. One refusenik stated: "Prime Minister Begin's words about the 'final solution' of the terrorist problem in Lebanon show why you cannot engage the Israeli soldier in this war." In a letter published in *Ha'aretz,* maverick scientist and philosopher Yeshayahu Leibovitz, who subsequently attributed a "Judeo-Nazi" mindset to Israeli soldiers, urged them to "refuse to serve in the occupied territories, so that your commanders do not turn you into a murderer." More than any other people, he warned, Israelis had reason to be wary of "obedience to orders" as sufficient justification for military action.

With the eruption of the Palestinian intifada in 1987 the focus of protest shifted from Lebanon to Judea, Samaria and Gaza. One hundred and sixty-five reservists had already been court-martialed for their refusal to serve in those territories, receiving one-to-three month sentences in military prison. The overwhelming majority—nearly ninety percent—had been active in leftist political and protest groups before their acts of refusal. One in five had already refused to serve in Lebanon. In a letter to Defense Minister Rabin, Adi Ophir condemned Israel's "repressive means" in "the twilight zone between law and evil." Occupation was "a far greater menace to Israeli democracy and to the rule of law" than refusal to serve. It was an indictment that he would embellish twenty years later in a book excoriating Zionist "colonization" of Palestinian land.

Although Israeli soldiers were restricted to using non-lethal teargas, rubber bullets and clubs, frequent street battles with young Palestinians throwing stones and Molotov cocktails took their toll on the IDF and public opinion. For the first time, soldiers confronted a substantial civilian uprising. The PLO decision to station women and children in the front lines of battle deeply upset many soldiers. Their vaunted "purity of arms" felt compromised once soldiers in full battle gear confronted Palestinian teenagers armed with slingshots, stones and firebombs. "The slightest deviation from the pure notion of self-defense," Linn observed, "seems to become an existential threat to the individual soldier's moral identity."

The extent of refusal was unprecedented, with nearly two hundred soldiers brought to trial and convicted in military tribunals. As in Lebanon, refusal predominated among a demographically identifiable segment of the population: secular, Ashkenazi, highly educated, from elite sectors of Israeli society. The majority of Israelis—especially at lower educational and income levels and from Mizrahi and religious backgrounds—accepted the view of political and military leaders that the intifada was "a continuation of the Arab war against Israel by different means." Young men from these cohorts willingly fulfilled their military obligations.

The Lebanon war had been opposed as a "war of choice" waged on foreign soil. But the Palestinian intifada, erupting only a few kilometers from Tel Aviv and Jerusalem, could hardly have been closer to home. (Indeed, for tens of thousands of Israelis living in Judea and Samaria it *was* home). Both conflicts provoked challenges from reservists who insisted that they must only be called upon to fight in "defensive and just" wars whose moral attributes they alone were empowered to assess.

Once a right-wing government came to power, and the IDF confronted Palestinian fighters and civilians in Lebanon, Judea, Samaria, and Gaza, the national consensus for military service crumbled. Dubi Hayun cited Martin Luther King's Birmingham Jail letter to justify his own imprisonment. Reserve officer Danny Zamir, a self-proclaimed "true Zionist democrat," lacerated "the all-knowing, primitive preachers and unbridled nationalists" who were "leading and misleading us to calamity." It was "a legitimate democratic act," he asserted, "to refuse when you're willing to pay the price."

While serving in Lebanon, Daniel Padnes recounted, he had begun to ask the question: "where should I draw the line?" With the outbreak of the intifada he realized "that my personal limit was the 'green line'"—Israel's temporary border under the 1949 Armistice agreement. Unwilling to serve in Gaza, he explained: "I was refusing for my friends on the left" and for his own years of work for "peaceful coexistence." Dudu Palma, the kibbutznik son of Holocaust survivors, had learned during thirty-five days in prison during the Lebanon war that he could "no longer share in undemocratic actions verging on war crimes." He would prefer to defend "a fragile democracy" against "a rising tide of nationalism and Khomeinist fundamentalism" within the recognized borders of Israel. A 1989 letter to Rabin signed by 280 high-school graduates cited the emotional toll exacted from soldiers who were obligated to violate their conscience by serving in occupied territories.

After five years of fighting in the streets and alleys of Palestinian towns and cities, 164 Israeli soldiers had been killed and nearly two hundred (mostly reservists) imprisoned for disobeying orders. More than one thousand young men had declared their refusal to participate in "an unjust occupation in defense of illegal Jewish settlements." Few military officers were persuaded by their justifications. General Yanush Ben Gal, who had served during the Lebanon war, stated bluntly: "Refusers? Kill them. . . . I see them as traitors . . . nobody has the right to decide when he wants to serve. . . . This is the beginning of anarchy."

The unprecedented extent of refusal during the wars of the 1980s revealed a deeply fractured Israeli society. For the first time, military service no longer was unanimously perceived both as a patriotic obligation and a defining rite of passage. Until then, Israel had been a "connected" society. Despite sharply contested political disagreements, it had prided itself on unbreakable bonds of national unity and shared responsibility for the defense of the state and protection of its citizens. Every Israeli soldier was taught to honor *tohar haneshek* (purity of arms), requiring the use of "weaponry and power only for the fulfillment of the mission and solely to the extent required; he will maintain his humanity even in combat." But the Lebanon war, and then the intifada, revealed an ominous schism in Israeli society that undermined the existing parameters of "moral legitimation." The abiding Israeli faith that its wars were "defensive and just" was sharply challenged.

For a growing number of young men, military service had become less a national responsibility than a personal choice. Relying upon the "black flag" doctrine (from the Kafr Qasim massacre), soldiers increasingly became their own arbiters of the legitimacy of military orders. A reserve lieutenant, sentenced to eighteen days in prison for refusing to guard settlements, denounced the "theft of land that isn't ours" by "a handful of fanatics, in the name of our 'historic right to ancestral land.'" A retired navy officer (who had departed for California) asserted that true Zionism was the "refusal to take part in the occupation." Once again, soldiers linked Israeli military responses to Nazi atrocities. A physician who declined reserve duty in a Palestinian prisoner camp stated: "My name is Marcus Levin and not Joseph Mengele, and by reason of conscience I refuse to serve in this place."

The growing appeal of universal values to young Israelis (as references to King and Gandhi suggest) challenged the once prevalent "tribal, isolated, emotional, and nationalistic" commitments that previously had been conspicuous attributes of Israeli identity. Surveys revealed that demands by young Ashkenazi Israelis for freedom of choice and personal fulfillment were undermining "the stigma of refusal." The politicization of military dissent and disobedience, invariably couched in moral language, was blatant and unprecedented. Refuseniks justified their decision as an "act of conscience" that "restored our moral backbone." But their identifiable political affiliation prompted a prescient warning from *Ha'aretz* lest left-wing disobedience become a precedent for future resistance by those on the political right.

The 1990s were a decade of euphoria and despair in Israel. The Oslo Accords, ratified with the famous handshake between Rabin and Arafat on the White House lawn, anticipated the exchange of "land for peace." But they provoked sharp protest within the religious Zionist community. Shortly after the agreement was signed an IDF reserve officer wrote to Prime Minister Rabin: "As a Jew faithful to the command of the God of Israel . . . I absolutely refuse to cooperate with any government, Gentile or Jewish, which takes steps to remove the people of Israel from its land." The Land of Israel, he asserted, "is an absolute value in national and religious terms." Consequently, there must be "a refusal to carry out orders which are inherently illegal." Another reserve officer wondered who might be evacuated from his own settlement, "where two colonels and two battalion commanders live."

Former Chief Military Rabbi Goren responded vehemently to the Accords, declaring: "It is forbidden to obey a military order which contradicts the command of settling the Land of Israel, which is equivalent to all the commandments of the *Torah*." He drafted an extensively annotated *halakhic* ruling prohibiting "the surrender of Jewish dominion over any portion of the Land of Israel" and the participation of religious soldiers in operations to transfer Israeli sovereignty. "A soldier who receives an order that is contrary to the laws of Torah," Goren asserted, "must observe the law of the Torah, and not the secular order." It was, he claimed, illegal to uproot settlements; indeed, "one is obliged to give one's life" to prevent it.

Precisely as prescient Israelis had anticipated, left-wing disobedience in the 1980s became the model for right-wing religious Zionist emulation a decade later. The regional council representing the settlers declared that any government prepared to relinquish territory was "an illegal government" whose orders should be disobeyed. Twenty high-school graduates sent a letter to Prime Minister Rabin indicating their intention to disobey orders to evacuate Israeli residents from the Golan Heights. "In the past we regarded the refusal of the left wing as a grave act." Now, however, "we understand that a refusal violates a law, but there are some things that you simply cannot pursue."

For the first time, Israeli soldiers in significant numbers confronted wrenching choices between loyalty to the laws of the state and loyalty to Torah. The Bnei Akiva religious youth movement advocated expansion of the "black flag" doctrine to include "orders that are contrary to traditional Jewish law," which are "blatantly illegal" and need not be obeyed. "On every serious question," it advised, a soldier would be expected "to consult his rabbi." Once again, if from a different sector of Israeli society, allegations of the "illegitimacy" of government policy became the justification for military disobedience.

Pursuant to the Oslo agreement, Rabin announced the impending evacuation of some IDF bases from Judea and Samaria and their transfer to the Palestinian Authority. His decision provoked a vehement response from a group of fifteen influential rabbis led by former Chief Rabbi Avraham Shapira, who had succeeded Rabbi Kook as head of the

Mercaz HaRav yeshiva. In a *halakhic* ruling he declared that evacuation of IDF bases, placing Jewish lives in jeopardy, was a forbidden violation of the biblical command to settle the land. Citing Maimonides ("Laws of Kings and their Wars," III:9), he ruled that "even if the King gives an order to transgress the words of the Torah, we do not listen to him." He urged the government not to place soldiers in a situation "in which they must struggle between their loyalty to the values which their lives are built on and army orders."

Rabin's critics claimed that his governing coalition, dependent upon the votes of five Arab Knesset members for its precarious ruling majority, lacked the legitimacy to issue such orders. Rabbi Jonathan Blass, leader of a program for *hesder* yeshiva graduates, asserted: "An Israeli soldier who will be violating his deepest religious principles by expelling Jews from the Land of Israel . . . is obligated to disobey those orders." One thousand reservists signed a statement to Rabin indicating that they would not obey orders to uproot settlements. Such action by the IDF, they declared, was "inhuman, anti-Zionist, and runs contrary to my conscience as a person, citizen, and Jew." Infuriated religious Zionists compared the Israeli government to the collaborationist Vichy regime in wartime France.

Rabbi Shapira's ruling provoked a vehement response from government officials who would not permit rabbinical edicts to negate government and military decisions. Rabin was incensed that rabbis would challenge his authority and command soldiers to disobey the government. Foreign Minister Shimon Peres warned: "There is no place for abandonment of the law." Environment Minister Yossi Sarid accused the rabbis of behaving "like the worst of the zealots who caused the destruction of the Second Temple." The rabbinical ruling, wrote Hillel Halkin, "has for the first time raised the specter of mass insubordination in Israel's citizens army." Jerusalem *Post* journalist Herb Keinan wondered: "Can brother drag away brother, and the house remain whole?"

The eruption of the Second Intifada in September 2000, with violent Palestinian riots following Prime Minister Sharon's visit to the Temple Mount in Jerusalem's Old City, quickly spiraled into waves of horrific terrorist attacks and suicide bombings throughout the country. A Hamas bomber exploded himself outside the Dolphinarium nightclub in Tel Aviv, killing twenty-one Israelis. A Palestinian terrorist targeted the Sbarro restaurant in the heart of downtown Jerusalem, murdering fifteen Israelis including parents and their children. In the deadliest attack, another Hamas suicide bomber killed thirty Israelis attending a Passover Seder in a Netanya hotel. Within a year, 130 Israeli civilians had been murdered in terrorist attacks.

As the IDF swept through Palestinian cities and towns in an attempt to root out terrorist cells, the nagging conflict between command and conscience and between the political left and right erupted once again. Yesh Gvul placed an advertisement in *Ha'aretz* castigating the IDF as "the Army of Defense of the settlements in the occupied territories." A "Combatant's Letter," initiated by two officers from an elite unit and eventually signed by hundreds of combat and reserve soldiers, lamented "the loss of IDF's human character and the corruption of the entire Israeli society." It challenged the legitimacy of "the Occupation."

The rhetoric of resistance and refusal became increasingly strident. Thirty-five years of "occupation," a refusenik claimed, had made Israeli society "violent and racist." Sergio Yahni, who had been sentenced to three prison terms during the First Intifada for his refusal to serve in the territories, was sentenced to another twenty-eight days during the Second Intifada for refusing to report for reserve duty. In a letter to the Defense Minister he accused the IDF of becoming "an armed wing of the settlement movement . . . the cancer which eats away at the Israeli social body." It was, he insisted, "both my Jewish and human duty to refuse to take part in this army . . . which commits crimes against humanity." Ilan Kaspari condemned the "cult of colonialist settlers, brutal and self-centered," who pursued a "colonialist-messianic fantasy."

The "immoral and non-legitimate" actions of the Israel Defense Forces in the West Bank and Gaza, critics alleged, expressed a government policy of "occupation, repression and colonization." Indeed, according to an eighteen-year-old whose letter to Prime Minister Sharon was published in *Ha'aretz* two days before his enlistment date, the IDF was guilty of "actions best described as 'terrorism.'" He preferred prison to service in "this army of occupation." According to a co-signer, the IDF symbolized the values of a nation that had descended to "an unprecedented moral low." He denounced the "militarization and racism among the Jewish population," demonstrated by its acceptance of "the occupation's crimes and ethnic cleansing," which had reached "a fascist level."

In September 2001, sixty-two high school students signed a letter to Sharon justifying their refusal to perform military service as an act of resistance to "Israel's pounding of human rights . . . in blunt violation of international conventions it has ratified." Several months later, more than four hundred reservists signed a letter declaring: "We shall not fight beyond the 1967 borders in order to dominate, expel, starve and humiliate an entire people." By then, more than one hundred conscientious objectors had been imprisoned.

Refuseniks frequently targeted Jewish settlers as the source of Israel's transformation into an oppressive and immoral nation. A Golani brigade sergeant who had signed the Combatant's Letter condemned the "cult of colonialist settlers, brutal and self-centered," with their "false slogans about security, Zionism and Judaism." Settlers, complained Major Rami Kaplan, the highest-ranking officer to sign the letter, "espouse the darkest of ideologies." A "Declaration of Refusal" castigated the government for making war to defend "the thugs of Itamar and Beit Hadassah in Hebron," for the "continued occupation" of Kiryat Arba by settlers, and for "continued [military] control" over Rachel's Tomb outside Bethlehem.

Once again, Nazi analogies proliferated. A 29-year-old graduate student in philosophy at Tel Aviv University, who rejected the settlers' "messianic-nationalist aspirations," saw "Germany right in front of me." To be "an accomplice to a crime," another refusenik understood, was forbidden. "You cannot be a Jew, the son of a refugee people," he claimed, "and oppress refugees." To Peretz Kidron, who gathered testimony from other refuseniks, selective refusal was "a reflection of the Jewish experience at the hands of [Nazi] soldiers who were 'just obeying orders.'"

Other scathing analogies were drawn from the spreading international delegitimization of Israel. "Our current situation," a refusenik claimed, "resembles that of apartheid South Africa." Israel's "colonial war to perpetuate the occupation" was compared to struggles there and in Algeria. To these examples a refusenik added "the torment of the slaves and the Indians in North America." With settlers holding a "fascist, fanatical ideology," and occupation "a moral crime," another claimed, "you can't be moral" while serving in the territories.

Some refuseniks proudly identified themselves as rebellious sons, "children of the mainstream who are breaking their consensus . . . because we have caused a terrible injustice to an entire [Palestinian] people." They assumed the "obligation to refuse" as their overriding moral imperative. Denouncing their government as illegitimate "occupiers," they rejected the "false belief in our ancestral right" to biblical Judea and Samaria, beyond the "legitimate" pre-1967 borders. A Tel Aviv University graduate (whose philosophy professor had been a refusenik during the First Intifada), defined refusal as "the most Zionist and patriotic thing one can do." Indeed, it not only was "a civic obligation" but the source of "the *democratic legitimacy* of our actions."

For increasing numbers of Israelis, the individual and not the state was empowered to determine national security needs and define the obligation of military service. Israeli efforts to suppress the Palestinian uprising, wrote Yigal Shochat, Surgeon General of the Air Force, were illegitimate "because the occupation is not legitimate." Conceding that he was not "a legal expert," and did not know "what is legal and what isn't," he nonetheless insisted that one must "refuse to obey an order that in your personal opinion is flagrantly illegal." In a democracy, "it is the right and duty of every citizen to oppose illegitimate warfare." Assaf Oron, who had received parental warnings that Arabs intended to throw Israelis into the sea, felt morally torn between competing obligations. "One was the ethical code and the other the tribal code, and I naively believed that the two could coexist."

In 2002, Major Rami Kaplan and Lt. Guy Grossman founded Courage to Refuse, based on the principle that "refusal to serve in the territories *is* Zionism." It claimed that soldiers had received orders "that had nothing to do with the security of our country, and had the sole purpose of perpetuating our control over the Palestinian people." The result was "the loss of IDF's human character and the corruption of the entire Israeli society." Insisting that "the Territories are not Israel," five hundred young men joined in declining "to fight this War of the Settlements . . . beyond the 1967 borders in order to dominate, expel, starve and humiliate an entire people."

Kaplan and Grossman explained that Israeli citizens of a technologically advanced and prosperous nation, in an increasingly globalized world, had witnessed "the dawn of individualistic values." In Israel, they noted, "the image of the successful businessman has recently replaced the courageous combat soldier as the subject of idealization and adoration." Grossman, a left-wing activist while a Tel Aviv University law student, favored the forcible evacuation of settlers. For their courage to refuse, nearly three hundred soldiers were court-martialed.

During the summer of 2003, a Hamas suicide bomber killed twenty-three Israelis, including seven children, on a Jerusalem bus. In retaliation, the IDF targeted a militant Hamas leader in his Gaza apartment building, dropping a bomb that also killed fourteen other residents. Civilian casualties (but only in Gaza) prompted twenty-seven active duty and reserve pilots to compose a "Pilots' Letter," declaring their opposition "to carrying out attack orders that are illegal and immoral of the type the State of Israel has been conducting in the territories." The pilots refused to participate in raids on population centers (precisely where Hamas leaders, willing to endanger civilians for their own protection, embedded themselves). Condemning such actions as "illegal and immoral," they blamed "the ongoing occupation, which is corrupting all of Israeli society." Immediately grounded by the Chief of Staff, they were rebuked by hundreds of Israel Air Force pilots who signed a petition deploring their refusal to serve.

Three months later, thirteen reservists from the elite commando unit *Sayeret Matkal* sent a sharp letter to Prime Minister Sharon stating their refusal to participate in "the occupation of the territories." They would not serve "as a shield in the crusade of the settlements" nor "corrupt our moral character in missions of oppression" that deprived Palestinians of "basic human rights." Their critique prompted Defense Minister Shaul Mofaz to accuse them of exploiting their elite military status to challenge government policy.

Among the refuseniks during the Second Intifada were five young men whose flamboyant disobedience riveted national attention. Haggai Matar was a leader of the *Shministim* high school students who had informed government ministers that they would not serve in the West Bank or Gaza. Insisting that Israel had reached "an unprecedented moral low," they deplored the "militarization and racism" that "have reached a fascist level." The letter declared: "We refuse to become the occupation's soldiers. . . . We call upon our contemporaries and upon the soldiers—whether conscripts, reservists or career military personnel—to do as we do." The IDF, Matar stated during his military trial, had committed "inhumane, immoral and in my opinion also illegal" acts.

His co-defendant Matan Kaminer left no doubt that the "occupation" was the source of their refusal. "If we leave the Occupied Territories completely, if we allow the establishment of a viable independent Palestinian state, and if we live in peace and equality alongside this state," he asserted, "there will be no suicide bombs and no violent actions committed by Palestinians against Israeli citizens." Grounding their refusal in "humanist, rationalist and democratic" principles, and protesting "the accumulating effects of militarization on Israeli society,"

Matar, Kaminer and their co-defendants acknowledged their obligation to obey the law but only in a democratic state (which Israel, by implication, was not).

Indeed, comparing Israel to South Africa under apartheid, they insisted that "a state ruling over 3.5 million people denied the right to vote cannot presume to be a state whose decisions are all reached in a democratic procedure." (Palestinians could, of course, vote in their own elections.) Matar, admitting that his "political views" had prevented him from enlisting in the IDF, conceded that he was "a traitor to the racist Israeli state that commits war crimes against the occupied Palestinians."

Judge Colonel Avi Levy, who presided over their trial, eviscerated the defendants' attempt to blur the distinction between conscientious objection and civil disobedience. Conscientious objection, the military judge declared, is "a purely personal act, carried out in silence, without publicity, aimed merely at getting exemption for one particular person from acts which he finds intolerable, incompatible with his personal conscience." But civil disobedience is "the complete opposite—a pernicious, seditious act of a group which seeks maximum publicity, maximum complicity and participation in its effort to hamper the elected government in carrying out its policies." Judge Levy described the defendants as "agitators" attempting "to overturn constituted authority." He warned: "If political refusal is legitimized, there will be chaos." The defendants were sentenced to an additional year in prison to the one they had already served.

The Second Intifada also prompted a group of soldiers who had served in Hebron to organize Breaking the Silence, which provided photographic images and testimony—mostly anonymous and unverifiable—to condemn Israeli "occupation" of the ancient Jewish city. After fourteen months of military service in Hebron, Yehuda Shaul, a yeshiva high-school graduate, could no longer endure "the moral erosion he saw in himself and his comrades." He removed his *kipa* to demonstrate that "my Judaism and the Judaism of the settlers isn't the same thing."

Financially subsidized by the New Israel Fund, Oxfam, and various politically sympathetic foreign organizations, Breaking the Silence opened a photography exhibit in Tel Aviv to display the (inhumane) consequences of Israeli rule. "We wanted," Shaul explained, "to bring Hebron to Tel Aviv." Why Hebron, he was asked. Because, he responded, "I know Hebron, because I have a score to settle with it, because it's the essence of the occupation."

With assistance from left-wing allies, Breaking the Silence published a volume of grievances from soldiers who had been commanded to serve in Hebron for no other reason, they alleged, than "to make the Palestinians' lives miserable." Their antipathy to Jewish settlers—"Jewish Nazis" one soldier labeled them—was undisguised. "You're mad at your country," another declared, "that the Jews are here" (where, to be sure, they had been since Abraham purchased the Machpelah cave to bury Sarah). Tours of Hebron, sponsored by Breaking the Silence and guided by soldiers, infuriated Jewish residents and elicited condemnation from the Hebron District Police Commander for their "severe and dangerous" provocation. *Ha'aretz* military journalist Amos Harel accused the group of embracing "a clear political agenda."

Anticipating the imminence of military service, groups of Israeli high-school students periodically expressed their refusal to enlist. Their critique was even more sweeping and radical than the protests from soldiers or reservists. A letter to Prime Minister Sharon in 2001 referred to Israel's "aggressive and racist policy," "pounding of human rights," and "illegitimate actions." The signees refused to participate in "acts of oppression against the Palestinian people that should properly be called terrorist actions." Another student group alleged that Israel had become "a militaristic, racist, chauvinistic and violent society."

Additional *Shministim* letters blamed the Jewish state for "the separation, control, oppression and killing policy . . . in the occupied territories," contradicting "the basic values a society that pretends to be democratic should have." In the end, they declared, "we cannot be moral and serve the occupation." An updated letter in 2009 asked: "Can military rule of a civilian population be considered anything other than a dictatorship?"

By then, conscientious objection had begun to cross gender lines. Young women complained that the IDF reflected and perpetuated the "militaristic" character of Israeli society in the service of "male hegemony." New Profile, a feminist group, encouraged young women to refuse the draft or, once in the IDF, to disobey orders. Several complied and were sentenced to two weeks in military prison for their refusal to serve. Mia Tamarin explained that she could not participate in an army whose purpose is "to fend off violence by violence. . . . There is always another, non-violent option, and it is this option that I choose." Idan Chalidi, claiming exemption on the ground that the army was a patriarchal institution that fostered a culture of sexual harassment, spent a month in prison for her refusal.

Two years into the Second Intifada, more than one thousand Israelis of military age had declared their intention to refuse to serve in the West Bank or Gaza. Several hundred others, choosing "selective refusal," had already rejected orders to do so. But even Peace Now, which had launched Israel's first mass anti-war protests during the Lebanon war, warned that "in a democratic regime, the refusal to serve is not only unlawful but immoral." What if religious soldiers, it asked pointedly, decided on the basis of their own claims of conscience to disobey orders to evacuate settlements?

Israeli law regarding selective conscientious objection had emerged during the First Intifada when a group of twenty-seven soldiers refused to serve in the territories, claiming that "a deliberate policy of repression" was implemented there. The Supreme Court summarily rejected the principle "whereby soldiers can dictate . . . where they will serve, whether for economic or social reasons, or for reasons of conscience." The Ministry of Justice explained: "the needs of the IDF must take priority over the personal preferences of its soldiers."

Fifteen years later, while the Second Intifada raged, the Court reaffirmed the distinction between conscientious objection, a valid ground for exemption from regular or reserve service, and selective objection. "Yesterday," it declared presciently, "the objection was against serving in South Lebanon. Today the objection is against serving in Judea and Samaria. Tomorrow, the objection will be against vacating this or that settlement." It was "a fine distinction," the Court observed, "between objecting to a state policy and . . . conscientious objection to carry out that policy." With evident concern, it anticipated a time when the IDF "may turn into an army of different groups comprised of various units, to each of which it would be conscientiously acceptable to act in certain areas, whereas it would be conscientiously unacceptable to act in others."

What had been a tiny and inconsequential trickle of refusal before Israel invaded Lebanon in 1983 had become widespread, entrenched, and highly politicized twenty years later. It hardly was coincidental that the commands of conscience had become ever more compelling during the tenure of right-wing Prime Ministers Menachem Begin and Ariel Sharon. For increasing numbers of young secular Israelis, traditionally the backbone of the IDF, military service had lost its power to define a fundamental obligation of citizenship. Echoing Israel's harshest foreign critics, and emulating young Americans during the Vietnam War era, they castigated the Jewish state as a source of evil undeserving of their commitment. To one young refusenik the army did not protect the nation; "it destroys, it damages society." To another, echoing the rhetoric of international denunciation, Zionism was "racist, colonialist and imperialistic."

Military service had become the newest arena for struggles over legitimacy. As judges had anticipated, justification for disobedience cut both ways. The stunning decision by Prime Minister Sharon in 2005 to evacuate settlers and soldiers from Gaza sharply divided the religious Zionist community. Some rabbis asserted that military orders contradicting God-given rights to the land must be disobeyed. Rabbi Shapira sharply warned: "An order to take part in the evacuation of Jews from their homes, in order to hand the land over to foreigners, contradicts our holy Torah faith and it is forbidden to obey it." More than fifty rabbis signed his call for disobedience, claiming that "the Jewish people possess an exclusive, God-given, and irrevocable right to possess the entire land of Israel." On the militant religious Zionist periphery, as previously on the political left, complicit Israeli soldiers were compared to the Gestapo; political leaders were branded as incarnations of Titus and Hitler.

Eighty respected rabbis vigorously dissented from Rabbi Shapira's statement, arguing that the risks and benefits of relinquishing territory were solely for political and military leaders to decide. Rabbi Eli Sadan, the founder of yeshivas designed to strengthen the commitment of religious youth to military service, assertively defended "our people," "our state," and the army but he did not include the sanctity of land. Rabbis Chaim Druckman and Yehuda Aviner, who had held prominent leadership positions in the settlement movement during its formative years, insisted on the supremacy of the state as an expression of divine will that required obedience. Rabbi Aviner, asserting the sanctity of both the Jewish state and the Land of Israel, called upon soldiers not to disobey orders while nonetheless insisting that the army must protect the land.

The evacuation of Gaza settlements was carefully prepared, with sensitivity to the issues it could raise both for settlers and religious soldiers. Chief of Staff Moshe Yaalon insisted on a policy of *yad le-achim* ("a hand to brothers"). Settlers were not to be considered enemies; they must be treated "firmly but with sensitivity." Concessions were extended to national-religious soldiers: none would be assigned to the front lines of evacuation; those with families living in settlements could request assignment elsewhere.

As many as one hundred soldiers indicated their intention to disobey orders and declined to engage in direct conflict with settlers; sixty-three were brought to trial. Captain Moshe Batavia, a career officer who had grown up in Kiryat Arba (adjacent to Hebron), refused to lead his soldiers during the evacuation. He told his commanding officer: "I can't get up in the morning . . . say prayers about the wholeness of the land and its sanctity, and in the afternoon do something that is the complete opposite." Following the evacuation, religious soldiers became more publicly assertive in demonstrating their support for settlements. A senior military officer declared that he would "rather give up Tel Aviv than Hebron," which he identified as "Jewish land [that] is promised to us by the Bible, by God. . . . I will not obey such an order."

During the first two decades of statehood, barely one hundred Israelis had claimed conscientious objector status. Yet by the time Israel celebrated its sixtieth birthday, it was estimated that more than one-quarter of those reaching the age of eighteen were claiming psychological disorders or political convictions to evade military service. Nearly one-third of military-age young women claimed religious exemptions, although many were not observant. In a decision that rejected the refusal of reservists to serve in the territories, Chief Justice Aharon Barak reiterated the increasingly frequent warning: "Today the objection is to serving in Judea and Samaria. Tomorrow the objection will be to removing settlements." His prediction was soon realized when more than one thousand religious soldiers signed a letter refusing to uproot communities in Judea and Samaria.

In the summer of 2007, pursuant to a court order, Defense Minister Ehud Barak mobilized the army and police to evict Jews from their homes in Mitzpe Shalhevet, the Hebron neighborhood named after a ten-month-old girl who had been murdered by a Palestinian sniper. Nearly forty IDF soldiers in an elite infantry unit, including two company commanders, refused to board buses to Hebron once they were informed that their mission was to evict civilians from their homes. A dozen, who remained adamant, were court-martialed and sentenced to one month in prison.

Referring to rabbis who had counseled the disobedient soldiers (all of whom were *hesder* yeshiva graduates), the Defense Minister declared that "soldiers receive their orders from their commanders and no one else, no matter how important or honorable he might be.... Refusing orders on ideological grounds is morally indefensible.... Just as it is wrong for the left to refuse to serve in the territories, it is wrong for the right to refuse to evacuate them."

A rabbinical spokesman responded: "The army shouldn't be drafting children of Judea and Samaria to throw their families out of their homes." The father of one disobedient soldier told Army Radio: "My son didn't join the army to expel Jews, but to protect them." Left-wing politicians and commentators who had vigorously justified military disobedience during the Lebanon wars and intifadas responded with a demand for harsh justice, claiming that "army service is not a buffet menu; you don't get to choose your assignments."

While a growing number of secular Israelis were evading military service, religious Zionist young men were avidly embracing it. The training ground for elite units once provided by kibbutzim was gradually relocated to the *hesder* yeshivot, serving as pre-military religious academies, and Nahal Haredi units, where Torah study was integrated with military service. Ironically, the plan to prepare Orthodox recruits for the IDF came from General Amram Mitzna, a secular kibbutznik who advocated the infusion of "deep values" into the IDF by Orthodox soldiers no less than the military socialization of religious young men. During the Second Intifada infantry soldiers wearing knitted *kippot* as the badge of their religious nationalist affiliation constituted twice their proportion in the national population.

Once religious soldiers adopted the protest tactics of their secular predecessors even minor incidents gained national attention. When four *hesder* yeshiva soldiers from settlements waved a banner opposing the demolition of two illegally built settler homes, Defense Minister Barak responded with a stern admonition. He distinguished freedom of expression from "subversive behavior," warning that Israel would not tolerate insubordination from its soldiers or the use of the IDF "to promote political viewpoints" that could "cause a tear in the fabric of society."

During a swearing-in ceremony at the Western Wall in 2009, two religious recruits in the Shimshon Brigade, which served in Judea and Samaria, raised a banner pledging their refusal to evacuate settlers. They were expelled from the brigade and sentenced to twenty days in prison. Religious soldiers from the Nachshon and Kfir Brigades publicly endorsed their statement. Brigade reservists asserted that the IDF should defend the country and its people, not remove Jews from their homes. Soon afterward, following an induction ceremony for the Golani Brigade, ten soldiers exposed their T-shirts bearing the message: "Golani fights the enemy and does not expel Jews." Their commander sentenced four of them to jail for expressing inappropriate "political opinions."

By then more than two-thirds of the recruits from settlements in Samaria were serving in elite IDF combat and Special Forces units (as opposed to the national average of 40 percent). Nearly one-third of their officers were religiously observant. Three years later, eighty-five percent of *hesder* yeshiva graduates, taught the unity of Jewish religion and nationality and the congruence of the State of Israel with the Land of Israel, were choosing to serve in combat units.

Military service, as Bar-Ilan University professor Stuart Cohen's illuminating studies reveal, had become "a religious imperative as well as a civic duty." It was a *halakhic* obligation, the Rabbinical Assembly ruled, for every Jewish male living in the State of Israel. Religious nationalist soldiers were taught that the failure to serve violated the obligation to participate in a commanded defensive war to protect one's neighbor and to save human life. According to Cohen's research, they demonstrated "a greater sense of purpose than do most secular recruits," whose sense of military service as a civic duty had waned.

This transformation was especially striking in the officer corps, where between 1990 and 2007 the presence of religious soldiers spurted from 2 to 30 percent. Three years later a majority of lieutenant colonels in the elite Kfir and Golani brigades wore *kippot*; religious company commanders constituted more than three times the percentage of the national religious community in the Israeli population. "It is hard to see," wrote Amos Harel, "how the company leaders who come from the settlements . . . will answer the call to remove Jews from their homes."

With the changing demography of the IDF, the language of religious Zionist rabbis became more strident. In 2009, a group of *hesder* rabbis issued a statement declaring that the IDF "has been used for purposes unrelated to Israel's defense and directly opposed to God's wishes. . . . We are committed to teach that loyalty to the Lord comes before any other loyalty, whether to the army or to the government." Some rabbis compared Palestinians to Philistines or even Amalek, the ancient nation that Israelites were commanded to destroy. Rabbi Eliezer Melamed, leader of the Har Bracha Hesder Yeshiva, published a book in which he insisted: "It is forbidden for any person, whether a soldier or an officer . . . to participate in the strictly forbidden act of expelling Jews from their homes and handing over any portion of the Land of Israel to enemies." Infuriated, Defense Minister Barak terminated the IDF's relationship with the yeshiva.

By now, unprecedented numbers of Israelis decide for themselves whether and where they will serve, which Jews they will protect, and which wars they will fight. To journalist Gershom Gorenberg, who has identified these trends as symptoms of the "unmaking" of Israel, "the risk of future insubordination or mutiny" from religious soldiers poses "a growing danger" (although disobedience by secular Israelis ever since the first Lebanon war had not elicited a similar dire warning). Gorenberg concedes that "there are moments when a person must obey a moral principle rather than a democratically elected law or policy," when "human life and dignity" were at stake. But "sacred territory" (meaning Jewish settlements) provides insufficient justification. For Gorenberg, the prospect of religious soldiers disobeying orders to evacuate settlers evokes the *Altalena,* when the government confronted "an armed faction dedicated to fantasies of power and expansion."

Disenchanted with the surge of religious nationalism, the transfer of political power from left to right, and the growth of settlements since the Six-Day War, secular Israelis in increasing numbers have challenged the virtually universal moral authority once enjoyed by the IDF. During the Second Intifada the IDF was pilloried, in Israel and worldwide, for its allegedly cruel indifference to human life in the battle against Palestinian terrorists embedded in Jenin despite extraordinary measures, at significant cost in soldiers' safety and lives, to limit civilian casualties. Speaking to Israeli youth groups, a soldier expressed his shock at allegations that the IDF had bulldozed houses with people inside, obstructed medical treatment, and used Palestinian civilians as human shields in a "massacre." Never before, he observed, had he encountered young Israelis who were so determined to find "a way out" of military service.

Inevitably, the fate of settlements in Judea and Samaria will turn on personal choices grounded in religious faith or political ideology no less than government decisions. Kiryat Arba Chief Rabbi Dov Lior, recognizing the national obligation to serve in the military and obey orders, nonetheless warned that should those orders contradict "the *mitzvoth* of the Torah, and this includes destruction of a community in Eretz Israel, it is forbidden to obey them." Above all, he asserted (citing the medieval sage Ramban), "It is forbidden to surrender parts of Eretz Israel to foreigners."

An army of citizen-soldiers, the IDF has long been the most deeply respected national institution among Israelis. But as Israel's wars have become increasingly divisive, the commitment of secular Israelis to military service has significantly waned. Relatively few young men have been convicted in court for their refusal to perform military service: 130 during the first Lebanon war; 165 during the First Intifada; 25 during the Second Intifada; and fewer than a handful during the second Lebanon war. But many more have communicated their intention to disobey, or have found ways to evade service by reaching agreements with their unit commanders for alternative postings (known as "gray refusal"). Increasing numbers of eighteen-year-olds seek and obtain psychiatric exemptions.

Amid the clouds of avoidance and disobedience that hover over the IDF, it has continued to search for ways to provide even ultra-Orthodox Israelis with a comfortable culture for military service. In 1999, the Netzah Yehuda battalion was formed within the Kfir Infantry Brigade, primarily for service in Judea and Samaria. From thirty recruits at the outset, it expanded to nearly one thousand soldiers a decade later and established an elite counter-terror squad. The only IDF unit without women, its soldiers must wear *kippot*, observe the Sabbath, eat kosher food, and have time allocated daily for Torah study and prayer. Eight years later another ultra-Orthodox track (*Shahar*) opened in the Air Force and Military Intelligence unit. Several hundred haredi young men have enlisted to become computer programmers, electricians and medical technicians. More than half have applied to extend their military service in the IDF Officers School.

The growing presence of religious soldiers has impacted gender relations in the IDF, where nearly one-third of the soldiers are women. A secular female soldier in a command position discovered to her astonishment that religious male soldiers would not even tolerate her touching their weapon, no less touching them, when she tried to demonstrate how to use it. Military service, she realized, meant "having to accept the burden of serving alongside thousands of individuals who see me as less than equal. For them, I could never be a soldier first; I would always be a woman, whose actions may spell danger to their most deeply held beliefs."

The disputed morality of military disobedience continues to polarize Israeli society. In the summer of 2012, as concern increased over Iran's nuclear capabilities and intentions, four hundred academics signed a petition circulated by Tel Aviv University professors calling upon Air Force pilots to refuse to obey orders to attack Iranian nuclear facilities. Those who obeyed, they warned, might jeopardize their military and civilian careers, and even be tried as war criminals. They would, however, be "rendering an important and vital service to the State of Israel and all who live here" by demonstrating that Israelis need not "blindly obey" orders to conduct such questionable missions. One hundred IDF reserve officers responded with a letter to Prime Minister Netanyahu sharply denouncing "any kind of call to refuse an order and breach the solidarity, as well as the social and national responsibility, upon which service in the IDF and its reserves rests."

The decisive battleground for defining the parameters of military disobedience, and Zionist legitimacy, is likely to be Jewish settlements. Their steady population growth, more than twice the national average, makes mass evacuation increasingly problematic. An ominous question looms: if orders are issued to remove tens of thousands of Jewish settlers from their homes and communities in the heart of biblical Judea and Samaria will religious soldiers comply? Or will they, like so many secular Israelis during the Lebanon wars and intifadas, evade the draft and refuse to serve or, once drafted, disobey the orders of their commanders? Ever more visible in command positions, will religious Zionist officers respect the decisions of political leaders or will they remain loyal to the commands of *halakha* as interpreted by their rabbis? If, according to the venerable principle, the law of the state is the law, when if ever may a soldier legitimately disobey it?

Ever since 1948, military service has been a source of both unity and division in Israel. Exemptions for yeshiva students (and Orthodox women) were a condition of rabbinical support for statehood and subsequent Labor Party rule. But they provoked deep resentment among those who honored the call to risk their lives by serving the state. Since the 1980s it has been secular Israelis, in unprecedented numbers, who have claimed exemptions, refusing to serve in "wars of choice" while asserting their own right to choose their battlefields.

The tension between *halakhic* and secular values that simmers in Israeli society inevitably suffuses the Israel Defense Forces. New inductees in the IDF have been instructed that the Bible they each receive is "our deed of tenure and charter of ownership to our land and to the estate of our fathers." But can Torah teachings, interpreted by rabbis, nullify national laws, duly enacted by the Knesset, and military orders, issued by IDF commanders?

Among potentially competing sources of authority—the state, military officers, individual conscience, *halakha*, God—what will Israeli soldiers honor, or reject? Who will determine the boundaries between compliance and disobedience: the government, soldiers, rabbis, settlers? If religious and secular soldiers ever turn against each other, or against the state that commands their allegiance, Israel would again confront the devastating tragedy of brothers at war—a tragedy, sadly, that is not without precedent in ancient Jewish and modern Israeli history.

4 Pariah Nation

From a Zionist perspective, Jewish history in exile from the Roman conquest to the birth of Israel constituted nineteen centuries of oppression, degradation, suffering, and tragedy. Driven from their ancient homeland, where they had enjoyed intermittent centuries of national sovereignty, Jews were dispersed among European Christian nations where they were confined to ghettos, denied citizenship rights, and expelled; and Middle Eastern Muslim lands where they were demeaned and degraded as *dhimmis*. Politically powerless, Jews were nonetheless accused of controlling the world through their shrewd—indeed malevolent—accumulation and manipulation of money: merchants who exacted their pound of flesh whether or not they resided in Venice. Maligned for their demonstrable weakness and imagined power, they were persecuted without fear of retribution or punishment.

Freedom, when and where it eventually occurred, was laced with ambivalence. The legal emancipation of Jews that began in France late in the eighteenth century eventually transformed life in the European diaspora, creating possibilities for integration into civil society with full citizenship rights. Yet their new freedom also intensified their vulnerability to perceptions of divided loyalty. In the debate over Jewish emancipation in the French National Assembly in 1789, the Bishop of Nancy, conceding that "it is necessary to grant [Jews] protection, security, liberty," nonetheless wondered: "must we admit into the family a tribe that is a stranger to oneself, that constantly turns its eyes toward [another] homeland"? The Count of Clermont-Tonnerre insisted that Jews "should be denied everything as a nation, but granted everything as individuals. . . . The existence of a nation within a nation is unacceptable to our country." A century later, Captain Alfred Dreyfus, sentenced to life imprisonment for the crime of treason that he did not commit, was dispatched to the Devil's Island penal colony—an appropriately named destination for a disloyal Jew.

In Russia, Jews were targeted for vicious pogroms, most notoriously in Kishinev (1903), described by poet Chaim Nachman Bialik as "the City of Slaughter." Dozens of Jews were murdered and hundreds injured for allegedly killing a Christian boy to obtain his blood for preparing Passover matzah. It was time, Max Nordau wrote, to replace fearful Jewish martyrs who merely "cried out in their dying prayers in the face of their executioners" with "deep-chested, sturdy, sharp-eyed men"—Zionist pioneers who would emulate the courage of the Maccabees and Bar Kokhba by restoring Jewish national sovereignty.

But in twentieth century Europe, when Jews became the chosen people for annihilation, Zionists in Palestine were powerless. During the Holocaust, a "tragedy unprecedented in history," wrote Polish Bund leader Shmuel Zygelboym in 1943, Western nations not only were passive observers but "accomplices of criminals." With the Nazi deportations to Auschwitz and Treblinka, and the destruction of the Warsaw ghetto and slaughter of its Jewish residents, Zygelboym—who had managed to escape to London—reached the limit of his endurance. In his suicide letter he wrote: "By my death, I wish to express my strongest protest against the inactivity with which the world is looking on and permitting the extermination of the Jewish people."

After the war England, which had expelled its Jews in 1290 and prohibited them from returning for 350 years, did what it could to prevent Holocaust survivors from reaching Palestine, ruled under British Mandatory authority. Granted statehood by the United Nations in 1947, Jews secured their independence by defeating the armies of neighboring Arab states that were determined to obliterate them. Israel joined the family of nations, earning widespread admiration for the historically unprecedented achievement that had finally restored Jews to their own homeland. Widely celebrated as heroic fighters for freedom, they basked in worldwide admiration. Implanting democratic institutions and absorbing more than a million refugees driven from their homes by Nazi terror and Muslim fury, Israelis demonstrated their fierce determination to defend themselves against the unremitting enmity of their Arab neighbors.

Nineteen years later, after its stunning victory in the Six-Day War, Israel was prepared to relinquish territorial gains that had reconnected Jews to their biblical homeland for peace with its hostile neighbors. But, as Foreign Minister Abba Eban astutely observed, "We found ourselves transformed from David to Goliath overnight. Israel had committed the dark sin of survival." The three "No's" at Khartoum that summer—no peace with Israel, no recognition of Israel, no negotiations with Israel—demonstrated unrelenting Arab determination to destroy the Jewish state within any borders.

The language of delegitimization had already been framed in the Palestinian National Covenant in 1964. Zionism, it proclaimed, "is a colonialist movement in its inception, aggressive and expansionist in its goals, racist and segregationist in its configurations and fascist in its means and ends." The Soviet state-controlled media, fusing the Star of David with the swastika, linked Israel to Nazi Germany. French President Charles De Gaulle lacerated Jews as "an elite people, self-assured and domineering," who had transformed "the very moving hopes of 1900 years into a burning ambition of conquest." Although the German government had been supportive of Israel, by 1969 the New Left in Germany was denouncing the Jewish state as the "spearhead" of Western colonialism in the Middle East; three years later it justified the Palestinian massacre of Israeli athletes at the Munich Olympics. The price for national self-preservation had become worldwide enmity.

In November 1975, one year after Yasser Arafat asserted the canard that "Zionism is an ideology that is imperialist, colonialist, racist . . . profoundly reactionary and discriminatory," the UN General Assembly approved Resolution 3379. Zionism, it declared, "is a form of racism and racial discrimination." With Jewish nationalism targeted for vilification, it marked the moment, as Israeli Ambassador Chaim Herzog bitterly noted, when the United Nations was "on its way to becoming the world center of anti-Semitism." The newly trendy vocabulary of defamation—"colonial," "imperialist," "racist"—identified Israel as the immoral equivalent of Nazi Germany and apartheid South Africa.

International calumny of the Jewish state became the newest campaign in the centuries-old unremitting war against the Jewish people. The venerable anti-Semitic defamation of Jews morphed into the anti-Zionist delegitimization of Israel. The state of the Jews, observed Israeli philosopher J.L. Talmon, had become the Jew of states. Israel was fulfilling the biblical prophecy of Balaam as "a nation that shall dwell alone and not be reckoned among the nations."

It is no small irony, but one seldom noted, that Palestinians (enabled by their allies worldwide) have so avidly plundered Jewish and Israeli sources in constructing their own national narrative as to warrant indictment for historical plagiarism. Without even a century of national history in the land they claim as the legacy of their ancient "Canaanite" inheritance, Palestinians have reinvented themselves as the "real" Jews, entitled to the land, history, holy sites, and symbols that have defined Judaism for three millennia.

Modern conceptions of "Palestine" began to emerge in the mid-nineteenth century when the Holy Land, as it became known to increasing numbers of European visitors, reentered Western consciousness. The veil of obscurity began to lift after Edinburgh-born artist David Roberts followed the trail of the ancient Israelites from Egypt through the Sinai wilderness to their promised land. During his journey Roberts sketched the drawings that filled *The Holy Land* (1842), his magnificent three-volume collection of lithographs. Riveted by ancient city gates and walls, barren wilderness landscape, and exotic local inhabitants, Roberts created unrivaled romantic depictions of sacred memory, now dismissively denigrated as "Orientalist."

A year after publication of *The Holy Land* another Scotsman, Rev. Alexander Keith, authored *The Land of Israel According to the Covenant with Abraham, with Isaac, and with Jacob*. Keith, too, had traveled to the Holy Land in 1839; there he came to believe that Christians should bring to fulfillment the biblical prophecy that Jews would return to their ancient homeland. His book included a phrase that would reverberate long afterward. The Jews, he wrote, are "a people without a country; even as their own land . . . is in a great measure, a country without a people." Slightly altered by a reviewer, it became the iconic phrase: "A land without a people and a people without a land."

Rev. Keith's words (with a sharp concluding reference to "those few" Arabs who "have but a slight hold on the land that is not theirs") were reiterated several years later in a letter from Lord Shaftesbury (Anthony Ashley-Cooper) to Lord Palmerston, the British Foreign Minister. Ashley-Cooper pondered the future of "Greater Syria" (as the land of the ancient Israelites was then commonly identified) following the Crimean War. He rephrased Keith's description as "a country without a nation" needing "a nation without a country." He wondered, "Is there such a thing?" before answering his own question: "the ancient and rightful lords of the soil, the Jews!"

Rev. Keith's phrase continued to recur in the writings of Christian Zionists, especially after pogroms erupted in Russia during the 1880s.

Evangelist William Blackstone, concerned over the plight of Russian Jews, referred to the "astonishing anomaly: a land without a people, and a people without a land." In 1897 John Lawson Stoddard published a travel guide exhorting Jews: "You are a people without a country; there is a country without a people. . . . Go back, go back to the land of Abraham."

Curiously, Rev. Keith's memorable phrase seldom appeared in Zionist literature. Israel Zangwill wrote in the *New Liberal Review* (1901) that "Palestine is a country without a people; the Jews are a people without a country." On the eve of World War I, Chaim Weizmann said: "there is a country which happens to be called Palestine, a country without a people, and, on the other hand, there exists the Jewish people, and it has no country. What else is necessary, then, than to fit the gem into the ring, to unite this people with this country?" But few other Zionists adopted the phrase, preferring to refer to Palestine more succinctly as the "Jewish national home."

From the end of the nineteenth century, Zionist land development exerted a strong pull on Arabs from Iraq, Syria, Trans-Jordan and the Arabian Desert who came to Palestine in search of a better life (and eventually became "Palestinians"). Despite the centuries-old presence of local Arab elites—the Husseini, Nashashibi and Khalidi families in Jerusalem prominent among them—there was little evidence of Palestinian national consciousness or cohesion. "Palestinian" identity fused Ottoman, Islamic, Christian, and local Arab sources. In their politics, social structure, land tenure, and public discourse Palestinian Arabs identified with Greater Syria and "the larger Arab people."

In her careful scrutiny of "land without a people" mythology, historian Diana Muir concludes that Arabs "neither perceived Palestine as a distinct country, nor Palestinians as a people." Testifying before the British Peel Commission in 1937, Syrian leader Auni Bey Abdul-Hadi had asserted: "There is no such country as Palestine. . . . Our country was for centuries part of Syria. 'Palestine' is alien to us. It is the Zionists who introduced it." Shortly before the State of Israel was born, Arab historian Philip Hitti conceded: "There is no such thing as Palestine in history, absolutely not."

Even historians sympathetic to the Palestinian national cause recognize that before World War I "Palestine" did not exist in Arab consciousness or self-definition. Rashid Khalidi, an expert on Palestinian identity (and an adviser to the Palestinian Authority), concedes that internal Palestinian politics were dysfunctional: leaders did not lead, nor could they mobilize public support or establish a Palestinian "state structure" or representative institutions. Even as late as 1964, when the PLO was founded, "the very idea of 'Palestine,'" Khalidi recognizes, "appeared to be in a grave, and perhaps in a terminal state."

Israeli sociologist Baruch Kimmerling and American scholar Joel Migdal, in their collaborative history of the Palestinian people, suggest that Palestinian national identity was the product of two centuries of encounters with European government administration and Zionist pioneering in Ottoman Palestine. But their narrative quickly reaches World War I with few signs of Palestinian national consciousness until the post-war years, and then only in response to "assertive Jewish nationalism." The Arab Revolt of 1936 finally marked "the creation of a national movement," but "the construction of a self-identified Palestinian people" did not emerge until the second half of the twentieth century. It was not until "the middle decades of the twentieth century," they conclude, that "Palestinians developed a self-identity as a people set apart."

A Palestinian people with a distinctive identity and consciousness was a product of the humiliating Arab defeat in the Six-Day War, which ended Jordanian control over West Bank Arabs. Why was it, wondered Walid Shoebat from Bethlehem, "that on June 4th 1967 I was a Jordanian and overnight I became a Palestinian. . . . We considered ourselves Jordanian until the Jews returned to Jerusalem. Then all of a sudden we were Palestinians."

Once Jordanian rule was terminated by King Hussein's aggression against Israel, West Bank Arabs began to construct a Palestinian national identity on the foundation of Jewish history in a land that never had been inhabited by a (previously non-existent) "Palestinian" people. But even Zuhair Muhsin, PLO military commander and member of the Executive Council, acknowledged: "There are no differences between Jordanians, Palestinians, Syrians and Lebanese. We are all part of one nation. . . the existence of a separate Palestinian identity serves only tactical purposes." The vision of a Palestinian state, he conceded, was merely "a new tool in the continuing battle against Israel."

That hardly was a recipe for nation building, but it may help to explain why Palestinians have defined themselves by relentlessly plundering Jewish history. What remains most striking about Palestinian identity is its derivation from, and persistent grounding in, Jewish sources. Like other Muslims, Palestinians claim Ishmael, Abraham's son by his servant Hagar, as the ancestral link to "their" biblical patriarch. The ancient Canaanites who were displaced by the conquering Israelites, according to a Palestinian archeologist, were the original Palestinian people. So, too, were the Jebusites, the biblical inhabitants of Jerusalem. With such fictions drawn from Jewish sources, a continuous "Palestinian" history of 5,000 years could be implanted in the Land of Israel. Palestinian identity thieves have seemed unfamiliar with, or determined to ignore, Koranic references to the Land of Israel as the sacred, blessed land of the People of Israel (*Qur: al-Maidah*, 5:21; *al-A'araf* 7:137; *Bani Israil*, 17:104).

Following Muslim precedent, Palestinians have persistently usurped ancient Jewish holy sites. Like the conquering Romans (who chose "Palestine" as the name to obliterate Judea from memory following the failed Bar Kokhba revolt), they have erased Jewish names and historical presence from the biblical land of Israel that they now claim as their own. More than a millennium ago, Jerusalem, nowhere mentioned in the Koran and never a Muslim capital, was designated as Islam's "third holiest" city after Mecca and Medina. It hardly was coincidental that the Dome of the Rock and *al-Aksa* Mosque were preemptively built on the site of the First and Second Jewish Temples, the better to prevent Jews from returning to their destroyed holiest site. The Western Wall, the sole remaining segment of the Temple enclosure, was identified (and degraded) as the tethering post for Muhammad's horse, Al-Buraq, before the Prophet ascended to heaven.

After the Muslim conquest of Hebron, *Me'arat HaMachpelah*, marking the ancient tombs of the Jewish patriarchs and matriarchs, was converted into a mosque that Jews were prohibited from entering for the next seven centuries. Rachel's Tomb outside Bethlehem, for millennia a place for Jews, especially women, to come for prayer and healing, also became a mosque, as did Joseph's Tomb in Nablus (biblical Shechem). Palestinians now claim these ancient Jewish holy sites as their own.

Modern history has provided a plethora of opportunities for Palestinian identity theft. If the Nazis inflicted the Holocaust on Jews, Palestinians cite their own equivalent tragedy, the Naqba of 1948, perpetrated by Israelis who drove them from their land. Children and grandchildren of refugees claim to be "the victims of the greatest act of horror of the twentieth century"—inflicted, of course, by Jews. As recompense they demand a state of their own in the Land of Israel. Predictably, their claimed "right of return" echoes Hebrew Psalm 137: "If I forget thee, O Jerusalem . . . ."

Holocaust denial, exemplified in the doctoral dissertation of Palestinian Authority President Mahmoud Abbas, pervades Palestinian symbols and rhetoric. In the inverted Palestinian narrative, Israelis are the new Nazis and Palestinians are their (Jewish) victims. The photo of twelve-year-old Muhammad al-Dura, allegedly killed in Gaza by Israeli bullets at the beginning of the Second Intifada, became a notorious symbol of Israeli brutality as the result of carefully edited French TV film footage. It instantly evoked ancient blood libels of Jews murdering Christian children. For a French journalist, the boy's (contrived) death "cancels, erases that of the Jewish child, his hands in the air before the SS in the Warsaw Ghetto." So, too, teen-age Palestinian girls have learned to equate their plight with that of Anne Frank. Abetting Palestinian identity theft, nations that indifferently witnessed the annihilation of Jews in Europe and their expulsion from Arab lands now loudly applaud the Palestinian usurpation of Jewish history and national identity, while castigating Israel for its cruel denial of spurious Palestinian claims to the Jewish past.

There are, to be sure, less corrosive—indeed, adulatory—examples of Palestinian reliance upon Israeli sources for national self-definition. Israel's Proclamation of Independence, accompanied by Ben-Gurion's appeal for "the immigration of Jews from all countries of their dispersion," was echoed by Arafat's claim that "The State of Palestine is the state of Palestinians wherever they may be." The Israeli Law of Return, enacted in 1950, frames the Palestinian claim of the right of a vastly inflated number of Palestinian "refugees" to return to the land they abandoned in 1948. The famous Jewish refugee ship *Exodus* has inspired Palestinian emulation with the notorious *Mari Marvara* flotilla to Gaza in 2010 that sparked a pitched battle with Israeli navy commandos. Emulating the Jewish settlers they despise for stealing "their" land, a group of Palestinians recently established their own "outpost" between Jerusalem and Ma'ale Adumim. Residential neighborhoods in the new city of Rawabi, under construction near Ramallah, have dismayed some Palestinians with their architectural resemblance to nearby Jewish settlements.

So it is that a people without its own national history has insistently plundered Jewish sources and claimed Jewish holy sites to persuade a gullible world audience that Palestinians are the rightful inheritors of Jewish land, history and traditions. Noting that "Palestinian Arabs shaped their national identity almost exclusively through usurped Jewish symbols and history," Harvard professor Ruth Wisse pointedly asks: "If the Palestinian Arabs consider themselves a nation, how and why do they represent themselves consistently as Jews?" Ironically and unwittingly, Palestinian identity thieves have cast themselves as the biblical Jacob, stealing Esau's birthright. It is Jews, after all, who are the surviving indigenous people in the Land of Israel—at least until Canaanites reappear to contest their claim.

In the emerging international delegitimization campaign against Israel following the Six-Day War, Holocaust denial became increasingly salient. It hardly was a new phenomenon: from Adolf Hitler's rise to power in Germany in 1933, the persecution and ultimate annihilation of European Jewry had been largely ignored. The august *New York Times,* self-proclaimed purveyor of "all the news that's fit to print," did not consider the murder of six million Jews as especially newsworthy. Guided by publisher Arthur Hays Sulzberger, an assimilated Jew of German descent who was exceedingly wary lest he be accused of special pleading for Jews or divided loyalty to the United States, the *Times* largely relegated Holocaust coverage to its inside pages while universalizing the identity of Jewish victims as "refugees" or "persecuted minorities."

To be sure, Zionists in Palestine had their own problems with Jews who went passively to their deaths "like lambs to the slaughter." Why were they not defending themselves, wondered heroic Zionists who scorned cowering *galut* Jews. Yet, as Tom Segev pointedly noted in *The Seventh Million*, "the new Jews, standing tall in Palestine, did just what the persecuted Jews of the Exile had always done, and were as powerless as they had been." Detailed information about Auschwitz and Nazi preparations to deport and gas 400,000 Hungarian Jews, provided by escapees Rudolf Vrba and Alfred Wetzler, reached Zionist officials who remained silent about the looming catastrophe.

Within a year after the war ended, some 350,000 Holocaust survivors reached Palestine. "Each new arrival," Segev wrote, "was a reminder that the Zionist movement had been defeated in the Holocaust." The survivors' bitterness was palpable. "The question lurks in our hearts," reflected Dov Shilanksy, who arrived on the *Altalena* (and forty years later became Speaker of the Knesset), "What did our brothers outside of hell do?" Yosef Rosensaft, with bitter memories of Bergen-Belsen, noted: "You danced the hora while we were being burned in the crematoriums." Yitzhak "Antek" Zuckerman, a leader of the Warsaw Ghetto uprising, believed that the Zionist Yishuv had abandoned the ghetto fighters, who "needed only one man who would bring them a word of good will from the Land of Israel. Just one man. And he did not come."

Nothing did more to educate Israelis and the world about the Holocaust, if belatedly and reluctantly, than the capture and trial of Adolf Eichmann in 1961. Predictably, there was harsh criticism of the decision by the Israeli government to claim to speak for the Six Million and prosecute Eichmann for crimes committed outside its jurisdiction. It exemplified "inverse racism" (*Time*); Israeli "jungle law" applied "in the name of some imaginary Jewish ethnic identity" (*Washington Post*); "immoral" and "illegal" Israeli actions—especially when applied to a "dull" bureaucrat who was "not worth hating" (*The New York Times*).

To Prime Minister Ben-Gurion, the Eichmann trial exposed "the profound tragedy of exile." But it also revealed Israeli discomfort with Jews who had rejected the opportunity to save themselves by leaving Europe for Palestine. The government simultaneously translated the trial proceedings into English, French and German—but not Yiddish, the primary language of Eichmann's victims and Israeli Holocaust survivors. Auschwitz escapee Rudolf Vrba, by then living in London, was not invited to testify although no one had risked as much to inform the world (and Zionist officials) of the unfolding Jewish calamity.

Just as Vrba's warning of impending horrors had been ignored in 1944, so his memoir *Escape from Auschwitz,* published in English in the mid-1960s, was not translated into Hebrew until thirty-four years later. Writing about the "culture of forgetting" in Israel that surrounded the Holocaust, Ruth Linn asks pointedly: "Could a narrative of an individualistic escape, by a non-Zionist Jew, critical of his Jewish leaders, ever be made to harmonize with the 'collective aura' that dominated the state of Israel?" Zionist passivity in the face of unprecedented Jewish tragedy long remained too discomforting for Israelis to confront.

By the 1970s, Holocaust denial had emerged from the cesspool of anti-Semitism to become another weapon of Israeli delegitimization. If, after all, there never was a Holocaust, what justification could there be for a Jewish state? Denial was constructed from a fabric of lies, beginning with the claim that no master plan for the "Final Solution" had ever been discovered—although Eichmann had conceded at his trial that at the Wannsee Conference, convened in 1942 to coordinate implementation of the Final Solution, Nazi leaders "spoke about methods of killing, about liquidation, about extermination." The existence of gas chambers for the mass murder of Jews (at least one million in Auschwitz alone) was denied. The postwar Nuremberg trials of Nazi war criminals were dismissed as "a farce of justice."

Even before the Six-Day War, France (a major supplier of military weapons and nuclear material to Israel) had become a favored nesting ground for Holocaust deniers. Literary critic Maurice Bardèche blamed the Jews for World War II and the Holocaust: "They were the ones who caused the world conflict and therefore bear responsibility for millions of dead." Exterminated Jews were the victims of disease, not gas chambers. "The alleged Hitlerian gas chambers and the alleged genocide of the Jews," claimed literature professor and outspoken Holocaust denier Robert Faurisson, "form one and the same historical lie." They constituted "a gigantic politico-financial swindle whose beneficiaries are the State of Israel and international Zionism." In France, as in much of Western Europe, the "new anti-Semitism" of anti-Zionism, with Holocaust denial as a fundamental component, became commonplace.

Across the Channel, British historian David Irving, author of a laudatory exculpation of Hitler, emerged as the most notorious denier. Labeling the gas chambers at Auschwitz, Treblinka, and Majdanek "a hoax" ("mock-ups build by the Poles"), he cited Auschwitz survivors as "testimony to the absence of an extermination programme." Predictably, it was all the fault of Jews, who "have exploited people with the gas chamber legend." To Northwestern University professor A.R. Butz, author of *The Hoax of the Twentieth Century*—as for Faurisson, Irving, and Palestinian leader Mahmoud Abbas—the Holocaust was a Jewish fabrication designed to further the Zionist cause. Israel, deniers alleged, depended upon an "invented" genocide to justify its existence.

Holocaust denial, aptly identified by historian Robert Wistrich as "this sickening effort of contemporary Jew haters to destroy memory," has served a dual purpose. Not only has it challenged the conventional justification for Jewish statehood; it has paved the way for Israelis to become the new "Nazis," guilty of perpetrating upon Palestinians the real Holocaust that had not annihilated six million Jews. By branding Israel a Nazi state, Wistrich suggests, "one is finally free to express in politically correct anti-Zionist language" the perennial hatred of Jews. Holocaust denial, observed Canadian jurist Irwin Cotler, "whitewashes the crimes of the Nazis, as it excoriates the crimes of the Jews. It not only holds that the Holocaust was a hoax, but maligns the Jews for fabricating the hoax."

Although the United Nations equation of Zionism with racism eventually was revoked (in 1991) following the initiation of the Oslo peace process, the international delegitimization of Israel surged a decade later during the World Conference against Racism in Durban, South Africa. Held under UN auspices, it embraced the conclusion of a preliminary regional conference (in Tehran) that the Jewish state was an "apartheid" state that perpetrated holocausts. NGOs in Durban organized their own forum and issued a declaration (endorsed, perversely, by Human Rights Watch) setting new parameters of malignant anti-Zionism. Sponsored by an array of states hardly renowned for their humanitarian concerns—Afghanistan, Cuba, Iraq, Syria, and Somalia, among them—it branded Israel "a racist, apartheid state" that committed "a crime against humanity" with its "segregation, dispossession, 'bantustanization' and inhumane acts." It identified "children, women and refugees" as "targeted victims of Israel's brand of apartheid and ethnic cleansing," including "acts of genocide" against Palestinians.

The Durban conference inspired the Palestinian call for a policy of Boycott, Divestment and Sanctions (BDS) against Israel for its "persistent violations of international law" and unwillingness "to respect fundamental human rights and to end its occupation and oppression of the people of Palestine." It had been fifty-seven years since "Israel was built mainly on land ethnically cleansed of its Palestinian owners," and thirty-eight years into its "occupation of the Palestinian West Bank (including East Jerusalem)." Yet Israel "continues to expand Jewish colonies" on Palestinian land. "Inspired by the struggle of South Africans against apartheid," Palestinians urged "people of conscience all over the world to impose broad boycotts and implement divestment initiatives against Israel similar to those applied to South Africa in the apartheid era."

Like so much else in the Palestinian narrative, the impetus for the BDS movement came from external sources. The idea had originated with Francis Boyle, an international law professor at the University of Illinois whose demonstrable hostility toward Israel included allegations of "Zionist control and domination of the American judiciary." Boyle, an adviser to the PLO between 1987-89 and 1991-93, accused Israel of "genocide" and proposed a divestment movement based on the "anti-apartheid model." Insisting "God had no right to steal Palestine from the Palestinians and give Palestine to the Zionists," he suggested that

Israel change its name to "Jewistan" and predicted that "this Bantustan for Jews" would "collapse of its own racist and genocidal weight."

Pro-Palestinian luminaries—including South African Archbishop Desmond Tutu, Israeli professor-in-exile Ilan Pappé, and prize-winning American poet Adrienne Rich (who decried "morally stone-blind" Israel)—enthusiastically endorsed the BDS movement. It received the imprimatur of former President Jimmy Carter, who proclaimed on National Public Radio that Palestinian land had been "occupied and then confiscated and then colonized . . . in many ways worse than it was in South Africa." By 2013, even the European Union had decided to boycott Israeli institutions and individuals across the 1949 armistice lines. That would include the Hebrew University (established on Mt. Scopus in 1925) and Jews living in Jerusalem's Old City.

Riffs (and rants) about the moral turpitude of Israel permeated American academic institutions, where sympathy for the plight of Palestinians converged with laceration of the Jewish state. The symbolic icons of the delegitimization of Israel were Edward Said, the aspiring Palestinian whose critical study of Western Orientalism framed his impassioned advocacy of the Palestinian cause, and Tony Judt, the renegade Jew whose youthful disillusion with Zionism and then Marxism eventually morphed into his embittered call for the disappearence of Israel.

No one did more to embrace and popularize the image of the wandering Palestinian victim, forced into exile from his homeland by Zionist aggression and conquest, than Columbia University professor Edward Said. His palpable identification with the Palestinian struggle after the Six-Day War and his denial of Zionist legitimacy transformed him into an international intellectual celebrity. From Said's uncompromising premise that Zionism was a colonial and racist movement, it followed that "a largely European people" would come to Palestine, "pretend that it was empty of inhabitants, conquer it by force, and drive out 70 percent of its inhabitants."

Said's self-identification as a victimized Palestinian refugee gave emotional resonance to his eloquent jeremiads against Israel. He passionately declared his "sense of belonging to the Palestinian people" and vividly articulated his "pain at their sufferings and defeats." As he claimed in an interview: "I am a Palestinian who was born in Jerusalem and was forced as a result of the 1948 Catastrophe to live in exile, in the same way as many hundreds of thousands of Palestinians were." In

1948, he wrote, "my entire family became refugees from Palestine." He repeatedly conflated his life as "a Palestinian in exile" with "a condition that ... includes the largest part of the Palestinian population."

Writing in *Harper's*, he noted succinctly: "I was born, in November 1935, in Talbiya, then a mostly new and prosperous Arab quarter of Jerusalem. By the end of 1947, just months before Talbiya fell to Jewish forces, I'd left with my family for Cairo." In a subsequent essay in *The New York Review of Books*, excerpted from his memoir *Out of Place*, he referred to the "wrenching, tearing, sorrowful loss [of Palestine] as exemplified in so many distorted lives, including mine."

But Said's oft-told tale of his Jerusalem boyhood and exile, his family's dispossession, and his lost home in Palestine was a self-constructed myth. The implication that between 1935 and 1947 Said and his family had lived in Jerusalem was false. And if the Said family left Jerusalem in 1947, as he recounted, how could it have been forced into exile "as a result of the 1948 Catastrophe"? To be sure, Said was born in Jerusalem in 1935. But on his birth certificate Said's parents identified Cairo as their permanent address, which it remained into his teen-age years. Throughout his boyhood, Edward Said's immediate family—parents, sister, retinue of servants, and Said himself—resided in luxurious comfort in Cairo, where his father owned a lucrative office supply business.

The Said family hardly departed from Jerusalem as fleeing "refugees." Late in 1947, amid accelerating inter-communal violence between Arabs, Jews, and British Mandatory authorities, they left Palestine of their own volition to return to their Cairo home. Said's anguished claim that "I lost—and my family lost its property and rights in 1948" in Jerusalem more accurately described the Saids' plight in Cairo, where revolutionary supporters of Gamal Abdel Nasser destroyed the family business in 1952 and subsequently nationalized family property.

Said's memoir revealed the identity confusion that permeated his family. His parents were Palestinian only by the accident of birth. Indeed, he noted, his father "never much liked" Palestine. Born in Jerusalem, which "he hated," he left as a teen-ager in 1911 for the United States, where he became a proud American citizen and lived for ten years, long enough to claim thereafter that America was "his country." Said's mother, born in Nazareth, was sent to boarding school and junior college in Beirut. With her marriage, she was "wrenched from a happy life in Beirut" to relocate in Cairo, where she lived for the next twenty years, returning to her true exilic home in Lebanon shortly before her death.

For Said's parents Palestine was a location of convenience and a place to visit relatives, but hardly their home or where they wished to live. Given the family's affluence, annual three-month summer respites from the brutal Cairo heat in the hills of Lebanon were welcomed. There also were visits to Jerusalem, which Said described as "off-and-on sojourns in Palestine." When Cairo was endangered during World War II, the Said family left Egypt for a lengthy vacation there. But once Palestine was besieged in 1947, they quickly returned to the safety of their Egyptian home.

Based on abundant evidence in his memoir, Palestine hardly was, as Said would claim, the place "I grew up in." Indeed, charming childhood photographs show Edward with his mother in the Mena House gardens in Cairo, with his father on the beach at Alexandria, with his family at the Giza pyramids, and with his sister Rosy on their Cairo apartment terrace dressed in Gezira Preparatory School uniforms.

Yet *The New York Review of Books*, when it published an excerpt from Said's memoir, and *The New York Times*, to accompany its laudatory review, chose to display a photograph of Edward and his sister captioned "in traditional Palestinian dress, Jerusalem, 1941." It is, to be sure, a fetching childhood photograph. Edward, age 6, wears a long robe with his head wrapped in a *keffiya*. Suggestively, his right hand rests on the handle of a knife tucked into his belt, while his left hand holds a pistol. This "traditional Palestinian" photo certainly affirms his own mythological narrative of his childhood. But the Gezira prep school photograph of young Edward, wearing his double-breasted school blazer, neatly pressed shorts, and knee socks, is a far more faithful depiction of his privileged, most un-Palestinian, boyhood in Cairo.

As compelling as his memoir might be in service to the Palestinian national cause—and, not incidentally, in elevating his own international stature as an intellectual-in-exile due to Zionist mistreatment of his family—it was a largely mythological construct. Based on his own recollections, Said's profound sense of identity dislocation and disorientation had nothing discernible to do with Israel. Those feelings, his book confirms, were far more attributable to the volitional wanderings of his rootless father, and the enduring yearning of his mother for Beirut, than to Zionist malevolence.

Only after the Six-Day War did Said, by then a tenured professor ensconced on Morningside Heights, finally reinvent himself as a Palestinian. Then, for the first time, he experienced the "wrenching, tearing, sorrowful loss [of Palestine] as exemplified in so many distorted lives, including mine. . . ." Nearly thirty years later he would tell an interviewer for *Al-Arabi*: "I am a Palestinian who . . . was forced as a result of the 1948 Catastrophe to live in exile, in the same way as many hundreds of thousands of Palestinians were." By then his own invented narrative of Israeli dispossession, like that of the Palestinian people to whom he claimed to belong, had become the conventional wisdom, contrived though it was, in the indictment of the Jewish state. Like Yasser Arafat, whose cause he loyally served, Edward Said was an Egyptian claiming to speak as a "Palestinian."

If Israel was to blame for the plight of Palestinians, there was an obvious remedy: eradicate it. Not by force, to be sure, but through delegitimization. That solution was the contribution of historian Tony Judt, like Said a world-renowned public intellectual, but unlike his "Palestinian" counterpart a Jew and disillusioned Zionist. Judt's adolescent infatuation with Marxism, in conjunction with his self-described "all-embracing engagement with left-wing Zionism," had inspired idyllic teen-age summers of joyous labor on Israeli kibbutzim. "I idealized Jewish distinction, and intuitively grasped and reproduced the Zionist emphasis upon separation and ethnic difference." He avidly embraced the "Muscular Judaism" (and "guilt-free sex") for which kibbutzim were then renowned. But disillusion soon followed: "Israel felt like a prison in those days, and the kibbutz like an overcrowded cell."

The Six-Day War sealed Judt's rejection and stoked his fury. His postwar "experience with the army on the Golan Heights" taught him that "most Israelis were not transplanted latter-day agrarian socialists but young, prejudiced urban Jews" whose "attitude toward the recently defeated Arabs shocked me . . . and the insouciance with which they anticipated their future occupation and domination of Arab lands terrified me." Their chauvinism, racism and militarism demolished his adolescent infatuation with the Jewish state; by the age of twenty, he "had become, been, and ceased to be a Zionist." Israel had taught him to be "suspicious of identity politics in all forms, Jewish above all."

Cambridge doctorate in hand, Judt became a highly respected scholar of French and modern European history. A self-described "universalist social democrat," he (like Said) eventually relocated to the United States, where he taught at New York University. His public recognition soared after his scathing essay, "Israel: The Alternative," appeared in *The New York Review of Books* (2003). Nearly four decades after leaving Israel behind, he became an anti-Zionist icon for branding the Jewish state an "anachronism" that was on the verge of becoming "neither Jewish nor democratic." Calling for its dissolution, the jilted lover of Zion finally gained his revenge.

In his despair over the crumbling Middle East peace process, Judt offered a scathing critique of Israel that passionately (and preposterously) enumerated what was so wrong with the Jewish state that it must cease to exist. There was, of course, the "occupation," with "illegal settlements" that "corralled" Palestinians into "shrinking Bantustans." Israel's "ethno-religious self-definition" made it an "anachronism" in the modern world of "individual rights, open frontiers, and international law"—Judt's idealistic fantasy, but hardly descriptive of the Muslim Middle East in which Israel is embedded.

Judt offered the familiar, dire and erroneous demographic projection that continued Israeli "occupation" of Judea, Samaria—and Gaza (which it soon abandoned)—would, within "half a decade," make it "neither Jewish nor democratic." To remain Jewish, it would be forced to "conduct full-scale ethnic cleansing" that "would condemn Israel forever to the status of an outlaw state, an international pariah," the status to which Judt had already consigned it.

It was time, he proclaimed, "to think the unthinkable." This once avid Zionist had become convinced that there was "no place in the world today for a 'Jewish state.'" With a two-state solution doomed, "the true alternative facing the Middle East in the coming years will be an ethnically cleansed Greater Israel and a single, integrated, binational state of Jews and Arabs, Israelis and Palestinians." Curiously but revealingly, no other nation in the world—least of all the prospective Palestinian state whose leaders proclaimed its *Judenrein* intentions—deserved replacement. But in the contemporary "'clash of cultures' between open, pluralist democracies and belligerently intolerant, faith-driven ethno-states," Judt asserted, Israel had become a "dysfunctional" anachronism. "Bad for the Jews," he concluded, it must disappear.

Shortly before his death, Judt reflected on his concededly "notorious" essay. Wrapping himself in the mantle of a Jewish protector of Israel, he proclaimed: "I do feel as a Jew that one has a responsibility to criticize Israel vigorously and rigorously, in ways that non-Jews cannot," lest they be accused of anti-Semitism. (Jews, to be sure, may be vulnerable to the charge of self-hatred.) He insisted that his "experience as a Zionist allowed me to identify the same fanaticism and myopic, exclusivist tunnel vision in others—most notably the community of American cheerleaders for Israel."

Judt proclaimed his own immunity from criticism because, as a Jew, he was "oblivious to moral blackmail from censorious fellow-Jews." After all, "I am also a Jew who has lived in Israel and been a committed Zionist" (even if only as a besotted teen-ager). Displaying his Jewish credentials, even as adult loathing for Israel replaced misguided youthful adoration, he claimed to be "deliberately trying to pry open a suppressed debate" as though there had been no calls for Israel's dissolution until the publication of his own diatribe.

Judt wanted everyone to know, despite impressions that he might give to the contrary, that "I was not, am not, and do not come across as anti-Israeli." Rather, he immodestly claimed, he was "more honest and outspoken" than others. (But, he conceded, "it took very little courage to publish a controversial piece about Israel in *The New York Review of Books* while holding a tenured chair at a major university.") Judt was merely objecting to the shift in Zionist political power "toward religious zealots and territorial fundamentalists" in a society increasingly dominated by "intolerant, belligerent, self-righteous, God-fearing irredentists."

The writings of Said and Judt popularized Palestinian grievances, underscored Israeli venality, and inspired a multitude of academic disciples. The University of California led the way in venomous denunciation of Israel. Initiated by Students for Justice in Palestine at Berkeley, an emerging academic hotbed of anti-Zionism, it sprouted chapters at Irvine, Riverside, San Diego and Santa Barbara. University-sponsored and funded student groups on the Irvine and Santa Cruz campuses harassed and assaulted Jewish students and defamed supporters of Israel. At their rallies and conferences, Muslim imams routinely praised suicide bombings that targeted Israel civilians while identifying Zionists as "the true and legitimate object of liquidation."

Stanford history professor Joel Beinin declared that Israel has "lost any moral justification for its existence." UC Irvine historian Mark LeVine accused Israel of "violence and terrorism" that emerges from "decades of occupation, discrimination and dispossession." At California State University (Northridge), a mathematician maintained a "Boycott Israel Resource Page" on his website, with a ten-page bibliography to support his claim that Israel is "the most racist state in the world at this time." Students on the Irvine campus prevented Israeli Ambassador Michael Oren from speaking; at San Francisco State University students verbally assaulted and threatened participants in a pro-Israel rally; the Berkeley Hillel Center was vandalized; and anti-Israel protesters on the Davis campus occupied a building and hoisted a sign reading "Davis + Gaza Are One Fist."

The plague of academic vilification spanned the nation. According to Noam Chomsky, the renowned MIT linguistic scholar, Israel's Jewishness "resides in discriminatory institutions and practices" whose source is "the genocidal texts of the Bible." It is "a place where racialism, religious discrimination, militarism and injustice prevail." An "escalating policy of apartheid" makes Israel a "rogue state" with a history of "war crimes" designed "to subdue the colonized population." Possessing a "Samson complex," its aggression (which Chomsky often described as "terrorism") creates the danger of "a final solution from which few will escape."

Zionists, claimed NYU philosopher Bertell Ollman in his "Letter of Resignation from the Jewish People," are "the worst anti-Semites in the world today, oppressing a Semitic people as no nation has done since the Nazis." Palestinians, wrote Marc Ellis of Baylor University, "are comparable to the Jews in the Warsaw Ghetto, awaiting annihilation." Norman Finkelstein, denied tenure at DePaul University, asserted that "Jews who do not stand against Israel are morally worse than Germans who did not oppose Hitler." Equating Israelis with Nazis, Finkelstein (the child of Holocaust survivors) could not imagine "why Israel's apologists would be offended by a comparison with the Gestapo."

Joel Kovel, who taught at Bard, wrote *Overcoming Zionism* "in fury about Israel and the unholy complicity of the United States and its Jewish community that grants it immunity." His remedy was to "annihilate" Israel: "No ethnic homeland, no Jewish state . . . because Zionism has meant recycling the negation that is Judaism into endless destruction." Northeastern University political scientist (and former adviser to the Palestinian Authority) Denis Sullivan achieved notoriety for framing his academic program around the demonization of Israelis as "basically Nazis."

Ivy League universities enthusiastically joined the chorus of denunciation. At the University of Pennsylvania, students sponsored a conference to promote "the growing global campaign to boycott, divest from and sanction the State of Israel until it complies with its obligations under international and human rights law." At Columbia, the Palestine Forum demanded the divestment of university funds from Israeli companies that profit from "occupation" and "illegal" settlements. Harvard president Lawrence Summers warned that "serious and thoughtful people" in "progressive intellectual communities . . . are advocating and taking actions that are anti-Semitic in their effect if not their intent."

Even Students for a Free Palestine at Oberlin College in Ohio, renowned for its liberalism ever since it became the first American college to admit female and African-American students, led a campaign to divest from six companies "that profit from the occupation and oppression of Palestinians." Support came from La Alianza Latina, the South Asian Students Association, the Queer Wellness Coalition and the Center for Women and Transgender People. Oberlin, proclaimed one proud student (without discernible irony), "lives up to its progressive history and reputation."

The Boycott Divestment and Sanctions movement was internationally contagious. Librarians from five countries, including the United States and Canada, called for a boycott of Israel to protest its "erasure of Palestinian culture and history." American Muslims for Palestine urged Chicago food shoppers to boycott dates grown by Israeli farmers. Salif Keita, the "Golden Voice of Africa," joined other popular entertainers in refusing to perform in Jerusalem. The age-old vilification of Jews had found its new language of defamation.

In England, where blood libels and brutal massacres had preceded the expulsion of Jews, and Shylock became the enduring stereotype of the venal Jew, a venerable tradition of anti-Semitism refocused on the Jewish state. More than one hundred British academics signed a letter in 2002 (initiated by a Jewish scholar and his non-Jewish wife) demanding a moratorium on cultural and research links with Israel and the denial of funding from the European Union to Israeli research and cultural institutions. Three years later the Council of the Association of University Teachers voted to boycott Bar-Ilan University because it offered courses at Ariel College, located in an Israeli city in Samaria. Even the Palestinian al-Quds University in Jerusalem condemned the Council vote.

The National Association of Teachers in England approved a boycott of professors and universities in Israel, with its "entrenched system of racial discrimination" and "apartheid policies." Jews and the Jewish state "are to be excluded from . . . the community of nations, because they are dangerous and malign." The Association sanctioned annual boycott proposals to condemn Israeli "annexation," "illegal settlement," and "the complicity of Israeli academia in the occupation." As Israel's deputy ambassador in London observed, "the last time that Jews were boycotted in universities was in 1930s Germany."

For Jacqueline Rose of Queen Mary University of London, perfidious Israel justified her rejection of Judaism. Maligning Zionism as "demonic" and "defiled," she was "appalled by what the Israeli state perpetrates on a daily basis in the name of the Jewish people" and "at what the Israeli nation perpetrated in my name": "a historic injustice against the Palestinians still awaiting redress."

Palestinians, asserted philosopher Tom Honderich of the University College in London, have the "moral right" to kill Jews; suicide bombers "who have killed themselves in the cause of their people have indeed sanctified themselves." Oxford professor (and poet) Tom Paulin, who proudly claimed that "I never believed that Israel had a right to exist at all," labeled the IDF the "Zionist SS"; Jewish settlers were "Nazis, racists" who "should be shot dead."

At the University of Manchester, Michael Sinnott described Israel as "the mirror image of Nazism" in its "atrociousness." His colleague Mona Baker dismissed two Israeli scholars from the editorial boards of academic journals because she "absolutely deplored the Israeli state" for going "beyond just war crimes" to "some kind of Holocaust" against the Palestinian people. Oxford professor Andrew Wilkie rejected the application of an Israeli graduate student because "I have a huge problem with the way that the Israelis take the high moral ground from their appalling treatment in the Holocaust, and then inflict gross human rights on the Palestinians." As he noted (in self-exculpation): "I am not the only UK scientist with these views."

England offered a congenial academic home for anti-Zionist Israeli scholars. To Oren Ben-Dor, a philosopher at Southampton University, Israel is "a terrorist state like no other." Ilan Pappé, who left the University of Haifa for Exeter, dismissed Arab declarations of war against Israel as mere rhetoric while accusing the Jewish state of "the ethnic cleansing of Palestine." To Akiva Orr, who founded an anti-Zionist publication in London, Zionism was "a heresy of Judaism." Uri Davis, an honorary fellow at Exeter (and a convert to Islam), argued in *Apartheid*

Israel that the Jewish state should be "dismantled" and replaced by a "democratic Palestine" that would end the "abomination" and "crime" of Zionism.

Israeli "atrocities" became a staple of British journalism. Writing in the *Guardian*, a favorite forum for anti-Zionist diatribes, Seumas Milne accused Israel of practicing South African-style "apartheid" and even Auschwitz-style "genocide." Any allegation of anti-Semitism, Milne wrote, is an "absurd slur which is being used as an apologia for Israel's brutal war of subjugation." The BBC, concluded the London correspondent for the *Jerusalem Post*, has persistently portrayed Israel as "a demonic, criminal state and Israelis as brutal oppressors," in effect "delegitimizing the Jewish state and pumping oxygen into a dark, old European hatred." Its "animus against Israel," another analyst wrote, is conspicuous for "its obsessive and visceral qualities."

England, wrote Melanie Phillips (among the few British journalists to defend Israel), has become "a kind of global laundry for the lies about Israel and bigotry toward the Jews churning out of the Arab and Muslim world," in effect "sanitising" them for foreign consumption and distribution. In his massively documented history of English anti-Semitism, Anthony Julius wrote that "to maintain that the very existence of Israel is without legitimacy," as so many British intellectuals and journalists seem determined to do, "is to embrace . . . a kind of anti-Semitism indistinguishable in its compass and consequences from practically any that has yet been inflicted on Jews." Indeed, Israel had become "the Jew among nations." With many pages of careful documentation, Robert Wistrich concluded that Great Britain has become "a world leader and innovator in promoting the 'new anti-Semitism," characterized by "a conscious attempt to 'Nazify' Judaism, Zionism and Israel."

As historian Efraim Karsh has documented, it is Arab and Muslim nations that are "the real perpetrators of Middle East apartheid." They, not Israel, practice religious intolerance (historically directed toward Jews and Christians and between Sunni and Shi'ite Muslims); ethnic discrimination (against Kurds and Berbers); racism (for centuries branding Jews as the ultimate source of evil); and gender discrimination (against women and homosexuals). After Israel won its war for independence in 1948, Arab rulers—supported by inflamed mobs—forced Jews to flee from their homes in Egypt, Syria, Iraq, Iran, Lebanon, Yemen and Morocco. Jordan, Lebanon and Syria still confine more than 600,000 descendants of Palestinian refugees in festering camps, without civic or political rights. Nearly 700,000 other Palestinians live in West Bank and Gaza camps under Palestinian Authority and Hamas rule.

The unrelenting assault on Israel represents what Ruth Wisse has aptly labeled "the liberal betrayal of the Jews." Critics ignore the inconvenient truth that she identifies: "Jews have more concurrent rights to their land than any other people on this earth can claim: aboriginal rights, divine rights, legal rights, internationally guaranteed rights, pioneering rights, and the rights of that perennial arbiter, war." Yet liberal academics dismiss these rights as spurious, especially when compared to contrived Palestinian claims designed to negate Jewish history and usurp Jewish land. Indeed, as Dutch scholar Ian Buruma observed, "the Palestinian cause has become the universal litmus test of liberal credentials."

This is no less true for Israeli writers, academics and artists on the left. Joining the international chorus of delegitimization of their own country, they have eluded guilt by association to gain respect as citizens of the world. Novelist Aharon Megged, writing in the *Jerusalem Post* in 1994 about "The Israeli Suicide Drive," observed that "the Israeli-Nazi equation" pervades Israeli film, poetry, painting, photography and other forms of cultural expression. He decried the "emotional and moral identification by the majority of Israel's intelligentsia with people openly committed to our annihilation."

Sparked by the "post-Zionist" revisionist critique of journalist Benny Morris, a kibbutznik born in the year of Israeli independence and a refusenik imprisoned during the First Intifada, a generation of "new historians" rewrote the past to implant left-wing stereotypes of Israeli venality. With his claim that Israel was "born tarnished, besmirched by original sin," Morris broke the mold of Zionist historiography that had provided moral justification for the establishment of the Jewish state. His scrutiny of the birth of the Palestinian refugee problem as an example of "ethnic cleansing" that launched the continuing practice of "oppressing the Palestinians" resonated among academic colleagues and journalists who rejected the patriotic pieties of their generational predecessors.

Morris eventually recanted, but post-Zionism still permeates Israeli academic culture. Avi Shlaim accused Zionists of "collusion" with King Hussein of Jordan in 1948 to divide Palestine at the expense of its Palestinian inhabitants. Shlaim subsequently blamed Israel for its "repression" of the Second Intifada, "an anti-colonial national liberation struggle." Ilan Pappé, who denounced the "ethnic cleansing" of 1948, has claimed that Zionism was more dangerous than militant Islam, and proposed a one-state solution that would eradicate Israel as a Jewish state. Sociologist Baruch Kimmerling, drawing upon an "invented past" in the Land of Israel to claim legitimacy, equated Zionism with colonialism, accusing Israel of "politicide": a movement "to destroy the political and national viability" of the Palestinian people through murders, massacres, land colonization, and ethnic cleansing.

Ben-Gurion University geographer Oren Yiftachel has defined Israel as an "ethnocracy" suffering from "creeping apartheid," a state "that maintain[s] a relatively open government, yet facilitate[s] a nondemocratic seizure of the country and polity by one ethnic group." By "Judaizing Israel/Palestine," he concluded, Zionism created a nation "that undermines the common perception that Israel is both Jewish and democratic." Therefore, "as a definable democratic-political entity, [Israel] simply *does not exist.*" (Ironically, his submission co-authored with an Israeli Arab was rejected by the English journal *Political Geography* because its authors were Israelis.) His colleague Neve Gordon, author of *Israel's Occupation,* actively supported the Boycott, Divestment and Sanctions movement and achieved notoriety with an article in the *Los Angeles Times* condemning Israel as "an apartheid state."

In his own distinctive revisionist challenge, Tel Aviv University historian Shlomo Sand concluded that Jews (but not Palestinians) were "an invented people" (of converts, no less), who had scattered through the Middle East and Eastern Europe without any historical connection to the ancient Land of Israel. From its birth, therefore, Israel was "a bastard child" that was "not entirely legitimate." Distinguished by its "ethnocentric nationalist character" (as a Jewish state), it became "progressively more nationalistic and hence much more racist." The very idea of a "democratic Jewish state," to Sand, is self-contradictory. Even if Israel were to abandon the settlements and its "apartheid territories," the "myth of the Jewish *ethnos* state" would endure, with "Jewish Israeli society" retaining its "deeply embedded image of the 'chosen people'" in the name of "a fanciful history or dubious biology."

"A sizeable group of [Israeli] academics, journalists, and commentators," concludes Efraim Karsh, "predicated their professional careers on rewriting Israel's history in an image of their own choosing so as to cast it in the role of the regional villain." Depicting the Palestinians as "hapless victims of Zionist/Israeli aggression," their work constitutes "a deliberate attempt at historical distortion." Identifying with the international consensus that proclaims Israeli venality, they shield themselves from the opprobrium directed at their pariah nation. Like generations of compliant diaspora Jews before them, they have chosen assimilation into the hostile culture that rewards their Zionist apostasy.

Admired Israeli writers with an appreciative international following have added their literary voices to the academic chorus of denunciation. Amos Oz, who lamented the return of Jews to their ancient homeland after 1967 as "occupation and capitulation and destruction," lauded the "marriage"—although intermarriage might be more apt—"between the Jewish heritage and the European humanist experience." Proud that he had "assimilated" this cultural fusion, Oz denounced the "fanatical tribalism, brutal and closed," of religious Zionist settlers. So, too, David Grossman proclaimed the moral equivalence of Palestinian and Jewish nationalism in their struggle over the same land. Arabs were like Jews in their aspirations for a homeland, Grossman observed, but Jews are "people who are able to harden their hearts" against their Palestinian Other. For Israeli writers, as for academics, defamation of their country is the price of admission and approval in Western intellectual circles.

The "betrayal of intellectuals," in French philosopher Julien Benda's memorable phrase, has become worldwide. Internationally renowned writers across the political spectrum, honored with Nobel Prizes, have venomously entwined anti-Semitism with anti-Zionism. Portuguese novelist José Saramago described Israel as "a racist state by virtue of Judaism's monstrous doctrines." Believing that they are the chosen people, he continued, Israelis claim justification for enacting "an obsessive, psychological and pathologically exclusivist racism." Günter Grass, who only recently had revealed his World War II service in the Wafen-SS, published a poem entitled "What Must Be Said." Mute for decades about his own loyalty to the Third Reich, he offered a self-righteous apology for ignoring the looming Zionist menace. "Israel's nuclear power," he wrote, "is endangering our already fragile world peace." About Iran's nuclear development he remained silent.

Alone among nations, Israel has been targeted by critics who deny its democratic character, falsely accuse it of "apartheid," and challenge its right to exist as a Jewish state. Anti-Zionism, with its "irrational Satanization" of Israel, has become the respectable contemporary expression of Judeophobia. With the demonization of Israel, Palestinians have been transformed into the world's exalted victims, embraced as "a chosen people transfigured by injustice and suffering beyond compare" inflicted by their Israeli conquerors and occupiers.

In traditional anti-Semitic rhetoric, the insidious power of Jews invariably lurked behind the thrones of their host nations. A contemporary variation on that hoary theme was an article on "The Israel Lobby," written by University of Chicago professor John Mearsheimer and Harvard professor Stephen Walt, published in The *London Review of Books* (2006). Why, they asked pointedly (and answered falsely), "has the US been willing to set aside its own security and that of many of its allies in order to advance the interests of another state?" Because, they concluded, the "Israel Lobby" has "managed to divert it . . . from what the national interest would suggest."

There was no "compelling moral case," Mearsheimer and Walt concluded in their article (and in their book of the same title a year later), for such favoritism toward Israel. Indeed, the costs—lavish financial support aside—far outweighed the benefits. Responding with ingratitude to American assistance, "Israel does not behave like a loyal ally." It builds settlements against American wishes and "conducts the most aggressive espionage operations against the US of any ally." The United States has "a terrorism problem," they argued, "because it is so closely allied with Israel," whose "past and present conduct offers no moral basis for privileging it over the Palestinians." Indeed, they wrote, "if backing the underdog were a compelling motive," the United States would support Israel's "opponents" (not identified as enemies). But the power of the Lobby, driven by "the neo-conservatives' devotion to Israel," rendered that impossible. "Thanks to the Lobby," they asserted, "the United States "has become the de facto enabler of Israeli expansion in the Occupied Territories, making it complicit in the crimes perpetrated against the Palestinians."

The Walt-Mearsheimer critique was widely and vigorously challenged for its hallucination of a menacing pro-Israel lobby, spearheaded by the American-Israel Public Affairs Committee (AIPAC). Eerily reminiscent of *The Protocols of the Elders of Zion*, it described in fulsome detail how powerful Jews conspired in secret to bend the American government to their malevolent will. It claimed that AIPAC's "stranglehold" on Congress tilted American policy in the Middle East decisively and dangerously toward the Jewish state. Branding the organization "a de facto agent for a foreign government," Walt and Mearsheimer tacitly accused its Jewish leaders and members of subverting the American national interest to benefit Israel.

Less noticed was their gratuitously derogatory characterization of the Jewish state, which cut far deeper than alleged ingratitude to its American protector and benefactor. "Some aspects of Israeli democracy," Walt and Mearsheimer asserted, "are at odds with core American values." Israel was "explicitly founded as a Jewish state and its citizenship," they erroneously alleged (by overlooking more than one million Israeli Arab citizens), "is based on the principle of blood kinship." Its democratic claims were undermined by its refusal to grant to the Palestinians, "a largely innocent third party" (whose repeated acts of terrorism the authors virtually ignored), "a viable state of their own or full political rights." In the end, Israel's peace-seeking record "is not distinguishable from that of its [Palestinian] opponents," who alone are widely accused of acting "with great wickedness." Israel, they concluded, "would probably be better off if the Lobby were less powerful and US policy more even-handed."

But it was Walt and Mearsheimer who were anything but even-handed. Their conspiracy-theory insinuations provided an updated riff on classic anti-Semitic allegations of devious Jews manipulating power behind the scenes for their own benefit and profit. Accused of inventing facts, twisting quotes, and selectively cherry-picking evidence to support their allegations, the authors confronted a prolonged barrage of criticism. But Mearsheimer, in particular, remained adamant. In a speech three years after publication of *The Israel Lobby*, he labeled Israelis "the new Afrikaners" whose nation was on its way to becoming "a full-fledged apartheid state."

The delegitimization of Israel is international in scope, unrelenting, and vigorously perpetuated by the United Nations, which has remained most united when targeting the Jewish state. Within a year after the UN Security Council approved Israel's application for admission, the UN established the United Nations Relief and Works Administration (UNRWA). Intended as a "temporary" agency, its sole purpose was to provide aid to a vastly inflated number of 860,000 Palestinian "refugees" (whose actual number, according to Karsh's meticulous research, was between 583,000 and 609,000). A "refugee" was defined as any person "whose normal place of residence was Palestine" between June 1, 1946 and May 15, 1948, "and who lost both home and means of livelihood as a result of the 1948 conflict."

In 1975, the year that the UN proclaimed Zionism as "racism," it also recognized "the inalienable right of the Palestinians to return to their homes and property from which they have been displaced and uprooted." Only for Palestinians, a "refugee" was redefined to include "descendants of fathers fulfilling the definition." The UN thereby created a permanent, ever-growing cohort of impoverished and dependent Palestinians whose grievances against Israel can be stoked in perpetuity by millions of people, descended from refugees, who were as yet unborn in 1948. Its double standard enables Palestinians alone to be citizens of another country yet still qualify as refugees, eligible for $1.23 billion of financial support annually from UNRWA.

By now, in addition to the estimated 30,000 genuine Palestinian refugees still living, the UNRWA policy of hereditary entitlement provides the protective cover of international legitimacy for five million "refugees" to assert claims on Israeli land they never inhabited. With its contrived and ever-growing number of Palestinian "refugees," estimated to reach 8 million by 2030, UNRWA stokes the fires of hatred against Israel for the Palestinian "refugee" crisis that the passage of time has all but obliterated. It thereby perpetuates and inflates the very problem that it was established to resolve while providing UNRWA with generous funding and its nearly 30,000 staff personnel with the assurance of continuing employment.

Human rights organizations, following the UN precedent, compete to provide aid to Palestinian "refugees." They would sacrifice one of their most compelling causes if Palestinians were removed from their roster of victims. "The occupation," wrote *Jerusalem Post* journalist Seth Frantzman, "is their raison d'etre and without it they cannot exist." Even if there is a State of Palestine, a Palestinian diplomat has acknowledged, Palestinians "are still refugees. They will not be considered citizens." Why not? Because once they became citizens of Palestine they would forfeit their "right of return" to Israel.

The International Criminal Court, established by the UN General Assembly in 1998, has catered to Palestinian victimization claims by classifying Jewish settlement (unlike Palestinian terrorism) as a "war crime." Israel (and the United States) quickly "unsigned" from the statute of authorization for the Court, which lacks jurisdiction over "crimes" committed before 2002. By then, however, virtually all currently existing Jewish settlements had already been established. That renders any designation of settlement as a "war crime" meaningless *ex post facto* rhetoric, although not without power to elicit ever more anti-Israel venom within the international community.

The UN may have reached its pinnacle of mendacity in 2009 with the notorious Goldstone Report on Israeli Operation "Cast Lead" in Gaza, authorized by its Human Rights Council. Chaired by respected South African Jewish jurist Richard Goldstone, it was charged with investigating the "grave violations" of human rights that Israel was accused of committing by targeting innocent civilians. The conclusion was reached even before the investigation began. The Israeli government, citing the demonstrable bias of the Council (nearly half its resolutions condemning a specific state during thirty-five years had targeted Israel), declined to cooperate.

Goldstone promised impartiality but the "investigation" was a farce. Defended by commission members as "diligent, independent and objective," it concluded that Israel had launched a "deliberately disproportionate attack designed to punish, humiliate, and terrorize a civilian population" for "its resilience and for its apparent support of Hamas." Its final report falsely accused Israel of collective punishment by intentionally targeting "the people of Gaza as a whole"; using Palestinians as "human shields"; and applying "excessive or lethal force" to quell Palestinian demonstrations. By pursuing "massive and deliberate destruction," Israel was found guilty of war crimes and possible crimes against humanity.

The commission made only passing reference to 8,000 Hamas rocket and mortar attacks, which admittedly had "caused terror in the affected communities of southern Israel preceding the launching of Cast Lead." It condemned Israel's "continuing occupation" of Gaza and the West Bank for its "violations of international humanitarian and human rights law," although all Israeli civilians and soldiers had been withdrawn from Gaza more than three years before the Israeli retaliation. It declined to investigate Hamas weapon storage sites in mosques, its transformation of Gaza's largest hospital into a military base, or—most damning—its use of local civilians as military shields. Nor did it cite Israeli warnings that preceded its retaliatory attacks in civilian neighborhoods where Hamas leaders and fighters were embedded. The Goldstone report ranked in mendacity with the invented "massacre" of Palestinian civilians in Jenin and the faked "murder" of 12-year-old Muhammad al-Dura in Gaza during the Second Intifada.

A year after the Commission report was released, Goldstone recanted. Writing in the *Washington Post,* he acknowledged: "If I had known then what I know now, the Goldstone Report would have been a different document." He had hoped, in vain as it turned out, that the inquiry would initiate "a new era of evenhandedness at the U.N. Human Rights Council, whose history of bias against Israel cannot be doubted." Instead, the Commission he chaired had flagrantly reinforced that bias. He claimed to have realized only belatedly that the damning centerpiece of his report was erroneous: Gaza civilians "were not intentionally targeted as a matter of policy" by the IDF.

But Goldstone's "duplicitous investigation," noted *Jerusalem Post* editor David Horovitz, had "poisoned Israel's name." "Like all previous blood libels against the Jews," wrote Melanie Phillips, the Human Rights Council's attempt to "delegitimise Israel as a global pariah" would have malignant consequences despite Goldstone's recantation: "the poison this one has injected into the global bloodstream has no antidote." The "apartheid" label, in conjunction with the denial of Israel's right to defend its own civilians against attack, Leslie Susser observed in *The Jerusalem Report*, would render the Jewish state morally opprobrious no less than militarily helpless. At the crest of a rising "tide of delegitimization," the Goldstone Report had provided nothing less than "a formula for Israel's dismantlement."

The UN, through its collateral organizations, enables Palestinian attempts to undermine Israeli sovereignty and erase Jewish history in the Land of Israel. UNESCO has a laudable "World Heritage" program to protect ancient historic and archeological sites of "outstanding universal value." But its animosity toward Israel is glaringly evident. In 1974 UNESCO stripped Israel of membership for its alleged (but nonexistent) damage to the Temple Mount in Jerusalem from nearby archeological excavations. Yet it averted its eyes and remained silent when the Muslim Waqf, to which Israel ceded control of the Temple Mount after the Six-Day War, authorized excavation of the underground "Solomon's Stables" area for construction of a mosque. The unmonitored removal of tons of bulldozed earth filled with archeological artifacts was obviously intended to obliterate evidence of the ancient Jewish presence there during the First and Second Temple eras.

UNESCO has long accused Israel of destroying the Palestinian past, for which there are no documents or archeological remains for the simple reason that no Palestinian "past" existed until its relatively recent invention. Yet UNESCO has authorized designation of two of the most ancient Jewish holy sites—*Me'arat HaMachpelah* in Hebron and Rachel's tomb outside Bethlehem—as mosques that are "an integral part of the Occupied Palestinian Territories." Palestinians seek World Heritage protection for the Qumran caves near Jericho, where the ancient Jewish texts known as the Dead Sea Scrolls were discovered, as their own inheritance. They claim the village of Battir, located in biblical Judea, as a Palestinian World Heritage site. "Battir" is better known to history as Beitar, site of the final battle of the Bar Kokhba revolt and the death of its leader in 135 CE.

In a mendacious inversion of truth, the old anti-Semitism has morphed into the new anti-Zionism, with Israel inexorably linked to the most depraved regimes of the twentieth century, its very right to exist constantly challenged. The delegitimization crusade, legal scholar Joel Fishman writes, is clearly designed "to obliterate the history, national identity, culture, and rights . . . [of Israel] as a sovereign state." It is, philosopher Bernard Harrison concludes, "seriously, even murderously, anti-Semitic."

How is this persistent and vitriolic campaign of delegitimization, which would require volumes to fully document, to be explained and understood? What transformed six million Jewish Holocaust victims into six million Israeli oppressors, with the nation-state of the Jewish people not only relentlessly vilified but also venomously criminalized? It can hardly be coincidental that the very people who for centuries were demonized as Christ-killers, Satanic devils, Shylock usurers, venal capitalist exploiters, Bolshevik revolutionaries, cowards and traitors, even worms and pigs—and accused of poisoning wells, ritual murder, bestiality, and plotting to control world finances—would encounter nearly worldwide loathing once they survived annihilation and built a state of their own.

As anti-Semitism became anti-Zionism, malevolent stereotypes of conquering Israelis as the world's new Nazis and racists replaced images of the venal Jews who were deservedly persecuted and exterminated over the centuries. "There are few better ways to get rid of guilt," observes Israeli writer Hillel Halkin, "than accusing the accuser of the crimes one is guilty of. The reversal of roles whereby Israelis are now cast as the Nazi aggressor and the Palestinians as their helpless victims has been a wonderful salve for the European conscience."

"The question of whether anti-Zionism can or should be equated with anti-Semitism," writes Robert Wistrich, "is one of those pivotal issues that refuse to go away." Not only is "anti-Judaism" deeply embedded in "the Western tradition," as historian David Nirenberg amply documents. Islamist Judeophobia, identified by Wistrich as "a deadly strain of genocidal anti-Semitism" that is constructed from "powerful Koranic stereotypes of Jewish depravity," has long been rampant throughout the Middle East. During the 1930s, Haj Amin al-Husseini, the British-appointed Mufti of Jerusalem, eagerly collaborated with Nazi Germany and traveled to Berlin to urge Hitler to eradicate the Jews. More recently, Iranian leader Mahmoud Ahmadinejad proclaimed at the UN Durban Review Conference Against Racism that Israel is a "totally racist state" that has established a "racist government in occupied Palestine" on "the pretext of Jewish sufferings." Repeatedly, and ever more assertively, he has called for its annihilation while defending Iran's nuclear development program for precisely that purpose.

Anti-Zionism, the "Judeophobia" of our time, has spread its malignant poison of delegitimization worldwide. Venomous hostility toward Israel has moved beyond demonizing rhetoric into deadly assaults on Jews. Beginning with the Munich Olympic massacre in 1972, followed ever since by terrorist attacks in the Rome and Vienna airports, the venerable Istanbul synagogue, the Jewish community center in Buenos Aires, the Chabad center in Mumbai, a Jewish school in Toulouse, and a Bulgarian airport, thousands of athletes, worshippers, school children, and tourists, to say nothing of Israeli civilians, have been murdered because they were Jews. While Muslim terrorists wreak their slaughter world opinion ignores the perpetrators and blames their Jewish victims.

Echoes of ancient blood-libels still resonate in the twenty-first century. The unrelenting international demonization of Israel, literary scholar Edward Alexander incisively observes, has transformed the "pariah people" into "the pariah state." That a liberal democracy—a rarity in the Middle East, Africa, and Asia—can be so harshly excoriated is as difficult to explain rationally, least of all to justify, as were the centuries of malevolent anti-Semitism that preceded it.

The hostility directed toward Israel is the contemporary expression of the world's most unremitting hatred, stretching across centuries, cultures and continents. It is hardly coincidental, Wistrich suggests, that "the current wave of globalized anti-Semitism that erupted at the beginning of the twenty-first century is fundamentally about Israel."

Anti-Zionism, he notes, "has become the most dangerous and effective form of anti-Semitism in our time, through its systematic delegitimization, defamation, and demonization" of the Jewish state. To wish for Israel's demise is nothing less than "to wish to destroy the Jews." All that has changed ideologically since the Hitler era, he concludes, is that the political left is now "deeply mired in the muck of anti-Semitic lies and anti-Zionist delusions" that proclaim Israel to be "the most racist, fascist, and criminal state on earth."

The most reviled state in the world is the nation of the most persistently reviled people in world history. The trajectory from anti-Semitism to anti-Zionism, from the age-old demonization of Jews to the current delegitimization of Israel, is fueled by the same Judeophobic hatreds that generated the persecution of Jews over the centuries. The world's longest enduring hatred is now the consuming "lethal obsession" of those who collaborate in the delegitimization of Israel as a pariah nation. Ancient history repeats itself. With the Babylonian destruction of Jerusalem and its Temple in 586 BCE, the Book of *Lamentations* records (*Lam.* 2-3): "all her friends have dealt treacherously with her, they have become her enemies." A world without hatred of Jews would finally be free, after two thousand years, from its consuming obsessions with Christ-killers and infidels. There are, regrettably, few signs of the imminence of that liberation.

Conclusion: Settling the Future

In Babylonian captivity, Psalm 137 records, Jews struggled to "sing the Lord's song in a foreign land." They pledged: "If I forget thee, O Jerusalem, let my right hand forget her cunning. If I do not remember thee, let my tongue cleave to the roof of my mouth; if I set not Jerusalem above my highest joy." Memory, as the perceptive scholar Yosef Hayim Yerushalmi writes, remained "a central component of Jewish experience." Replacing sovereignty, it provided the key to Jewish survival in exile.

During centuries of dispersion, Jews never forgot their past in the Land of Israel. In the language of prayer, celebration and mourning, they continued to express their yearning to return. With the rebirth of Jewish nationalism in the late nineteenth century, Zionists were determined to bring that enduring vision to fruition. The Balfour Declaration of 1917, then the League of Nations Mandate in 1922, and finally the United Nations in 1948, recognized "the historic connection of the Jewish people with Palestine" that the State of Israel affirmed in its Proclamation of Independence.

Nineteen years later, Israel's precarious borders were challenged by Arab aggression. The stunning Israeli military victory in the Six-Day War became a transformative moment for the convergence of Zionism and Judaism—and for the struggles over legitimacy, both internal and external, that have confronted Israel ever since. Galvanized by their unexpected opportunity, religious Zionists sought to restore what Hebrew University sociologist Gideon Aran discerned as "the duality of nation and religion [that] had existed within Judaism from its very beginnings, and has accompanied it through history as its distinguishing feature."

More than 350,000 Israelis now live in 121 communities built in Judea, Samaria and the Golan Heights since the Six-Day War. They constitute as diverse a demographic mix as does the population of Israel. The two largest settlements, abutting Jerusalem, are the ultra-Orthodox enclaves of Betar Illit and Modi'in Illit with 90,000 residents, for many of whom Zionism remains a misguided secular faith. For many other settlers, especially in Samaria to the north, religious Zionist ideology is overshadowed by the opportunity for affordable housing and a better quality of life than could be found in the expensive and overcrowded urban centers they left behind. Perhaps one hundred thousand Israelis comprise the religious Zionist core that tenaciously claims the land as Israel's biblical birthright and inheritance.

To their Israeli critics, concentrated on the political left, settlers personify the "xenophobic nationalism" and "God-sanctioned violence" that have provoked justifiable international ostracism of Israel for its illegal occupation of "Palestinian" land. Religious settlers have been branded "Zealots for Zion" whose messianic fanaticism poses a challenge to Israeli democracy that will inevitably undermine the Jewish state. By avidly promoting settlements, concludes Ehud Sprinzak (among the more moderate Israeli critics of the convergence of Zionist nationalism and religious Judaism), religious Zionists have initiated the "erosion of Israel's democratic culture."

The "mix of messianism and nationalism," writes Gershom Gorenberg in *The Accidental Empire*, has the ominous potential for elevating "the settlement imperative" above democracy. Settlements express the spirit of "illegalism" carried over from the pre-state years, when "breaking the law for the sake of [Zionist] ideals was proof of true dedication." Young religious Zionists have attempted to compensate for their "illegitimacy complex" when they measure themselves against their heroic secular forebears. But their determination to build new communities in the Land of Israel, Gorenberg concludes, has imperiled democracy in the State of Israel.

In *Lords of the Land*, a comprehensive—and unremittingly hostile—survey of forty years of Jewish settlement, Israeli historian Idith Zertal and *Ha'aretz* journalist Akiva Eldar lacerate settlers for their illegal occupation, plunder, destruction and lawlessness. In a tragic twist of irony, the "pragmatist philosophy" of settlement ("another acre and another goat") that had once guided secular Zionists to statehood "had now been confiscated by the new alliance of the Revisionists and the national-religious." The "malignancy of occupation," the authors write, "in contravention of international law," has "brought Israel's democracy . . . to the brink of an abyss."

In his review of *Lords of the Land*, Hebrew University professor Gadi Taub blames "a small group of zealots" for provoking a "struggle over the very soul of the Jewish State." In his own book, *The Settlers*, Taub has condemned settlement as "Israel's most glaring violation of democratic rights and liberal values." In what has become the mantra of settlement critics, he predicts that continued "occupation" must inevitably confront Israel with two intolerable options: either "Jewish apartheid," if it continues to rule over Palestinians who are denied the right to vote in Israeli elections; or a "non-Jewish democracy" ruled by an (imagined) Arab majority between the Jordan River and the Mediterranean. Either result would undercut "a great deal of Judaism's moral heritage" while erasing the main achievement of Zionism: "a sovereign, democratic Jewish state." At best, Taub concludes (with a damning—and false—historical analogy), "Zionism and the occupation can live uneasily together as liberalism and slavery did in the United States."

"The goal of the Zionist project since its inception," write Ariella Azoulay and Adi Ophir, has been "the Judaization of the Land of Israel . . . by colonization of its frontier." Beginning with the confiscation of abandoned Palestinian property after the establishment of the state, and continuing with Israeli community building in the Galilee, it extended into the West Bank and Gaza following the Six-Day War. Not even the Israeli withdrawal from West Bank cities under the Oslo Accords, and from Gaza a decade later, could alter the authors' perception of Israel as a "tyrannical regime" of "ethnocratic and racist" occupation.

The refrain of religious fanaticism in the settlement movement is the conventional wisdom of secular Zionist critics. To University of Pennsylvania political scientist Ian Lustick, Jewish settlement represents virulent fundamentalism: a "distinctive blend of messianic expectation, militant political action, intense parochialism, devotion to the Land of Israel, and self-sacrifice that characterized the Jewish Zealots of Roman times." Once again, as in the first century, "the seductive but perilous temptations of redemption" threaten to destroy Jewish sovereignty from within. For journalist Peter Beinert, whose popular book *The Crisis of Zionism* pillories Jewish settlements, there are "two Israels": "a flawed but genuine democracy" within its pre-1967 borders and "an ethnically-based nondemocracy" beyond, where Israel "systematically oppresses" Palestinians.

The endlessly reiterated critique of Jewish settlements rests on two fundamental claims. First, by occupying and colonizing "Palestinian" land they violate international law. Second, retention of the settlements must inevitably undermine Israel's Jewish majority, identity and democratic values. But neither assertion, whether grounded in law or demography, is valid.

The persistent indictment of settlements for violating international law cites provisions of the Hague Regulations (1907) and the Fourth Geneva Convention (1949). Article 42 of the Hague Regulations defines "occupation" as the illegal authority exercised by the army of one country over the territory of another. According to Article 43, however, its application requires "the authority of the legitimate power" to have "passed into the hands" of the occupying power. Between 1949 and 1967, however, Jordan was not recognized internationally as the "legitimate power" with sovereign rights in the West Bank. Under the terms of the Hague Regulations, therefore, Israel is not an illegal occupier.

The relevant provisions of the Fourth Geneva Convention were grounded in international revulsion over the forced population transfers instigated by Nazi Germany (and the Soviet Union) during World War II. Conducted for "political and racial reasons," they were followed by the transfer of their own civilians into newly occupied territory. Accordingly, Article 49(1) prohibits "individual or mass forcible transfers, as well as deportations of protected persons from occupied territory to the territory of the Occupying Power. . . ." Article 49(6) declares: "The Occupying Power shall not deport or transfer parts of its own civilian population into the territory it occupies."

Israel did not violate either provision. It neither deported Palestinians from the West Bank after the Six-Day War, nor transferred Jews to it. Indeed, the Jewish right of settlement there had been protected under international law ever since the end of World War I. It gained explicit recognition at the San Remo Conference in 1920, when Great Britain received the League of Nations Mandate to govern Palestine. Incorporating language from Lord Balfour's Declaration three years earlier, the Mandate cited "the historical connection of the Jewish people with Palestine and the legitimacy of grounds for reconstituting their national home in that country." Jews were guaranteed the right of settlement throughout "Palestine," which under the original terms of the Mandate comprised the land east and west of the Jordan River—including present-day Jordan, the West Bank, Gaza and Israel.

Jewish settlement was limited by the Mandate in one respect only: Great Britain, the Mandatory power, acting in conjunction with the League of Nations Council, retained discretion to "postpone" or "withhold" the right of Jews to settle east—but not west—of the Jordan River.

Consistent with that solitary exception, Colonial Secretary Winston Churchill decided to separate Trans-Jordan from Palestine to provide a kingdom for England's wartime ally Abdullah, son of the Sharif of Mecca.

Upon the establishment (in 1922) of Transjordan, comprising three-quarters of the land originally designated as Mandatory Palestine for the Jewish national home, the British government withheld the right of Jewish settlement in that territory. But Article 6 of the Palestine Mandate explicitly protected "close settlement" by Jews in the land west of the Jordan River, thereafter to be called "Palestine." That guarantee, never rescinded or superseded, remains the enduring international legal foundation for the legitimacy of Jewish settlements and the right of Jews to build their homes in the land west of the Jordan River.

The Charter of the United Nations, successor to the League of Nations after World War II, explicitly protected the rights of "any peoples or the terms of existing international instruments to which members of the United Nations may respectively be parties." Drafted by Zionist representatives, Article 80 became known as "the Palestine clause" for preserving the right of the Jewish people to settle throughout their historic homeland west of the Jordan River. It was flagrantly violated when Jordan invaded the fledgling Jewish state, asserted sovereignty over the West Bank, and prevented Jews from living anywhere within the land illegally occupied by the Hashemite kingdom.

Following the Six-Day War, UN Security Council Resolution 242 permitted Israel to administer its newly acquired territory—the West Bank, Gaza, and Golan Heights—until the achievement of "a just and lasting peace in the Middle East." Even then, however, Israel would only be required to withdraw its armed forces (civilians were not mentioned) "from territories"—not from "the territories" or "all the territories."

The absence of "the," the famous missing definite article, was neither an accident nor an afterthought. It resulted from what American Undersecretary for Political Affairs Eugene V. Rostow, who played a major role in drafting Resolution 242, described as more than five months of "vehement public diplomacy" to decisively clarify its meaning. He insisted that "the Jewish right of settlement west of the Jordan River . . . was made unassailable" by the League of Nations Mandate. It applied to the West Bank no less than to Tel Aviv and Haifa. And, as Rostow subsequently noted, Jewish settlers were not "deported" or "transferred" to the West Bank (prohibited by the Geneva Convention), least of all by force. They moved there entirely of their own volition. Nor did the Israeli government remove Palestinians from their homes to enable their presence.

No restriction on Jewish settlement, wherever it had been guaranteed by the League of Nations Mandate forty-five years earlier, was adopted by the United Nations. Proposals requiring Israel to withdraw from all the territory it had acquired in the Six-Day War were defeated in both the Security Council and the General Assembly. "The Jewish right of settlement in the area," Rostow asserted, "is equivalent in every way to the right of the existing Palestinian population to live there."

Three months after the Six-Day War, Theodor Meron, Legal Counsel to the Israeli Foreign Ministry, advised Prime Minister Levi Eshkol's political secretary: "My conclusion is that civilian settlement in the administered territories contravenes the explicit provisions of the Fourth Geneva Convention." Its prohibition on forced population transfers, Meron wrote, was "categorical and is not conditioned on the motives or purposes of the transfer." But the government did not accept Meron's assumption of a forced transfer; his report was filed and forgotten.

Several years after the war, Attorney General Meir Shamgar (who subsequently served as president of the Supreme Court between 1983 and 1995) declared that the Geneva Convention was inapplicable to Jewish settlements. Under international law, he noted, any restriction must be based "on the assumption that there has been a sovereign who was ousted and that [it] was a legitimate sovereign." But Jordanian claims of sovereignty over the West Bank had never been recognized internationally (except by Great Britain and Pakistan). Israel could not, therefore, be considered a "belligerent occupier."

Judge Stephen Schwebel of the International Court of Justice concluded that territory acquired in a war of self-defense, waged by Israel in 1967, must be distinguished from territory acquired by "aggressive conquest," such as that launched by Nazi Germany in 1939. The provisions of the Palestine Mandate that allocated the land west of the Jordan River to the Jewish people for close settlement would remain in force until sovereignty was determined in a peace treaty between Israel and the Palestinians.

International law expert Julius Stone has described the persistent attempts to undermine the legitimacy of Jewish settlements as a "subversion ... of basic international law principles." Application of the Geneva Convention provisions to Judea and Samaria, he writes, would require that "these areas, despite their millennial association with Jewish life, shall be forever *judenrein*," constituting "irony" pushed to "absurdity." Hebrew University law professor Yehuda Z. Blum, who served as Israeli Ambassador to the United Nations, declared: "Jews are not foreigners anywhere in the Land of Israel." In his comprehensive study of Jewish territorial rights, international lawyer Howard Grief documents the enduring significance of the San Remo Resolution as the legal foundation of Jewish national sovereignty west of the Jordan River. Indeed, Grief suggests that Prime Minister Ariel Sharon's removal of Israeli settlers from Gaza and four northern West Bank communities in 2005 might itself constitute an illegal "forcible transfer" under the terms of the Geneva Convention.

The Supreme Court of Israel has not ruled decisively on the legality of settlements. In one of its early decisions the Court declared that uncultivated West Bank land had been illegally requisitioned for the settlement of Elon Moreh and ordered its return to Arab owners. Justice Landau conceded that government claims of the right to settle in the entire Land of Israel were "well based in Zionist philosophy." But the Court found insufficient security interests to justify the seizure of private land. On state and unclaimed land, however, settlement has remained largely unimpeded by the Israeli judiciary.

In a 1982 opinion, Justice Aharon Barak declared that "Judea and Samaria are held by Israel by way of military occupation or belligerent occupation," derived from "the rules of public international law." This constraint, he asserted, even included the 1907 Hague Regulations, to which Israel was not a party but whose guidelines for military administration and deference to local (Jordanian) law and private property rights the Israeli government has nonetheless respected. But the Supreme Court, concludes Hebrew University legal scholar David Kretzmer, has walked a fine line between legitimizing settlements and restraining government authorities, declining to issue a definitive ruling on settlement legality.

Justice Barak's restrictive interpretation was rejected in the 2012 report of Israel's Levy Committee, authorized by Prime Minister Netanyahu's Cabinet to investigate the legal status of unauthorized settlement construction. The Committee, chaired by retired Justice Edmund Levy, reiterated that ever since 1922 Jews have held the internationally guaranteed legal right, never revoked, to "close settlement" west of the Jordan River. The provisions of the Fourth Geneva Convention regarding occupation and population transfers, it concluded, "cannot be considered to be applicable and were never intended to apply to the type of settlement activity carried out by Israel in Judea and Samaria." Because Jordanian sovereignty in the West Bank was not recognized under international law, Israel cannot be considered a "belligerent occupier." Israelis, the Commission concluded, "have the legal right to settle in Judea and Samaria."

The international drumbeat of settlement illegality remains unrelenting. The UN Security Council and General Assembly have repeatedly passed resolutions declaring settlements to be illegal under international law. The Rome Statute, adopted by the International Criminal Court in 1998, reiterated that "the transfer, directly or indirectly, by the Occupying Power of parts of its own civilian population into the territory it occupies" constitutes a war crime.

According to the International Court of Justice, "no territorial acquisition resulting from the threat or use of force shall be recognized as legal." A three-member panel of the UN Human Rights Council has accused Israel of a war crime by violating the Geneva Convention prohibition on population transfers to occupied territory. But "the illicit effort to use international law to delegitimize the settlements," law professor David M. Phillips perceptively observes, "is the same argument used by Israel's enemies to delegitimize the Jewish state."

International law aside, settlement critics have repeatedly warned of a looming demographic disaster for Israel, eventually depriving it of a Jewish majority, if it retains control over the West Bank. But such Jewish "demographic panic," concludes Yakov Faitelson of the Institute for Zionist Strategies, has a long history of gloomy and erroneous predictions. In 1898, prominent Jewish historian Simon Dubnow warned that only 500,000 Jews would live in the ancient homeland a century later (a number already exceeded when Israel declared independence in 1948). Roberto Bachi, founder of Israel's Central Bureau of Statistics, significantly underestimated Jewish immigration and fertility rates, while inflating projected Arab population growth during the second half of the twentieth century. By 2001, the Jewish population west of the Jordan was more than twice his most optimistic forecast, while the Arab population was nearly 40 percent lower than he had anticipated.

During the First Intifada, Haifa University geography professor Arnon Sofer issued the dire—and erroneous—prediction that "in the year 2000, Israel will become non-Jewish." (He underestimated the number of Jews by nearly one million while inflating the Arab West Bank population by an equivalent number.) Early in the new century the increasingly contentious struggle over the future of Jewish settlements prompted a similarly exaggerated warning from Israeli demographer Sergio DellaPergola that "before the end of this decade, Jews will become a minority in the lands that include Israel, West Bank and Gaza Strip." It did not happen.

Israeli apprehension was heightened by a census conducted by the Palestinian Central Bureau of Statistics (PCBS) in 2007, claiming that 2,300,000 Arabs inhabited the West Bank and Jerusalem. The consequences seemed ominous. With its continued rule over a growing Palestinian population between the Jordan River and Mediterranean, Israel must inevitably lose its Jewish majority and identity or cease to be democratic. But even the Palestinian Bureau head conceded that these numbers were exaggerated, representing "a civil intifada," a demographic weapon against Israel to undermine Jewish settlement. The double counting of 208,000 Jerusalem Arabs as both Israeli and West Bank residents, and the inclusion of Palestinian emigrants—to say nothing of West Bank population inflation—assured demographic distortion. Other Palestinian ministries, rejecting the bloated PCBS numbers, acknowledged the reality of a considerably lower West Bank population of 1.6 million Palestinians.

Despite the litany of "demographic calamity projections," Faitelson has noted, the Jewish population west of the Jordan River has grown from a tiny 5 percent minority a century ago to more than a 60 percent majority. In recent years that majority has expanded because of unanticipated immigration (one million newcomers from the Soviet Union), rising Jewish and declining Arab fertility rates, Palestinian emigration, and the withdrawal from Gaza, which removed one million Arabs from Israeli authority.

"Beware of Palestinians Bearing Demographic Numbers," warns Yoram Ettinger, a critical Israeli analyst of "demographers of doom" who rely upon distorted population trends. His data suggest that the PCBS vastly exaggerated the West Bank Arab population by over-reporting births, under-reporting deaths, and ignoring emigration. Propelled by Yasser Arafat's gleeful prediction that "the womb of the Palestinian woman will defeat the Zionists," it disregarded rising Israeli Jewish fertility rates. "The suggestion that Jews are doomed to become a minority between the Jordan River and the Mediterranean," Ettinger concluded, "is either dramatically mistaken or outrageously misleading."

When Israel celebrated its sixty-fifth anniversary of independence in 2013, 6 million Jews (including 350,000 settlers) comprised 75.3 percent of its population, which also included 1.6 million Arab citizens (20.7 percent). Even including 1.6 million West Bank Palestinians, Israel still enjoyed nearly a 2:1 Jewish majority west of the Jordan River. With birth-rate projections indicating continued Jewish population growth (with settlements currently, and substantially, exceeding the nation's growth rate), a declining Arab share of Israeli births, and an ultra-Orthodox fertility rate in Judea and Samaria that is now two-and-a-half times that of the local Arab population, it is highly unlikely that Jews will be outnumbered in the foreseeable future, except in the forebodings of settlement critics.

Yet ominous warnings, based on inflated Palestinian demographic projections and driven by criticism of Jewish settlers, have become the conventional wisdom. "Given the demographics west of the Jordan River," President Obama declared in Jerusalem in April 2013, "the only way for Israel to endure and thrive as a Jewish and democratic state is through the realization of an independent and viable Palestine." That, however, is a *non sequitur*. Demographic data confirm a substantial (and increasing) Jewish majority west of the Jordan River in conjunction with abundant evidence of a thriving and diverse Israeli democracy that no Middle Eastern Arab or Muslim state comes close to matching.

But Jewish settlements continue to provoke contentious disagreement among Israelis—and worldwide calumny—over demography, democracy, and legality. It reveals the still unresolved struggle over the meaning of Zionism, the identity of the Jewish state, and the conundrum of Israeli legitimacy. The dismay of secular Zionists over the challenge from religious Zionist settlers was poignantly expressed thirty years ago by writer and left-wing political activist Amos Oz. Visiting the pioneering settlement of Ofra, a Gush Emunim stronghold, he vigorously rejected the settlers' claim to be "authentic Jews" who had seized the mantle of Zionism from "rootless Israelis" aspiring to be "a satellite of Western culture."

Oz insisted upon the validity of "the rendezvous between a Jew like me and Western humanism," which secular Zionists had "assimilated" (a revealing word choice) but religious Zionist settlers challenged. Yet there was a palpable note of nostalgic regret in his description of Gush

Emunim pioneers, "running around on hilltops with submachine guns and walkie-talkies, who had adopted the mannerisms and the slang of the kibbutz," claiming to be "heirs of the pioneering spark that had dimmed." Indeed, that was precisely who they were.

Ever since the first *halutzim* arrived in Ottoman Palestine in the 1880's, Zionism has been defined by settlement. For the post-1967 generation of religious Zionists, no less than for their secular predecessors, settlement was a national homecoming grounded in the biblical narrative, nurtured by centuries of Jewish yearning and decades of unrelenting Zionist struggle against unremitting hostility from neighboring Arab states and peoples. The newest settlers, as historian Michael Feige recognizes, were engaged in "a symbolic reenactment of the conquering of the land in ancient times and a reproduction of the pioneering Zionist practice."

It is often forgotten that although Zionism, in significant measure, was a secular rebellion against Orthodoxy, it drew heavily upon Jewish religious tradition, history, and symbols, without which its own claim to legitimacy would have been suspect. But the unanticipated convergence of nationalism and religion, which challenged the parameters of secular Zionism after 1967, posed fundamental questions about national identity that lie at the unresolved core of Israel's legitimacy struggles.

These conflicts, both internal and international, are likely to remain entwined with Jewish settlements for the foreseeable future. Disagreement over their legitimacy has even dredged up the *Altalena* from dim historical memory to become, once again, a subject of acrimonious political debate. During the countdown to the removal of Jewish settlers from Gaza in 2005, *Altalena* memories were repeatedly cited to condemn or justify the expulsion. Knesset Speaker Reuven Rivlin compared the besieged Gaza settlers to Irgun members on board the doomed ship confronting Ben-Gurion's determination to use military power to force their surrender. A left-wing Knesset member, echoing Ben-Gurion, responded: "We must fight extremist settlers by all possible means . . . if need be we'll open fire . . . the sovereign authority must announce that in order to preserve itself it too is ready to kill."

On the secular left, Israeli journalists, academic intellectuals, and politicians vigorously defended Prime Minister Sharon's decision to use force if necessary to expel Gaza settlers. Legal commentator Moshe Negbi complained that "Ben-Gurion's successors have demonstrated total limpness in imposing law and order on extremists. . . . It is this limpness that has brought down upon us the malignancy of the Jewish settlements" and their resident "fanatics." Sinking the *Altalena*, wrote Yoel Marcus in *Ha'aretz*, "established the principle of one army and one authority," a precedent that must be followed in Gaza. Tommy Lapid, leader of the staunchly secular Shinui party, insisted that when "a popular movement imbued with treasonous faith and incited by messianic rabbis challenged the law," the state must assert its power to assure the triumph of "democracy" over a "faith-inspired agitated mob."

In the Jewish state, writes Hebrew University political scientist Shlomo Avneri, "only one legitimate body is authorized to enforce political decisions." Ben-Gurion's order to attack the *Altalena* might have demonstrated "ruthless determination," Avneri concedes, but it secured for the Israel Defense Forces "a monopoly on the legitimate use of force." Historian Yosef Salmon defends the right of the state to exercise "its power and authority" over minorities threatening "its legitimate right to maintain control."

But ninety-one year-old Shmuel Katz, a member of the Irgun high command in 1948, dismissed the claims of those who were "conjuring up the *Altalena* myth of a revolt that was never planned and never took place." The "memory of the *Altalena*," he said, "is being manipulated for political purposes" to justify the expulsion of Jewish settlers from Gaza. Settler groups, claiming that Sharon welcomed "a second *Altalena*" so that he, too, could "fire the 'holy cannon,'" declared: "You will not get a civil war from us, because we . . . will not fight against our brothers." Conflicting memories of the primal struggle over legitimacy in June 1948 still roiled the Jewish state nearly sixty years later.

For many Israelis, and for Israel's critics worldwide, Jewish settlements remain the primary "obstacles to peace." The international delegitimization of Israel focuses incessantly on the theft of "Palestinian" land and the malevolent settlers who illegally "occupy" it. But history suggests otherwise. Even Kimmerling and Migdal, in their history of the Palestinian people, recognize that Judea and Samaria comprised "the center of ancient Jewish civilization." Now protected under international law for nearly a century, settlement in the Land of Israel west of the Jordan River affirms the right of the Jewish people to inhabit their own homeland. Settlements may infuriate Israel's ever-growing multitude of critics, but settlement in the Land of Israel has been deeply embedded in Zionism—to say nothing of Jewish history—since its inception, long before Palestinians appeared to contest it.

Like the future of Zionism a century ago, the future of the State of Israel remains inseparable from Jewish settlement. Less the expression of "illegalism" than the fulfillment of Jewish national striving, settlements ultimately rest on memories of biblical promise and ancient Jewish sovereignty, expressed in millennia of yearning to return to the Land of Israel. There would have been no Jewish state within any borders had not generations of pioneering Zionists—overcoming seeming insuperable obstacles set by hostile neighbors, an arid and inhospitable landscape, antagonistic foreign powers and apprehensive diaspora Jews—settled the ancient homeland and restored national sovereignty there.

The return to biblical Judea and Samaria following the Six-Day War marked the convergence of Zionism and Judaism, biblical promise and twentieth century international guarantees. Only in one essential respect did post-1967 settlers differ from the pre-1948 pioneers who inspired them: they were Zionists who forged the unity between nationalism and religion that their secular predecessors had rejected. In that convergence lies the source of the calumny to which they have been subjected by secular Israelis (and diaspora Jews) ever since.

Comprising a minority of the settlement community, religious Zionists nonetheless remain its cutting edge and impassioned advocates. Vilified by secular Israelis—most conspicuously intellectuals, academics, writers and journalists on the left—they are calumnied by Israel's hostile critics and demonized by the international organizations whose paternalism, under the guise of protection, effectively consigns Palestinians to perpetual dependence.

With their right to inhabit the Land of Israel constantly challenged from within and outside the State of Israel, Jewish settlers are located at the vortex of Israel's legitimacy struggles for the foreseeble future. Precisely how the ethnic cleansing of 350,000 Jews (whose numbers continue to rise) from the Land of Israel by any government of Israel can be justified, no less implemented, remains unclear. It would be a national tragedy of catastrophic proportions if Israelis were once again to approach the precipice of civil war over competing definitions of Zionist legitimacy, with the battlefield shifting from the shores of Kfar Vitkin and Tel Aviv to the hills of Judea and Samaria.

Amid the obsessive focus on Jewish settlements it is rarely noticed that the demands of both Palestinians and Jews for independent statehood, in the historic borders of Palestine, could be satisfied with relative ease. Geographically and demographically, a Palestinian state already exists in two-thirds of the land defined as Mandatory Palestine by the League of Nations after World War I. The Kingdom of Jordan is home to the world's largest percentage of Palestinians, who comprise more than half its population. But the Hashemite monarchy, supported by a Bedouin minority (which dominates the military), has always ruled the country. King Abdullah, increasingly apprehensive about his growing Palestinian majority, began to revoke the citizenship of Jordanian Palestinians in 2007, classifying them as "stateless refugees" and vigorously supporting their "right of return" to Israel.

But Jordanian Palestinians are already at home, in Palestine. Together with fellow Palestinians now living in Ramallah, Nablus, Jenin, Hebron, Bethlehem and elsewhere in the West Bank, they would comprise an overwhelming majority of the Jordanian population. Surely the ambitions of an autocratic Hashemite monarch, whose great-grandfather in Mecca received the gift of two-thirds of Palestine from Great Britain, should not be permitted to impede Palestinian statehood within the borders of their national home. Similarly, Jews living in Maale Adumim, Gush Etzion, Ariel, Kiryat Arba, Hebron, and more than one hundred other communities in Judea and Samaria would remain within the borders of Israel. With Palestinians in their Jordanian and West Bank homeland in Palestine, and Jews in their biblical homeland in the Land of Israel, two independent nations could define their own terms of independence and co-existence.

For now and the foreseeable future, however, Israel is likely to remain the pariah state of history's pariah people, "a people that dwells alone, and is not counted among the nations." Whether other nations can relinquish their venomous delegitimization of the world's solitary Jewish state seems—based on two thousand years of history—unlikely. Centuries of anti-Semitism have made Israel the perfect target, with Jewish settlements providing the currently fashionable justification for the malignant expression of this ancient hatred.

In its Proclamation of Independence the fledgling state looked to Jewish antiquity to validate its existence. "The Land of Israel was the birthplace of the Jewish people," its opening sentence reminds the world, where "their spiritual, religious and national identity was formed." Embedded in its past in that land are the deepest sources of Zionist legitimacy. Yet sixty-five years later Jews continue to struggle with their own internal demons of history, memory, and identity no less than with venal enemies for whom the largest (and most despised) Jewish "settlement" in the Middle East, ever since 1948, remains the State of Israel.

Those who predict Israel's moral demise based upon its presumed inability to remain Jewish and democratic are false prophets of doom. More than a century of Zionist history confirms that only by settling the land can Jews reconnect to their ancient past and assure their national future in an increasingly hostile world. No settlements existed before the Six-Day War, yet Arab hostility to the existence of a Jewish state within any borders was unyielding. Even as settlements stoke the current international crusade to delegitimize the Jewish state, they strengthen the fusion of nation, land and religion that defines Zionism as the distinctive expression of Jewish national identity in the ancient promised homeland of the Jewish people.

Acknowledgments

I am deeply grateful for the generous assistance and encouragement that I received during my preoccupation with Israel's legitimacy struggles. My valued research assistant Sarah Trager (Wellesley College 2013) located important sources for the *Altalena* and military disobedience. Nathan Ehrlich carefully scrutinized the chapter on military disobedience, offering many helpful insights and suggestions drawn from his own experience. Not for the first time, Daniel Horowitz was a supportive and insightful critic. Danielle McClellan's copy editing skills are greatly appreciated. Alan Childress, publisher of Quid Pro Books, once again facilitated my journey into print with ease and pleasure, as did Michele Veade. Responsibility for the result is, of course, entirely mine.

Portions of this book, originally published elsewhere, are reprinted with permission: *Brothers at War: Israel and the Tragedy of the Altalena* (Quid Pro Books, 2011); *Hebron Jews: Memory and Conflict in the Land of Israel* (Rowman & Littlefield, 2008); "Edward Said's Silence," *Congress Monthly*, published by the American Jewish Congress (Nov-Dec 1999), 12-14; "Inventing 'Palestine,'" *The Jewish Press* (August 10, 2011), 1.

Susan has once again endured my idiosyncratic preoccupations as a writer; her love has been sustaining. Amid the solitude of writing, my children Jeffrey, Pamela, Shira and Rebecca, and grandchildren Cole, Dalia, Jonah, and Sophia Caroline (born the day this manuscript was completed) are a beloved presence in my life, no matter how geographically distant they may be. Pasha has been a delightful, if occasionally demanding, companion. Rebecca gently asked a pointed question that forced me to rethink the place of Jewish settlements in this book. Most of all, I am grateful to Jeff for his meticulous scrutiny, critical astuteness, probing questions, and unfailing encouragement, especially during difficult times.

JSA
January 2014

Bibliographical Essay

This is a selective guide to the many and varied sources I consulted, citing those that were especially helpful in sharpening, or challenging, my own analysis.

Chapter 1. War of Brothers

My *Brothers at War: Israel and the Tragedy of the Altalena* (New Orleans, 2011) was the first history of this tragic episode and its lingering memories by a historian. A full bibliography can be found there. The Jabotinsky Archives, Beit Ha-Palmach Archives and Haganah Archives in Tel Aviv, and the Central Zionist Archives and Menachem Begin Heritage Center Archives in Jerusalem contain valuable documents. Revealing published sources include Menachem Begin, *The Revolt* (Tel Aviv, 1977); David Ben-Gurion, *Israel A Personal History* (Tel Aviv, 1971); Eliahu Lankin, *To Win the Promised Land* (California, 1992); Saul Friedlander, *When Memory Comes*, Tr. Helen R. Lane (New York, 1979); Uri Milstein, *The Rabin File: An Unauthorized Exposé* (Jerusalem, 1999), 357-69. For a fascinating video that includes interviews with still troubled participants: *Altalena*, Written and Directed by Ilana Tzur, Keshet Broadcasting Ltd. (1994). For definitions of legitimacy, see Max Weber, "Politics as a Vocation," in H.H. Gerth and C. Wright Mills (eds.), *From Max Weber: Essays in Sociology* (New York, 1958), 78; Bernard Lewis, *Faith and Power: Religion and Politics in the Middle East* (New York, 2010), 142.

Chapter 2. God and State

Thoughtful analysis of the origins, paradoxes and consequences of secular-religious conflict can be found in Zalmon S. Abramov, *Perpetual Dilemma: Jewish Religion in the Jewish State* (Rutherford, N.J., 1976); Charles S. Liebman and Eliezer Don-Yehiya, *Civil Religion in Israel:*

Traditional Judaism and Political Culture in the Jewish State (Berkeley, 1983); Liebman, "Cultural Conflict in Israeli Society," in Liebman and Elihu Katz (eds.), *The Jewishness of Israelis* (Albany, 1997); Ehud Luz, *Parallels Meet* (New York, 1998); Asher Cohen and Bernard Susser, *Israel and the Politics of Jewish Identity* (Baltimore, 2000); Aviezer Ravitzky, *Messianism, Zionism, and Jewish Religious Radicalism* (Chicago, 1996). See also Michael Walzer, Menachem Lorberbaum, Noam J. Zohar (eds.), *The Jewish Political Tradition*: Volume I *Authority* (New Haven, 2000), xxiii, 3-4, 247-48.

Responses to Ben-Gurion's request for a definition of "Who is a Jew?" appear in Eliezer Ben-Rafael, *Jewish Identities: Fifty Intellectuals Answer Ben-Gurion* (London, 2002). Ehud Sprinzak, *Brother Against Brother* (New York, 1999) explores violence and extremism in Israeli politics. See also Sprinzak, *Ascendance of Israel's Radical Right* (New York, 1991); Menachem Friedman, "The State of Israel as a Theological Dilemma," in Baruch Kimmerling (ed.), *The Israeli State and Society* (New York, 1989); Menachem Klein, *The Shift: Israel-Palestine from Border Struggle to Ethnic Conflict* (New York, 2010); Menachem Mautner, *Law & the Culture of Israel* (New York, 2011); Shmuel Almog, Jehuda Reinharz, Anita Shapira (eds.), *Zionism and Religion* (Hanover, N.H., 1998), especially the essays by Shlomo Avineri, Israel Kolatt, Israel Bartel and Aviezer Ravitzky; Noah J. Efron, *Real Jews: Secular Versus Ultra-Orthodox and the Struggle for Jewish Identity in Israel* (New York, 2003); Nadav G. Shelef, *Evolving Nationalism: Homeland, Identity, and Religion in Israel, 1925-2005* (Ithaca, 2010).

Secular Israeli apprehension over the place of religion in a Jewish state is expressed in Shulamit Aloni, *The Arrangement: From a State of Law to a Halakhic State* (Tel Aviv, 1970).

Leora Bilsky, *Transformative Justice: Israeli Identity on Trial* (Ann Arbor, 2004) provides a fascinating analysis of the competing definitions of legitimacy that pervaded the trial of Yigal Amir for his assassination of Prime Minister Yitzhak Rabin. See also Yoram Peri (ed.), *The Assassination of Yitzhak Rabin* (Stanford, 2000).

Insightful scrutiny of cultural conflict in Israel can be found in Myron J. Aronoff, *Israeli Visions and Divisions: Cultural Change and Political*

Conflict (New Brunswick, 1989); Laurence J. Silberstein, *The PostZionism Debates* (New York, 1999); Robert Wistrich and David Ohana (eds.), *The Shaping of Israeli Identity: Myth, Memory and Trauma* (London, 1995); Anita Shapira (ed.), *Israeli Identity in Transition* (Westport, CT, 2004); Yaacov Shavit and Shoshana Sitton (Tr. Chaya Naor), *Staging and Stages in Modern Jewish Palestine* (Detroit, 2004); Dan Urian and Efraim Karsh (eds.), *In Search of Identity: Jewish Aspects in Israeli Culture* (London, 1999), especially the essays by Eliezer Schweid, "Judaism in Israeli Culture" and Baruch Kimmerling, "Between Hegemony and Dormant *Kulturkampf* in Israel"; Oz Almog, *The Sabra: The Creation of the New Jew* (Berkeley, 2000); Dov Waxman, *The Pursuit of Peace and the Crisis of Israeli Identity* (New York, 2006). For an overview: Eva Etzion-Halevy, *The Divided People* (Lanham, MD, 2002).

For the Americanization of secular Israeli culture: Uzi Rebhun and Chaim I. Waxman, "The 'Americanization' of Israel: A Demographic, Cultural and Political Evaluation"; Maoz Azaryahu, "McIsrael? On the 'Americanization of Israel," *Israel Studies*, 5 (Spring 2000), 41-91. Recent religious conflict in Israel is examined in Mati Wagner, "The Ultra-Orthodox on the Warpath," *Commentary* (February 2012), 33-36; Ben Sales, "Religious Conflict in Beit Shemesh," *JTA* (February 18, 2013).

Israel's constitutional struggles are explored in Amnon Rubinstein, "Israel's Partial Constitution: The Basic Laws" (April 2009) http://jewishvirtuallibrary.org/source/isdf/text/Rubinstein. See also Aharon Barak, "A Constitutional Revolution: Israel's Basic Laws" (1993), Yale Law School, *Faculty Scholarship Series* (Paper 3697); Gila Stopler, "Religious Establishment, Pluralism and Equality in Israel—Can the Circle Be Squared?" *Oxford Journal of Law and Religion*, 1 (October 17, 2012), 1-25.

For the Tal Law and efforts to enlist haredi men in the IDF see Elli Fischer, "Tal Tales," http://www.jewishideasdaily.com/4619/features/tal-tales (July 31, 2012); "Ministers Approve New Universal Conscription Law," timesofisrael.com (July 7, 2013); Isabel Kershner, "Service Brings Scorn to Israel's Ultra-Orthodox Enlistees," *The New York Times* (July 7, 2013).

For Women of the Wall: Jeremy Sharon, "Historic Victory in Court for Women of the Wall," *Jerusalem Post* (April 25, 2013); Maayana Miskin, "Women of the Wall: We're Liberating the Kotel," *Arutz-7* (May 10, 2013); Jodi Rudoren, "Standoff at Western Wall Over Praying By Women," *The New York Times* (May 11, 2012); Arnold Eisen, "Jews of the Wall," *mosaicmagazine.com* (June 26, 2013). For a perceptive critique of Women of the Wall, see Evelyn Gordon, "Provocation at the Wall," *Commentary* (September 2013) http://commentarymagazine.com/article/provocation-at-the-wall.

A variety of perspectives on Israel's stuggles as a democratic Jewish state can be found in Nachman Ben-Yehuda, *Theocratic Democracy: The Social Construction of Religious and Secular Extremism* (New York, 2010); Yuval Elizur and Lawrence Malkin, *The War Within: Israel's Ultra-Orthodox Threat to Democracy and the Nation* (New York, 2013); Guy Ben-Porat, *Between State and Synagogue: The Secularization of Contemporary Israel* (Cambridge, 2013); Gershom Scholem, "Israel and the Diaspora," in *On Jews and Judaism in Crisis: Selected Essays*, ed. Werner J. Dannhauser (New York, 1976), 257. Yossi Klein Halevi, *Like Dreamers: The Story of the Israeli Paratroopers Who Reunited Jerusalem and Divided a Nation* (New York, 2013), explores the post-1967 conflict between kibbutz and settlement visions of Zionism.

Chapter 3. Conscience and Country

Among analytical studies of the Israel Defense Forces and military disobedience Stuart A. Cohen's writings are indispensable. See *The Scroll and the Sword* (Amsterdam, 1997); "Dilemmas of Military Service in Israel: The Religious Dimension," in Lawrence Schiffman and Joel B. Wolowelsky, *War and Peace in the Jewish Tradition* (New York, 2007); "Tensions Between Military Service and Jewish Orthodoxy in Israel: Implications Imagined and Real," *Israel Studies*, 12:1 (Spring 2007), 103-26; and *Israel and its Army: From Cohesion to Confusion* (London, 2008).

See also Ruth Linn, "Conscientious Objection in Israel During the War in Lebanon," *Armed Forces & Society* 12 (1986), 489-512, and *Conscience at War: The Israeli Soldier as a Moral Critic* (Albany, 1996);

Reuven Gal, *A Portrait of the Israeli Soldier* (New York, 1986); Geoffrey B. Levy, "Judaism and the Obligation to Die for the State," in Michael Walzer (ed.), *Law, Politics, and Morality in Judaism* (Princeton, 2006), 182-203; Yigal Levy, Edna Lomsky-Feder, Noa Harel, "From 'Obligatory Militarism' to 'Contractual Militarism'—Competing Models of Citizenship," *Israel Studies*, 12:1 (Spring 2007), 127-48; Yulia Zemlinskaya, "Between Militarism and Pacifism: Conscientious Objection and Draft Resistance in Israel," *Central European Journal of International and Security Studies*, Vol. 2 (2008), 9-35; Yoram Shachar, "The Elgazi Trials-Selective Conscientious Objection in Israel," *Israel Yearbook on Human Rights*, 12 (1982), 214-58; Sara Helman, "Negotiating Obligations, Creating Rights: Conscientious Objection and the Redefinition of Citizenship in Israel," *Citizenship Studies*, 3 (1999), 45-70; Jaclyn Blumenfeld, "Conscription and the Marginalization of Military Values in Modern Israeli Society," unpublished B.A. thesis, Department of Middle Eastern Studies, Emory College (2010).

For soldiers' testimony: *The Seventh Day: Soldiers Talk About the Six-Day War* (New York, 1971); Peretz Kidron (ed.), *Refusenik! Israel's Soldiers of Conscience* (London, 2004); Ronit Chacham, *Breaking Ranks: Refusing to Serve in the West Bank and Gaza Strip* (New York, 2003); Aviv Lavi, "Hebron Diaries," *Ha'aretz* (October 10, 2006) for Yehuda Shaul's experiences that led to the founding of Breaking the Silence; Tom Segev, *1967* (New York, 2005), 362-68; Roane Carey and Jonathan Shainim, *The Other Israel: Voices of Refusal and Dissent* (New York, 2002); *Soldiers' Testimonies from Operation Cast Lead, Gaza 2009*, www.breakingthesilence.org.il; *Our Harsh Logic: Israeli Soldiers' Testimonies from the Occupied Territories 2000-2010* compiled by Breaking the Silence (New York, 2012); Eyal Press, "Israel's Holy Warriors," *The New York Review of Books* (April 29, 2010), 33-35; Marc H. Ellis, *Israel and Palestine: Out of the Ashes* (London, 2002). See also: http://www.refusingtokill.net/Israel/ShministimLetter2008.htm; http://www.refusingtokill.net/Israel/israeltrialofthefive.htm; http://www.refusingtokill.net/Israel/Israelindex.htm; www.jewishpeacefellowship.org/Objection.htm; "Interview with Israel's Refuseniks," *New Internationalist*, 380 (July 2005); Pilots' Letter (September 24, 2003); Commandos' Letter (December 2003); Lev Luis Grinberg, *Politics and Violence in Israel/Palestine* (London, 2010). For a critique of disobedient religious soldiers for doing what secular soldiers had already done, see Gershom Gorenberg, *The Unmaking of Israel* (New York, 2011), ch. 5. Judge Colonel Levy's distinction between conscientious objection and civil disobedience can be found at www.wri-irg.org/news/2004/Israel0204-en.htm.

According to the Military Justice Law (1955), Section 125: "A soldier shall not bear criminal responsibility . . . when the order given him is manifestly unlawful." (I am grateful to Avinoam Sharon, Lt.Col [IDF ret.] for this citation.) Israeli government policy on selective conscientious objection was issued by the Ministry of Justice, Human Rights and International Relations Department (May 25, 1993): http://www.mfa.gov.il/MFA/Government/Law/LegalIssues.

For women in the IDF: Aryeh Tepper, "Women in Arms" *Jewish Ideas Daily* (December 2, 2010); Shani Boianjiu, "What Happens When the Two Israels Meet," *The New York Times* (September 7, 2012).

For the disproportionate service of religious soldiers in combat units: Gil Ronen, "Samaria Gives Twice Its Share of Combat Soldiers," *Arutz-7* (January 27, 2012) and "85% of Hesder Recruits—in Combat Units," *Arutz-7* (July 31, 2012). For the increasing enlistment rate of ultra-Orthodox Israelis: David Lev, "IDF to Establish Top 'Sayeret' Unit for Haredi Soldiers," *Arutz-7* (October 18, 2012). For concern lest religious soldiers follow the precedent of disobedience set by secular soldiers: Amos Harel, "Has the IDF Become an Army of Settlers?" *Haaretz.com* (May 9, 2010).

The rising rate of draft dodging among secular Israelis is explored in Gil Ronen, "Israeli Society Debates Draft Dodging," *Arutz-7* (August 20, 2007) and "IDF Manpower Chief Says 28% Dodging Draft," *Arutz-7* (November 6, 2007).

Chapter 4. Pariah Nation

For analysis and criticism of the delegitimization campaign: Robert Wistrich, *From Ambivalence to Betrayal: The Left, the Jews, and Israel* (Nebraska, 2012); Edward Alexander and Paul Bogdanor (eds.), *The Jewish Divide Over Israel* (New Brunswick, 2006), especially the essays by Bogdanor, "The Devil State: Chomsky's War Against Israel" and Cynthia Ozick, "The Modern 'Hep! Hep! Hep!'"; Edward Alexander, *The State of the Jews* (New Jersey, 2012). Two essays by Joel Fishman offer important contributions: "'A Disaster of Another Kind': Zionism=Racism, Its Beginning, and the War of Delegitimization Against Israel," *Israel Journal of Foreign Affairs*, 5:3 (2011), 75-92; and "The Relegitimization of Israel and the Battle for the Mainstream Consensus," *Israel Journal of Foreign Affairs*, 6:2 (2012), 9-20. Also, Efraim Karsh, "The Middle East's Real Apartheid," *Jerusalem Post* (March 5, 2013); Ehud Sprinzak, "Anti-Zionism: From Delegitimization to Dehumanization," *Forum on the Jewish People, Zionism and Israel*, 53 (May, 1984), 2-3; Phyllis Chesler, *The New Anti-Semitism* (San Francisco, 2003); Pierre-André Taguieff, *Rising From the Muck: The New Anti-Semitism in Europe* (Chicago, 2004); Bernard Harrison, *The Resurgence of Anti-Semitism: Jews, Israel, and Liberal Opinion* (Lanham, MD, 2006). The Boycott, Divestment and Sanctions movement is carefully tracked by Shurat HaDin-Israel Law Center, whose reports appear on www.israellawcenter.org. A useful survey of the "anti-Israel discourse" in contemporary Europe is provided in Robin Shepherd, *A State Beyond the Pale: Europe's Problem with Israel* (London, 2009).

Aspects of the delegitimization campaign are explored in Gil Troy, *Moynihan's Moment: America's Fight Against Zionism As Racism* (New York, 2013); Adam Horowitz, Lizzy Ratner, Philip Weiss, *The Goldstone Report: The Legacy of the Landmark Investigation of the Gaza Conflict* (New York, 2011); Douglas Davis, "Hatred in the Air: The BBC, Israel and Anti-Semitism," in Paul Iganski and Barry Kosmin (eds.), *A New Anti-Semitism? Debating Judeophobia in the 21st Century* (London, 2003); Melanie Phillips, *The World Turned Upside Down* (New York, 2010); Elhanan Yakira, *Post-Zionism, Post-Holocaust*, Tr. Michael Swirsky (Cambridge, 2010); Manfred Gerstenfeld, *Demonizing Israel and the Jews* (New York, 2013).

The delegitimization of Israel has become a cottage industry, especially for the Pluto Press in London. For a sampling: Uri Davis, *Israel: An Apartheid State* (London, 1987); John Rose, *The Myths of Zionism* (London, 2004); Jonathan Cook, *Blood and Religion: The Unmasking of the Jewish and Democratic State* (London, 2006); Jacqueline Rose, *The Question of Zion* (Princeton, 2005) and *The Last Resistance*

(London, 2007); Joel Kovel, *Overcoming Zionism* (London, 2007); Ben White, *Israeli Apartheid* (London, 2009). See also Michael Neumann, *The Case Against Israel* (Petrolia, CA, 2005).

For American contributions, John J. Mearsheimer and Stephen M. Walt, *The Israel Lobby and U.S. Foreign Policy* (New York, 2007) stands alone. See also Peter Berkowitz, *Israel and the Struggle Over International Laws of War* (Stanford, 2011) and "Lawfare," a review by Jeremy Rabkin, *Jewish Review of Books*, 3:2 (Summer 2012), 29-32. Anthony Julius, *Trials of the Diaspora: A History of Anti-Semitism in England* (New York, 2010), locates the current delegitimization of Israel in England within the long history of British anti-Semitism. For linkage between the history of anti-Semitism and the demonization of Israel, see David Nirenberg, *Anti-Judaism: The Western Tradition* (New York, 2013); also, Hillel Halkin, "Cause for Grief?" *Mosaic* (August 2013).

For contributions to delegitimization by Israeli scholars: Ilan Pappé, *The Ethnic Cleansing of Palestine* (Oxford, 2006); Jeff Halper, *An Israeli in Palestine: Resisting Dispossession, Redeeming Israel* (London, 2008); Gabriel Piterberg, *The Returns of Zionism: Myths, Politics and Scholarship in Israel* (London, 2008); Oren Yiftachel, *Ethnocracy: Land and Identity Politics in Israel/Palestine* (Philadelphia, 2006); Yiftachel, "'Creeping Apartheid' in Israel-Palestine," *Middle East Report*, no. 253 (Winter 2009); Baruch Kimmerling (ed.), *The Israeli State and Society* (Albany, 1989); Neve Gordon, *Israel's Occupation* (Berkeley, 2008). For the short history and modern construction of Palestinian national identity, see Baruch Kimmerling and Joel Migdal, *The Palestinian People: A History* (Cambridge, MA., 2003).

A useful anthology of Israeli academic revisionism is Laurence J. Silberstein, *Postzionism: A Reader* (New Brunswick, 2008), especially Kimmerling, "Academic History Caught in the Cross-Fire," 102-20. Benny Morris's path-breaking revisionist essay, accusing Israel of having been "born tarnished, besmirched by original sin," appears in Morris (ed.), *Making Israel* (Ann Arbor, 2007).

For critical scrutiny of revisionism, see Efraim Karsh, *Fabricating Israeli History: The 'New Historians'* (London, 2000). Steven Plaut, "Israel's Tenured Extremists," *Middle East Quarterly* (Fall 2011), 61-70, is an extensively documented analysis. See also Edward Alexander, "Hitler's Professors, Arafat's Professors," *Judaism*, 52 (Winter/Spring, 2003), 95*ff;* Solomon Socrates, "Israel's Academic Extremists," *Middle East Quarterly*, 8:4 (Fall 2001), 5-14; Shlomo Saran, "Our Inner Scourge: The Catastrophe of Israel Academics," Ariel Center for Policy Research, Policy Paper No. 171 (2007).

For the academic convergence of anti-Semitism and anti-Zionism: Gerstenfeld, "Anti-Israelism and Anti-Semitism: Common Characteristics and Motifs," *Jewish Political Studies Review*, 19:1-2 (Spring 2007). "Israel: The Alternative," Tony Judt's call for the dissolution of Israel, appeared in *The New York Review of Books* (October 23, 2003), sparking a vigorous response (and self-defense) in the December 4 issue. My analysis of Edward Said draws upon my "Edward Said's Silence," *Congress Monthly* (Nov-Dec 1999), 12-14. For an extensive survey and sharp critique of academic anti-Zionism and anti-Semitism, see Richard L. Cravatts, *Genocidal Liberalism: The University's Jihad Against Israel & Jews* (Sherman Oaks, CA, 2012). For one blatant example: Nadia Abu El-Haj, *Facts on the Ground: Archeological Practice and Territorial Self-Fashioning in Israeli Society* (Chicago, 2001).

For Palestinian usurpation of Jewish history and symbols, see Wisse, *Jews and Power*, 160-61, and David Meir Levi, *Stolen History: How the Palestinians and Their Allies Attack Israel's Right to Exist* (Sherman Oaks, CA, 2011). A nuanced assessment of Israel's precarious international legitimacy appears in Efraim Inbar, "Jerusalem's Decreasing Isolation," *Middle East Quarterly* (Spring 2013), 27-38.

Conclusion: Settling the Future

For critiques of Jewish settlers: Ehud Sprinzak, *The Ascendance of Israel's Radical Right* (New York, 1991); Robert I. Friedman, *Zealots for Zion: Inside Israel's West Bank Settlement Movement* (New York, 1992); Gershom Gorenberg, *The Accidental Empire* (New York, 2006); Idith Zertal and Akiva Eldar, *Lords of the Land* (New York, 2007); Gadi Taub, *The Settlers and the Struggle Over the Meaning of Zionism* (New Haven, 2010); Ami Pedahzur and Arie Perliger, *Jewish Terrorism in Israel* (New York, 2009); Ian Lustick, *For the Land and the Lord: Jewish*

Fundamentalism in Israel (New York, 1988); Peter Beinert, "To Save Israel," *The New York Times* (March 18, 2012). Legal aspects of the Israeli presence in Judea and Samaria are scrutinized in David Kretzmer, *The Occupation of Justice* (Albany, 2002). For the Elon Moreh ruling: "The 'Elon Moreh' High Court Decision of 22 October 1979 and the Israeli Government's Reaction," www.archives.gov.il/ArchiveGov_Eng/Publications/ElectronicPirsum/Elon Moreh/. Kretzmer is sharply critical of settlements in "The Chickens Come Home to Roost," *The Jerusalem Report* (August 26, 2013), 6-7. For a critique of his position, see "Inbox," 2, and Peter Wertheim, "The Complex Legality of Settlements," *The Jerusalem Report* (September 23, 2013), 30.

For his revealing debate with the settlers of Ofra, see Amos Oz, *In the Land of Israel* (New York, 1983), "An Argument on Life and Death (B)," 134-35, 138-39. See also Michael Feige, *Settling in the Hearts: Jewish Fundamentalism in the Occupied Territories* (Detroit, 2009); Ari Shavit, "The Settlers' Aim: Occupy Israel," *Ha'aretz* (January 3, 2013). For examples of the embrace of secular Western values by Israeli intellectuals: Yaron Ezrahi, *Rubber Bullets: Power and Conscience in Modern Israel* (New York, 1997) and Zeev Sternhell, *The Founding Myths of Israel* (Princeton, 1998). An especially vehement critique of Israel's settlement-guided "ethnic democracy," or "Judeocracy," is Ariella Azoulay and Adi Ophir, *The One-State Condition: Occupation and Democracy in Israel/Palestine*, Tr. Tal Haran (Stanford, 2013). For Tommy Lapid's response to the Gaza evacuation, see Yair Lapid, *Memories After My Death: The Story of Joseph 'Tommy' Lapid*, Tr. Evan Fallenberg (London, 2011), 382-83. Ilan Peleg and Dov Waxman argue in *Israel's Palestinians: The Conflict Within* (Cambridge, 2011) that Israel "suffers from a legitimacy crisis vis-à-vis its Palestinian citizens," with Jewish "ethno-nationalism" triumphant ever since 1948 over "liberal democracy." See also Kimmerling and Migdal, *The Palestinian People*, ch. 6, for a historical summary of Arabs in Israel.

On the legality of settlements under international law: Eugene V. Rostow, "Bricks and Stones," *The New Republic* (April 23, 1990), 19-23 and "Resolved: Are the Settlements Legal? Israeli West Bank Policies," *The New Republic* (October 21, 1991), 14-16; David M. Phillips, "The Illegal Settlements Myth," *Commentary* (December 2009), 32-37; Howard Grief, *The Legal Foundation and Borders of Israel Under International*

Law (Jerusalem, 2008); Grief, "Misconceptions Regarding Israel's Legal Foundation Under International Law," *Outpost* (July/August 2010), 7-8 and "The Transfer of Jews Under Prime Minister Sharon's Unilateral Disengagement Plan," *Jerusalem Post* (October 22, 2004); JHH Weiler, Yaffa Zilbershats, and Avi Bell, "What are Israel's Rights in Judea and Samaria? Two Views," *Jewish Ideas Daily* (August 9, 2012).

For the Levy Commission report: The Commission to Examine the Status of Building in Judea and Samaria "Conclusion and Recommendations" (July 13, 2012), http://unispal.un.org/UNISPAL.NSF/0/D9D07DCF-58E781C585257A3A005956A6; Editorial, "Settling Truths," *Jerusalem Post* (September 7, 2012). See Ted Belman, "Settlements Are Not Illegal," *Israpundit* (July 11, 2012); Daniel Mandel, "Israel, Settlements, and The Rewriting of Law and History," *The Iconoclast* (March 4, 2013); Joshua Teitelbaum, "Israel as the Nation-State of the Jewish People," Jerusalem Center for Public Affairs, #579 (September-October 2010).

For scrutiny of demographic distortions: Yakov Faitelson, "The Politics of Palestinian Demography," *Middle East Quarterly* (Spring 2009), 51-59; Yoram Ettinger, "Demographic Trends in the Land of Israel, by Yakov Faitelson," Jerusalem Cloakroom #239 (February 6, 2011); and Ettinger, "Jewish-Arab Demography Defies Conventional 'Wisdom,'" *Israel Hayom* (October 19, 2012). A critique of their methods and conclusions appears in Ian S. Lustick, "What Counts is the Counting: Statistical Manipulation as a Solution to Israel's 'Demographic Problem,'" *Middle East Journal*, 67 (Spring 2013), 185-205. Current demographic trends are explored in Paul Moreland, "Israel's Fast Evolving Demography" *Jerusalem Post* (July 21, 2013). The geography and demography of Jordan as Palestine is thoughtfully analyzed by Mudar Zahran, "Jordan is Palestinian," *Middle East Quarterly* (Winter 2012), 3-12.

Index

Abbas, Mahmoud 112, 115
Abdul-Hadi, Auni Bey 109
Abdullah, King 143, 152
Abramov, S. Zalman 46
Accidental Empire, The (Gorenberg) 140
Achimeir, Abba 8
Agnon, S.Y. 50
Agreement, Armistice (*see* Armistice Agreement)
Agreement, Status Quo (*see* Status Quo agreement)
Agudat Yisrael 45, 46
Ahmadinejad, Mahmoud 136
AIPAC 130
Al-Dura, Muhammad 112, 133
Alexander, Edward 136
Alexandroni Brigade 23
Al-HaMishmar 64
al-Husseini, Haj Amin 136
Allon, Yigal 27, 28, 29
Altalena 3-4, 8, 15-37, 61, 62, 67, 78, 100, 115, 149-150, 155
Alterman, Nathan 61
Altneuland (Herzl) 40
Amir, Yigal 67, 68
Amitzur, Bezalel 32
Antiquities of the Jews 1
apikoros 3
Arab Revolt (1936) 10, 110
Arab riots (1929) 7-8, 57, 64
Arafat, Yasser 4, 65, 81, 86, 107, 112, 120, 147
Aran, Gideon 60, 139
Arch, Robinson's (*see* Robinson's Arch)
Argov, Shlomo 81
Ariel, Yisrael 80
Arlosoroff, Chaim 8-10, 15, 21, 29, 36
Armistice Agreement (1949) 52, 85
Ashley-Cooper, Anthony 108

Auschwitz 106, 113-115, 126
Aviner, Yehuda 96
Avneri, Shlomo 150
Ayalon, Zvi 26
ayin tachat ayin 10
Azoulay, Ariella 141
Bachi, Roberto 146
Baker, Mona 125
Balfour Declaration 139, 142
Bar Kokhba 77-78, 106, 111, 135
Barak, Aharon 69, 97, 145
Barak, Ehud 97, 98, 100
Bardèche, Maurice 115
Bar-Ilan, Meir 47
Basic Law 69
Batavia, Moshe 97
BBC 18, 126
BDS Movement 116, 117, 124, 128
Begin, Menachem 4, 10-16, 18-25, 27-31, 33, 34, 36-37, 47, 52, 62-64, 80-83, 95
Beinert, Peter 141
Beinin, Joel 122
Ben Gal, Yanush 85
Ben-Ami, Yitzhak 15, 24, 25
Benda, Julien 129
Ben-Dor, Oren 125
Ben-Gal, Michael 27
Ben-Gurion, David 3, 7, 9-17, 19-38, 41-48, 50, 52, 55, 59, 62, 63, 70-71, 112, 114, 128, 149, 150
Bentov, Mordechai 26
Ben-Yehuda, Nachman 75
Berenson, Julian 24
Bergen-Belsen 113
Berlin, Isaiah 50
Bernstein, Peretz 32
Betar 9, 24, 139
Betar Illit 139
Bialik, Chaim Nachman 106

Bilsky, Leora 45, 67, 68
biryonim 10
Bishop of Nancy 105
"black flag" doctrine 79, 86-87
Blackstone, William 109
Blass, Jonathan 88
Blau, Amram 46
Blum, Yehuda Z. 145
Bnei Akiva 61, 87
Boyle, Francis 116
Breaking the Silence 93-94
Brit Habirionim 8
Britain (*see* Great Britain)
British Mandate 7
British Broadcasting Company (*see* BBC)
British Peel Commission 42, 109
British Secret Service 13
Brother Daniel (Rufeisen, Oswald) 49
Buruma, Ian 126
Butz, A.R. 115
Camp David Accords 80
Canaanite 77, 108, 111, 113
Carlebach, Azriel 30
Caro, Joseph 3
Carter, Jimmy 117
Casear 2
"Cast Lead" 133
Chalidi, Idan 94
Chomsky, Noam 123
Churchill, Winston 12-13, 143
"cinema riots" 48
Clermont-Tonnere, Count of 105
Cohen, Stuart 99
Combatant's Letter 89-90
Committee for National Liberation, Hebrew (*see* Hebrew Committee for National Liberation)
Committee, Levy (*see* Levy Committee)
Convention, Geneva (*see* Geneva Convention)
Cotter, Irwin 115
Count of Clermont-Tonnere (*see* Clermont-Tonnere, Count of)
Courage to Refuse 91
Crisis of Zionism, The (Beinert) 141
Dathan 1
Davis, Uri 125

"Declaration of Revolt" 11
DeGaulle, Charles 107
Deir Yassin massacre 37
Della-Pergola, Sergio 147
Der Judenstaat (Herzl) 40
Dilesky, Hilary 30
din moser 66
din rodef 66-68
dina d'malkhuta dina 3
Dreyfus, Alfred 40, 105
Dror, Amnon 29
Druckman, Chaim 96
Dubnow, Simon 146
Eban, Abba 59, 107
Egypt 1, 108, 119-120, 126
Eichmann, Adolf 114
Eilat 30
Eldar, Akiva 140
Elgazi, Gad 80
Ellis, Marc 123
Elon Moreh 61, 63, 145
Elon, Amos 56
emancipation 3, 105
epikoros 39
Eritrea 13, 17
Esau 4, 113
Escape from Auschwitz (Vrba) 114
Eshkol, Levi 16, 144
Ettinger, Yoram 147, 148
Etzel (*see* Irgun; IZL)
Even, Dan 23-25, 32, 54-55, 59
Exodus 18, 22, 112
Faitelson, Yakov 146, 147
Faurisson, Robert 115
Fein, Monroe 15, 17-19, 22, 25-26, 30-32
Final Solution 114
Finkelstein, Norman 123
Fisch, Harold 44, 55
Fishman-Maimon, Yehuda Leib 12, 32, 45, 46, 50
Frank, Anne 112
Frankfurter, Felix 50
Frantzman, Seth 132
French National Assembly 105
Galilee 2, 59, 81, 82, 141
Galili, Yisrael 16, 19, 20-21, 23, 26-27, 29
General Zionist Party 12

Geneva Convention 142-146
Geva, Eli 82
Ghandi 83, 86
ghetto, Warsaw (see Warsaw ghetto)
Golan Heights 58, 60, 87, 120, 139, 143
Goldstein, Baruch 64
Goldstone Report 133-134
Goldstone, Richard 133-134
Golomb, Eliahu 11, 12
Gordon, Neve 128
Gorelnik, Israel 31
Goren, Shlomo 50, 53-54, 64, 71, 87
Gorenberg, Gershom 100, 140
Gouri, Haim 61
Grass, Günter 129
Great Britain 11, 13, 126, 142, 144, 152
Grief, Howard 145
Grossman, Guy 91, 129
Groznick, Abba 29
Gruenbaum, Yitzhak 12, 26, 29, 32
Gur, Mordechai "Motta" 53, 62
Gush Emunim 60-63, 75, 80, 81, 148
Gush Etzion 4, 58, 60, 152
Ha'aretz 83, 86, 89, 94, 140, 150
HaCohen, Zecharya 50
Haetzni, Elyakim 58, 63, 65
Haganah 10-14, 16-17, 19, 20, 27, 30-31, 34, 37-78
Hague Regulations 142, 145
halakha 45, 49-51, 64, 65-68, 77, 102-103
Halevi, Binyamin 79
Halkin, Hillel 88, 135
halutzim 149
Hamas 88-89, 91-92, 127, 133
Hammer, Zevulon 67
haredi/haredim 39, 47-48, 69-75, 98, 101
Harel, Amos 94, 99
Harel, Isar 19, 20
Hashemite kingdom 143, 152
Hashomer Hatzair 31
Hason, Moshe 32
Hatikvah 18
ha-totach ha-kadosh ("holy cannon") 36-37, 150
havlaga 10
Hayun, Dubi 85
Hazit Haam 8-9

Hazon Ish 46
Hebrew Committee for National Liberation 15
Hebron 4, 7, 39, 52, 55, 57-59, 63-65, 90, 93-94, 97, 135, 152, 155
Herut party 47
Herzl, Theodore 40-42
Herzog, Chaim 107
hesder yeshiva 71
Hibbat Zion 41
Histadrut 12, 14
Hitler, Adolf 7-9, 96, 113, 115, 123, 136-137
Hitti, Philip 109
Hoax of the Twentieth Century, The (Butz) 115
Hoffman, Anat 73, 74
Holocaust 13, 24, 44, 53, 70, 83, 85, 106, 111-116, 123, 125, 135
"holy cannon" 36-37, 150
Holy Land, The (Roberts) 108
Honderich, Tom 125
Horovitz, David 134
Hussein, King 53, 81, 110, 127
IDF 4, 16, 19-21, 24-26, 29-32, 34, 53-54, 62, 65, 67, 71, 80, 82, 84, 86-89, 91-95, 97, 98, 99-103, 125, 134
illegitimacy 87, 140 (see also legitimacy)
Independence, Proclamation of (see Proclamation of Independence)
International Court of Justice 144, 146
International Criminal Court 132, 146
Intifada, First 89, 91, 95, 101, 127, 146
Intifada, Second 88-89, 92, 93, 95, 98, 100-101, 112, 127, 133
Irgun 3, 8, 10-14, 15-37, 78, 149-150 (see also IZL)
"iron wall" (Jabotinsky) 7
Irving, David 115
Isaac 4
Ishmael 4, 110
Israel Defense Forces (see IDF)
Israel Lobby, The (Mearsheimer and Walt) 130-131
Israel's Occupation (Gordon) 128
IZL 20, 23, 27-29, 34 (see also Irgun)
Jabotinsky, Eri 29

Jabotinsky, Vladimir "Ze'ev" 7, 10, 15, 36, 42-43, 52
Jewish Agency 8, 11-13, 46, 76
Jewish settlers 4, 59-68, 81, 87, 89-91, 93, 94, 96-98, 100, 102-103, 112, 125, 129, 140-141, 143, 145, 148-151 (*see also* settlements, legitimacy of)
Jewish Social-Democratic party (*see* Poale Zion)
Jordan Valley 58 (*see also* Transjordan)
Josephus 1-2, 24
Jotapata 2
Judea 4, 33, 52, 56, 58-60, 63, 80-84, 87, 90, 95, 97-98, 100-102, 111, 121, 135, 139, 144-146, 148, 150-152
Judt, Tony 117, 120-122
Julius, Anthony 126
Kaminer, Matan 92, 93
Kaplan, Rami 90, 91
Karelitz, Abraham Isaiah 46
Karsh, Efraim 126, 128
kashrut 46, 71
Kaspari, Ilan 89
Katz, Shmuel 15-16, 20-22, 25, 150
Kaufmann, Yehezkel 50
Keinan, Herb 88
Keita, Salif 124
Keith, Alexander 108, 109
Keren, Moshe 28
Kfar Vitkin 20-21, 23-25, 27, 32-36, 151
Khalidi, Rashid 109, 110
Khartoum 59, 107
Kibbutzim 7, 13, 42, 55, 56, 58-59, 71, 98, 120
kiddush 71
Kidron, Peretz 80, 90
Kimmerling, Baruch, 110, 128, 150
King David hotel bombing 37
King, Jr., Martin Luther 83, 85-86
Kiryat Arba 59-60, 63-64, 90, 97, 100, 152
Kishinev pogrom 42, 106
Knesset 45, 48, 50-51, 58, 61-62, 65, 66, 68-69, 71-72, 88, 103, 113, 149
Koestler, Arthur 32
Kohn, Joe 28, 30
Kook, Hillel 20, 31
Kook, Abraham Isaac 43

Kook, Tzvi Yehuda 53, 56, 58, 60-63, 81, 87
Korah 1, 2
Kovel, Joel 123
Kretzmer, David 145
Kugel, James L. 1
Labor Party 4, 9, 12, 14, 47, 60, 63, 102
Labor Zionist political cooperation 8-9, 12-13, 36, 42, 56, 61, 78
Land of Israel 7, 14, 41, 43-45, 52-53, 57, 59, 60-61, 63, 66, 78, 81, 86-88, 96, 99, 108, 111, 113-114, 128, 134, 139-141, 145, 150-152, 155
Land of Israel According to the Covenant with Abraham, with Isaac, and with Jacob, The (Keith) 108
"land without a people" 108-109
Landau, Chaim 16
Lankin, Eliahu 15, 17-21, 23-25, 29-32
Lapid, Tommy 150
Law of Return (1950) 48-49, 112
League of Nations Mandate 139, 142-144, 152
Lebanon 4, 81-86, 95, 98, 100-102, 119, 126
legitimacy 1, 3-5, 14, 21, 34, 36, 42, 45, 47, 51-52, 56, 58-60, 63-68, 70, 75, 81, 83, 86, 88-89, 91, 96, 102, 117, 126, 128, 132, 139, 142-144, 148-150, 152, 155
   democratic 91
   dual 52
   international 75, 132, 165
   of Irgun 36
   political 38
   religious 52
   of settlements (*see* settlements, legitimacy of)
   Zionist 14, 42, 58-59, 102, 117, 157
Lehi 11-13, 16, 34, 78
Leibovitz, Yeshayahu 83
Levin, Nahum 48
Levin, Itzhak Meir 48
LeVine, Mark 122
Levinger, Moshe 58, 61, 63
Levinstein, Meir David 45
Levite family 1
Levy Committee 145
Levy, Avi 93
Levy, Edmond 67, 68

Levy, Zipporah 18
Lewis, Bernard 38
Likud Party 4
Linn, Ruth 83, 84, 114
Lior, Dov 100
Lord Moyne (*see* Moyne, Lord)
Lords of the Land (Zertal and Eldar) 140
Lustick, Ian 141
Ma'ariv 30
Maimon, Yehudah Leib (*see* Fishman-Maimon, Yehuda Leib)
Maimonides 77, 88
Majdanek 115
Mandatory Palestine 7, 13, 37, 43, 52, 106, 118, 142-143, 152
"Manifesto of the Sicarii" 8
Mapai Party 8-9, 36, 48
Marcus, Yoel 150
Mari Marvara 112
massacre, Deir Yassin (*see* Deir Yassin massacre)
Matar, Haggai 92, 93
Mea Shearim 48, 72
Me'arat HaMachpelah 52, 111, 135
Mearsheimer, John 130, 131
Megged, Aharon 127
Meir, Golda 80
Melamed, Eliezer 99
Menuchin, Ishai 82
Mercaz HaRav 53
Meretz party 69
Meridor, Yaakov 16, 24, 32
Meron, Theodor 144
Migdal, David 29
Migdal, Joel 110, 150
milchemet achim 29
Military Justice Law (1955) 79
Milne, Seumas 126
Mitzna, Amram 98
Mizrahi Party 12, 32, 41, 47-48, 84
Modi'in Illit 139
Mofaz, Shaul 92
Morris, Benny 127
Moscowitz, Haimito 56
Moses 1, 2
Moyne, Lord 12
Mt. Sinai 1, 68

Mudrick, Oded 68
Muhsin, Zuhair 110
Muir, Diana 109
Munich Olympics 107
Nahal 71
Nahal Haredi 71, 98
Nasser, Gamal Abdel 118
National Religious Party 50, 61, 65, 67
Naturei Karta movement 46
Nazi 4, 8, 10, 12-13, 49, 83, 86, 90, 106-107, 111-115, 123, 125-127, 135-136, 142, 144
Negbi, Moshe 149
Netanya 20, 22-23, 72, 74, 89
Netanyahu, Benjamin 72, 74, 102, 145
Netzah Yehuda 101
Neuman, Geora 80
New Profile 94
Nirenberg, David 136
Nordau, Max 41, 106
Nuremberg trials 115
Obama, Barak 148
Ollman, Bertell 123
"Operation Purification" 32
Ophir, Adi 84, 141
Orientalism 117
Oron, Assaf 91
Orr, Akiva 125
Oslo Accords 64-65, 67, 86, 141
Overcoming Zionism (Kovel) 123
Oz, Amos 56
Paglin, Amihai 23
Pa'il, Meir 19
Palestine 3, 7-8, 10-13, 15-18, 24, 32, 39, 42-43, 52, 57, 59, 106, 108-122, 124-128, 131-132, 136, 139, 142-144, 148-152, 155
Palestine Clause 143
Palestine Post 32
Palestine Liberation Organization (*see* PLO)
Palestinian National Covenant 107
Palma, Dudu 85
Palmach 11-12, 16, 19, 22, 26-29, 31, 34, 37, 56, 62, 78
Pappé, Ilan 117, 125, 128
Paulin, Tom 125

PCBS 147
Peace Now 81, 95
Peres, Shimon 60, 61, 88
Peri, Yoram 79
Perpetual Dilemma (Abramov) 46
Pharoah 1
Phillips, David 146
Phillips, Melanie 126, 134
Pilots' Letter 92
PLO 4, 65, 81-82, 84, 110, 117
Poale Zion party 42
Polish Free Army 10
political sovereignty 2
Porat, Hanan 58, 63
Proclamation of Independence (1948) 38, 44-45, 112, 139, 152
Protestrabbiner 39
Provisional Government 11, 16, 33
putsch 3, 37
Rabbinical Council of Jewish Settlements 66
Rabbinical Court 49-51, 69
rabbinical legal authority 2, 40
Rabin, Yitzhak 28, 30-31, 54-55, 61, 62, 64-68, 84-88
Rabinowitz, Zadok HaCohen 40
Red Sea 1
religious Zionists 4, 32, 41, 44, 47, 53, 56, 58-66, 86-88, 96, 98-99, 102, 129, 139-140, 148, 149, 151
Revisionism 7, 10
Revolt, The (Begin) 11
Rich, Adriennne 117
Rivlin, Reuven 149
Roberts, David 108
Robinson's Arch 73-74
Rose, Jacqueline 125
Rosenblatt, Tzvi 9
Rosenblum, Doran 64
Rostow, Eugene V. 143, 144
Rubenstein, Amnon 68, 69
Rufeisen, Oswald 49
Sadan, Eli 96
Sadat, Anwar 80, 81
Said, Edward 117-120, 122, 155
Saison ("The Season") 12, 13
Salmon, Yosef 150

Samaria 4, 52, 56, 58-61, 63, 80-84, 87, 91, 95, 97-102, 121, 124, 139-140, 144-146, 148, 150-152
San Remo Conference 142
San Remo Resolution 142
Sand, Shlomo 129
Sanhedrin 68
Saramago, José 129
Sarid, Yossi 88
Sarna, Nahum 2
Sassover, Israel 13
Sayeret Matkal 92
Schiff, Ze'ev 82
Schneerson, Menachem Mendel 50
Scholem, Gershom 75
Schwebel, Stephen 144
Second Temple 33, 88, 134
Secret Service, British (*see* British Secret Service)
Segev, Tom 48, 113
Senior, Boris 24
settlements, legitimacy of 3, 59-68, 75, 81, 85-91, 95-100, 102, 112, 121, 124-125, 128, 130, 132, 139-153
Settlers, The (Taub) 141
Seventh Million, The (Segev) 113
Shahar 101
Shalit, Benjamin 51
Shamgar, Meir 144
Shapira, Anita 28
Shapira, Avraham 87, 88, 96
Shapira, Moshe 32
Sharansky, Natan 74
Sharon, Ariel 61, 64, 82, 88-89, 92, 94-96, 145, 149-150
Shas party 65
Shaul, Yehuda 93
Shehehiyanu 45, 54
Shertok, Moshe 21, 26-27, 37
Shilanksy, Dov 113
Shinui party 150
Shlaim, Avi 127
Sh'ma 53, 73
Shministim 92, 94
Shochat, Yigal 91
Shoebat, Walid 110
Shulhan Arukh 3, 50

Shulman, Paul 22, 23
sinat hinam 68
Sinnott, Michael 125
Six-Day War 4, 41, 53-56, 58-59, 75, 80-81, 100, 106, 110, 113, 115, 117, 120, 134, 139, 141, 143-144, 151, 153
Sneh, Moshe 11, 14
Sofer, Arnon 146
Soloveitchik, Joseph Dov 50
Sprinzak, Ehud 9, 12-13, 66, 140
Status Quo agreement 46, 52, 70-71
Stavsky, Avraham 9, 15, 19, 25-26, 29, 31
Stern, Avraham 12
Stern, Yedidiah 72
Stone, Julius 144
Stopler, Gila 74
Students for a Free Palestine 124
Sullivan, Denis 123
Sulzberger, Arthur Hays 113
Summers, Lawrence 124
Supreme Court 49-51, 63, 69-71, 73, 80, 95, 144-145
Susser, Leslie 134
Tal Law 71, 72
Talmon, J.L. 107
Talmud 2, 39, 41, 46, 49
Tamarin, Mia 94
Tammuz, Benjamin 64
Taub, Gadi 140, 141
Teitelbaum, Joel 45
Tel Aviv 7, 9, 13, 18, 20-21, 25-28, 31-36, 43-45, 53, 62, 67, 84, 88, 90-91, 93, 97, 102, 128, 143, 151
Tel Rumeida 64-65
Ten Commandments 1
tohar haneshek 85
Torah 2-3, 39-41, 43-46, 50, 54, 60-61, 63, 67-68, 70-71, 73-74, 77, 80-81, 87-88, 96, 98, 100-101, 103
transfer agreement (Arlosoroff) 8, 10
Transjordan 143
Treblinka 106, 115
Tsur Yisrael 44
Tutu, Desmond 117
UN (*see* United Nations)
UN Durban Review Conference Against Racism 116, 136
UN General Assembly 107, 132, 144

UN Human Rights Council 133, 134, 146
UN Resolution 242 143
UN Resolution 3379 ("Zionism is Racism") 107
UN Security Council 131, 143, 144, 146
UNESCO 134-135
United Nations (UN) 4, 14-15, 18-19, 24, 36, 44, 106-107, 116, 131-133, 136, 139, 143-146
United Resistance Movement 13-14
UNRWA 131-132
Vespasian 2
Vrba, Rudolf 113, 114
Walt, Stephen 130, 131
Warsaw ghetto 106, 112, 114, 123
Warshavsky, Eli 30
Waxman, Dov 70
Weber, Max 38
Wedgwood 30
Weiss, Shalom 30
Weizman, Ezer 80
Weizmann, Chaim 10, 12, 13, 41, 109
West Bank 4, 52, 60, 63, 66, 83, 89, 92, 95, 110, 116, 127, 133, 141-148, 152
Western Wall 52-57, 62, 73-74, 98, 111
Wetzler, Alfred 113
Wilkie, Andrew 125
Wisse, Ruth 113, 127
Wistrich, Robert 115, 126, 136
Wolffsohn, David 41
Women of the Wall 73-74
World War II 13, 18, 24, 36, 115, 119, 129, 142-143
World Zionist Organization 10
Yaalon, Moshe 96
Ya'ari, Ehud 82
yad le-achim 96
Yadin, Yigael 16, 23, 26-28, 30, 32, 57-58
Yahni, Sergio 89
Yanai, Shmuel 26
Yarimi, Yeshayahu 25
Yarom, Uri 31
Yesh Gvul 82, 89
yeshiva 46, 48, 53, 56-58, 61, 65, 67, 70-73, 88, 93, 96-100, 102
Yiftachel, Oren 128
Yishuv 3, 10-12, 35, 40, 46, 78, 114

Yom Kippur War 60, 63, 80
Zamir, Danny 85
Zangwill, Israel 109
Zealots 2, 8, 57, 141
Zertal, Idith 140
Zerubavel, Arbel 29
Zichroni, Amnon 79

Zionism, as racism 4, 89, 92, 107-136
Zionist Congress 41
Zionist Revolution, The (Fisch) 55
Zionists, religious (*see* religious Zionists)
Zizling, Aharon 29
Zuckerman, Yitzhak "Antek" 114
Zygelboym, Shmuel 106

About the Author

Jerold S. Auerbach is the author of ten previous books, including *Unequal Justice: Lawyers and Social Change in Modern America* (1976), a *New York Times* Noteworthy Book; *Justice Without Law?* (1983); *Rabbis and Lawyers: The Journey From Torah to Constitution* (1990, 2010); *Jacob's Voices: Reflections of a Wandering American Jew* (1996, 2010); *Are We One? Jewish Identity in the United States and Israel* (2001); *Explorers in Eden: Pueblo Indians and the Promised Land* (2006); *Hebron Jews: Memory and Conflict in the Land of Israel* (2009); *Brothers at War: Israel and the Tragedy of the Altalena* (2011); and *Against the Grain: A Historian's Journey* (2012).

His articles have appeared in *The Wall Street Journal, Commentary, Harper's, The New York Times, Jerusalem Post, The New Republic, New York Sun, The Jewish Press, American Thinker,* and *The Algemeiner*. His published essays about Israel are accessible at www.jacobsvoice.tumblr.com

Auerbach has been a Guggenheim Fellow, Visiting Scholar at the Harvard Law School, Fulbright Lecturer at Tel Aviv University, and recipient of two College Teachers Fellowships from the National Endowment for the Humanities. He is Professor Emeritus of History at Wellesley College, where he taught for forty years.

Visit us at *www.quidprobooks.com.*

www.ingramcontent.com/pod-product-compliance
Lightning Source LLC
Chambersburg PA
CBHW070314240426
43663CB00038BA/2278